COMMUNITY THAT IS CHRISTIAN

COMMUNITY THAT IS CHRISTIAN

A HANDBOOK ON SMALL GROUPS

JULIE A. GORMAN

VICTOR BOOKS
A DIVISION OF SCRIPTURE PRESS PUBLICATIONS INC.
USA CANADA ENGLAND

Copyediting: Pamela T. Campbell
Cover Design: Joe DeLeon
Interior Illustrations: Tom Shumaker

Library of Congress Cataloging-in-Publication Data

Gorman, Julie.
   Community that is Christian: a handbook on small groups / by Julie A. Gorman.
      p. cm.
   Includes bibliographical references.
   ISBN 0-89693-260-5
   1. Church group work. 2. Small groups. I. Title.
BV652.2.G569 1993
253'.7—dc20   93-29655
                                                                       CIP

---

1   2   3   4   5   6   7   8   9   10   Printing/Year   97   96   95   94   93

VICTOR BOOKS
A division of SP Publications, Inc.
Wheaton, Illinois 60187

To all those
who have been
community
to me

CONTENTS

FOREWORD

Small groups emerged clearly in the last two decades as one of the most potent instruments available to the Christian church for growth, renewal, service, and outreach both in the United States and throughout the world. From the cell groups energizing the growth of the largest congregation in the world in Seoul, Korea, to the discipleship and Bible study groups of an inner city church in Philadelphia, Christian small groups provide important opportunities for evangelism and new member assimilation, for involvement with contemporary needs such as homelessness or world hunger, and for building relationships in an individualist and often lonely culture. A recent national study led by sociologist Robert Wuthnow of Princeton University documented the astonishing fact that approximately one in four adult Americans is involved in a small group which includes spiritual purposes. The largest percentage of these groups are church based.

Yet for all the importance of the small group movement, little has been written for Christian leaders, whether lay or clergy, to help them better understand the sometimes complex dynamics and critical issues at work whenever people gather together in Christian small groups. This book performs that useful function from a solidly Christian, biblically-grounded framework which will provide encouragement and insight for Christians seeking to begin or develop small groups in their church.

Author Julie Gorman brings solid qualifications to provide such a resource. As a pastor in several congregations and as a professor at Fuller Theological Seminary, she has taught thousands of Christians in the art and science of building Christian community through small groups. She has not only studied the relevant research literature on small groups, but she has also visited, examined, and probed hundreds of church programs to gain increased knowledge of what makes groups work. She is a gifted teacher who demonstrates her commitment to the challenge of equipping the people of God to know and do the will of God in the world. With her biblical understanding of discipleship, she provides practical help to beginners and experienced leaders alike. I have been privileged to work alongside her as a

9

colleague and friend for many years. I am grateful for the work she has done to make her experience and learning available to an ever larger audience.

Roberta Hestenes
President of Eastern College and Professor of Spirituality
St. Davids, Pennsylvania

CLOSE ENCOUNTERS
OF THE HUMAN KIND

Imagine the Lone Ranger setting up housekeeping and becoming a part of the community. Or the Marlboro Man leaving his lonesome vigil on the range to become a member of a small group. To many persons in our crowded, competition-driven society, belongingness in community seems as far-fetched. Biblical passages that are based on corporate togetherness are subconsciously read in suspiciousness because our cultural filters are trained to pick up independence and individual feats. Even the church has settled for independent living and individualized worship experiences as being the norm.

This book is a call to believers to explore a community that is distinctively theirs by covenant and calling. If we are ever to think and act Christianly we must take into account the heritage that is a part of our uniqueness as children of God. That heritage is community oriented more than individually focused. It is *cooperative* rather than *competitive.* We have been endowed with "family"; we function in a system called "body." *His family. His body.* Our individual worth is enhanced, not diminished, by this systemic relationship. ᐧThis is a call to recognize that we will never realize the likeness of Christ in our aloneness; we will never transform the world as individuals; we will never discover the fullness of life in Christ if we stay solo. We are distinct as people of God because we were made to live in relationship with the Head and the parts of the body—with the Father and the rest of the family. While today groups are often formed to enhance the individual, the biblical model reminds us that the individual enhances the group. Distinction comes from contributing to the advance of the group. Community that is distinctively Christian will have group dynamic elements that are good. But it will embrace more. Community that is distinctively Christian will host the presence of God in the midst of it! Such existence appears radical in our present culture.

11

COUNTERCULTURE

As Americans we pride ourselves on our ability to take care of ourselves. The Declaration of Independence is more than a political document. It is a personal manifesto. From our youth we have been taught such axioms as, "Don't depend on anyone else," "Decide on your own," "If you don't look out for yourself, nobody will," "Stand on your own two feet." We have embraced freedom as the highest virtue. We prize the freedom to move in and out of relationships as our own individualized choices determine. The choice to have children, to stay married, and a host of other free choices common today underscore this freedom. If the relationship does not fulfill us—whether friendship, group, church, marriage, or other—we can opt out.

"Rights language" is our native tongue. We make decisions now based on rights—our personal rights—rather than on absolutes and virtues. Persons quit jobs, break rules, and abdicate responsibilities with no other explanation than "I felt (or didn't feel) like doing it." Self-fulfillment accentuates our personal autonomy and separateness. Individualism is king and generates pride in our culture. Our heroes are those who "made it on their own" or survived to make it to the top of the heap by standing on others. The pressure of success grips us in all spheres of society. We evaluate each relationship by "What can I get out of it?" "In general, Americans do not join groups for what they can contribute, but for what they can get out of them" (Dyrness, 98-99). Even groups have "become for us a collection of individuals created by individuals for their own individual advantages" (Kraus, 76–77).

As a result, the small group movement today is seen as something to be used to another advantage (such as church growth) or as an optional ornament that is added to our collection of socially approved activities. *Newsweek* in its cover story of February 5, 1990 estimates there are some 15 million Americans in about 500,000 support groups in our country today. We are a nation preoccupied with taking care of ourselves and such groups provide a self-help forum. They also provide someone to listen to us in a world that moves too fast and remains too independent to spend time caring about a person. Christian education with its emphasis on personal felt need and individualized growth has

12

contributed to this cultural cult of narcissism. Christianity in general has gravitated toward a privatized cultivation of the faith. The "free" church model with its emphasis on the voluntary association and commitment of individuals is founded on an individual's Christian experience. It is "me and Jesus," "my faith," "my God," "my relationship with Him," "the church of my choice." The subjective question around which our faith revolves is "Have you come to know Jesus Christ as your personal Savior?" Personal piety is the benchmark by which we evaluate a person's faith. "Subjective criteria become the norm for reality and truth in religious profession. Spirituality is defined in terms of personality characteristics, belief patterns, and personal piety" (Kraus, 110).

While this personal emphasis has merit, it must always be in balance with the equally valuable corporate emphasis. In the Puritan era the development of a personal relationship with Christ, where it occurred at the expense of community, was identified as anti-Christian. Puritan Thomas Goodwin declared,

> To be proficient in "holy duties" is indeed more sweet to a man's own self, but to be proficient in our calling is more profitable to others—to the Church, the commonwealth, or the family—and so may glorify God more.
>
> (quoted in Horton, 167)

When scriptural interpretation is left to the individual, it often is shaped by that which supports the individual's lifestyle. When moral values are determined by the individual they become relative, based on the feelings of one. When Christian graces are seen as *my achievements* we undermine their godly foundations by cultivating a sense of pride. When the corporate element is missing we lose more than numbers. We become self-focused.

Created to be an interdependent, integral part of community, persons cannot abdicate this role without numerous consequences both to themselves and to the system which they comprise. Our culture exalts in its freedom, choices, and personally earned achievements. But it also lives with loneliness, competition, and fear of not being accepted.

Community is not just small groups—it is a mind-set. A mind-set that values the corporate as much as the individual. A mind-set that does not pride itself so much on individual accomplishment as on the community growth effect on all. A mind-set where the greatest fulfillment is in the enabling of others. A mind-set that contributes its strength toward the good of the whole, not hording it for self. A mind-set wonderfully depicted by Jesus (Philippians 2). A mind-set where the person is comfortable with weakness because that is a reminder there is a connectedness to the whole which can never be replaced with self-sufficiency.

This sense of living in interconnectedness with persons whom you didn't choose and who may not enhance one's personal achievements (indeed may even hamper them) does not set well with most evangelical Christians. Self-realization on your own, individual freedom and privacy, and autonomy have been bred into our being. We have identified such achievements and powers with being a Christian. Thus we can move into the church easily, with little change. We simply modify biblical frameworks to embrace our cultural philosophy. And "God helps those who help themselves" becomes a principle for Christian living. Pride is fostered in individualized spiritual growth, outdistancing the others who lack determination and perseverance. Groups become techniques for sharpening our own skills and coping with our own needs. They are useful so long as we feel they help us as individuals or move us in the direction of our personal goals. They are to be embraced only as we feel comfortable and ignored when we don't. Responsibility for others is nice as long as it doesn't interfere with our personal development and we can choose whom to be responsible for.

As Christians living in America we have our "rights." Groups will do fine as long as they know their boundaries and realize that it really is the individuals who run the church. And each individual must determine what is best for him or her. With these kinds of values in mind, Lee and Cowan question, "Can we redeem our precious individuality by transforming it into a radically relational form?" (Lee and Cowan, 61) Can Christians who have been bombarded with cultural mores extolling American individualism be recreated to value the sanctity of the individual within an over-arching sphere of community? That is the hope that has

14

spawned this book. Can those who are born of God reframe their thinking in operational spheres that are opposed to this widely accepted private individualism? Will we settle for a semblance of godliness in this area but deny the power of God to transform us into and through community?

COUNTERFEITS VERSUS THE REAL THING

As children of the Heavenly Father we wrestle with another small group dilemma. In an age of prolific counterfeits and designer copies, are we tempted to settle for a semblance of community by simply adding small groups to our church or classroom menu? Community takes commitment and effort for it cuts across many of our culturally embraced standards. But community is the norm in Scripture. It is part of the reflected image of God still stamped upon our nature. Its cultivation is part of the fulfillment of Christ in us. Its realization is an echo of God's nature in earthly surroundings. We will never "grow up into Him" without it. It is a reflection of our relatedness to God as Father. "Everyone who believes that Jesus is the Christ is born of God; and everyone who loves the Father loves His child as well" (1 John 5:1).

How can we love our Father but not His other children? Indeed, it never occurred to John or anyone else in apostolic times that it was possible to be in communion with God without being in community with men.

We are called to an inheritance of "community." But it is also a call to commit to the realization of this standard and that doesn't just happen. It takes work and patience. Living in community requires cultivation of concepts of mutuality, service, and corporate responsibility. It implies receiving and pursuing, increasing self-disclosure, and interdependency. There is no "lite" relational commitment for those who find it difficult to be in a group relationship. In what ways are our Christian classrooms actually different from the typical university classroom? The distinctives must be more than the content we teach.

When we commit to shared life and the work of interconnected community we endorse the importance and inclusiveness of our lives as being related to one another. We acknowledge that life is essentially *us* and not just *me*. We exist in webs of relationships. Whatever I become reshapes my networks. This corporate connection has a reciprocal effect on us as individuals. We become as the networks affect us. Because we are locked into this relational dance no person exists outside of the system, unaffected by and isolated from others. We are marked by the patterns of our systems and we in turn form the vision, esteem, and operational procedures of our corporate webs.

Within an intentional Christian community which is consistently committed to becoming one body in its praxis of mutuality:

- Every act of authentic self-disclosure makes one person's story a gift to the becoming of another.

- Every act of genuine understanding of another's story enhances the size of the listener's spirit.

- Every act of responsible challenge in the spirit of understanding is an invitation to an increase in stature.

- Every act of non-defensive exploration in response to challenge reflects a commitment to a life of larger dimensions.

(Miller, 95)

We cannot play at community development — it is essential to who we are and profound enough in its implications to keep us pursuing it until it climaxes in that great communal celebration of Lamb and Bride. It is not an optional choice for those more relational by nature. It is not possible to set it aside to pursue private gain and find the blessing of God upon us. The Old and New Testaments are filled with reminders of our connectedness to others and our fruitlessness without that awareness. Nor is it possible to grow up in Him by simply embracing the concept without allowing the reality of the needs and presence of others to cut across our lifestyles. Dietrich Bonhoeffer incorporates community into his *Cost of Discipleship*. He speaks of "people who love the idea of community more than the experience of community."

Community is a way of life. We don't like to think of being responsible for others. I like not being my brother's keeper. Nor do I want any other having responsibility for me. Dependency is on the most feared list today. Self-disclosure is relegated to the professionals whom I pay to listen. Vulnerability and weakness are dangerous. Commitment is too binding and controlling. It is easy to settle for a counterfeit or substitute because of the cost to ourselves of pursuing real community. We must not settle for small group times that are as good as the garden club or the local Alcoholics Anonymous meeting. Community is distinctively Christian.

CONFUSING SKILL DEVELOPMENT AND COMMUNITY

Because groups have been recognized to bring some benefit to people and to play a part in the accomplishment of desired goals, they have been incorporated into every organization known. They are "user friendly." It is impossible to find a person who has never had any group experience. Education utilizes them, business incorporates them, volunteers participate in them, and children form them in early years. Such a tool has not escaped the scrutiny of this world's experts. Our inborn creativity wants to analyze the functioning of groups and reduce such functioning to logic, combining principles with techniques in a system of group rules and rights. The problem confronting us is that community is not programmable — it is not possible to reduce it to a system of techniques.

While educational, sociological, psychological, and anthropological sciences can contribute much insight into descriptive workings of a group, they are always limited to the systems within which they operate. God's motivational rules for relationships supercede anything the technological experts can deliver. Just as the person who knows and operates on the basis of the Word of God will be wiser than his or her teachers, so the person who operates out of the values given in Scripture will be "group dynamically" effective — not on the basis of controlling a situation through a technique but out of a heart that is acting in obedience and love toward the related Creator and Lord. Thus kingdom persons who are "walking in the truth" naturally put into practice right responses and Spirit-directed skills of supporting,

17

caring for, and building up others in the body relationship. And such occurrence is as integral to the relationship as the hand being raised to rub the head in response to the interconnections of the nerves which are in the body together. "Equipping" by its very nature is not just teaching skills, but holistically growing persons up in Christ's way of living and loving so that the whole body ends up increasing in maturity in Him. The building of community will never be achieved by the perfection of better techniques but by the development of better men and women who realize and respond to the interconnected system of relationships into which they have been placed by God Himself. We must not let techniques and skills become uppermost in small groups. Community is developed not only by insight into relational skills but also by cultivation of a heart that knows and loves God and His people as they love themselves.

There is nothing sinful about methodology and research. Much is included in this book to give insight and explanation. When it comes to community they can enhance and enlighten those who seek to know God's design. But community as God envisioned it can never be reduced to dynamics and skills. We can teach expressions and cultivations of caring but we can't give members hearts that care — especially when that caring expressed may cost them comfort. We can help members understand principles and priorities of commitment but we cannot generate commitment within them, a commitment that takes precedence over their own self-interests.

We can acquaint persons with the value and skills involved in esteem building in another, but that does not guarantee that those persons will promote another's well-being at their own expense.

There are no shortcuts to Christ as Lord, only a recognition that community is forged by God as He indwells a people open to that vision of corporate connection with each other and with Him. Because He indwells His people, there is the possibility of community being experienced wherever they are together. Christian small groups must never become subverted into thinking that the sciences have the answers. We borrow from them anything that does not contradict our theological superstructure. But when it comes to community — to whom shall we go? Not to the latest guru. Peter's words remain true, "You alone have the words of life." To live community is to live His life.

It is in community that I am most challenged to grow up in Jesus Christ. It is easier to be holy alone. But I do not lose my identity when in community—I find it. I am uniquely me in the presence of others who need me to complement and fulfill the total picture we become together. None of us takes on the other's identity. Together we become what we could not become alone. It is God's unique plan that it be so.

CONCEPTUAL DESIGN

This book is prepared for pastors, congregational leaders, and all who seek to explore and to implement community in their congregations. It is a text for those who equip persons who will or who presently lead small groups. It contains plan design and instructions for setting up a ministry of groups. It is intended to stimulate and inform the people of God as they facilitate community and work in covenant relationships with others. It is an interactive manual for transformation of community living in home, school, church, or marketplace.

Part I frames the big picture of community. It includes chapters on the biblical evidence of corporate togetherness and belonging, a chapter on the major mind-set that undermines community—individualism—and how that philosophical framework pervades and shapes our thinking today. The fourth chapter in this section targets relational conditions in society that foster a deep-seated hunger for groups today. Part II utilizes two chapters to sketch desirable goals, and describe true community and the process of transformation that enables a changed people. Chapter 7 is gateway to Group Development which comprises Part III of the book. Topics dealt with include the principles important to the beginning of a group, self-disclosure that causes a group to bond, contribution of individual uniquenesses to the formation of a group, communication facilitating, inevitability of conflict in community settings and how to respond, and a chapter on Turning Points which mark the growth cycles of groups. Part IV works with specialized concerns and their relationships to community ministry. Chapter 13 poses the question "So What's the Difference?" and examines what is known of gender differences and their impact on and implications for small groups. Leadership, its role and development, comprise chapter 14 while 15 offers overall perspectives and principles for putting together a small group program made up of multiple groups. Boundary Crossings finishes the book with distinctives involved when groups cross cultures, generations, and neighborhoods as the church seeks to provide community for those who are in specialized groups. Community exists in many special focus groups today, but the three selected for examination are Crosscultural groups, Intergenerational clusters, and Home churches. As you begin this journey through *Community That Is Christian* why not invite a friend to read another copy so you can discuss and shape your ideas in community with another of likeminded interest?

PART I
THE BIG PICTURE
OF COMMUNITY

1

BIBLICAL FOUNDATIONS OF COMMUNITY

*The most conspicuous weakness of evangelical
Protestant theology has been its lack of understanding
and witness to authentic community as the fulfillment of
the believer's personal relation to God.*
C. Norman Kraus, 109

However much we may think of our relationship to God in individual terms, we are always seen by God as family, networked, honeycombed, related to one another as His children, His bride, His building.

And that relationship is not just a collective. Not single ribbons tied to a central maypole. Not solo strings on a piano playing one tuneful but monotonous note. We are corporate, a whole concerto of harmony and chording. TOGETHER we are in Christ Jesus.

Richard Halvorsen declares that Jesus Christ, by putting us in His body, determined that we would need each other as much as we need Him (Halvorsen, *Perspectives*). And the only way our corporate body can function is by being tuned to Him. A.W. Tozer wisely observes, "One hundred pianos are never more closely tuned to each other than when they are tuned to the same tuning fork."

Relating is at the heart of knowing God. Relating is also at the heart of becoming the people of God. Our faith journey is one we make together. Community is the context for our growth. It is a distinctively Christian concept.

GOD IS A PERSON

We sing it in our hymns. It is etched deeply into our creeds. "God in three Persons, blessed Trinity." God is a Person. He encounters and relates to Himself. He relates to others in the Godhead. He communicates. He creates personal community.

Contrary to modern Hollywood epics, God is not a force or a principle or an impersonal dynamic. God is a Person enjoying and pursuing relationships. The entire account of Scripture is a record of His commitment to developing encounters with others. The Son came to make known the Father and open up a way of relationship with Him. Jesus' direct and profound relationship with God as His Father forever affects our understanding of relationship from now on.

Now life is defined by our encounter with the Son. For those who live in Christ Jesus the bonding is eternal. Nothing can separate us from that personal relationship with God (Rom. 8:39). God is a Person. God is a Person in Community.

THE COMMUNITY OF GOD

The doctrine of the Trinity has been called a contrived doctrine. In other words, nowhere in Scripture is the doctrine of the Trinity specifically "spelled out" compared to the way that the doctrine of God's holiness is declared. The Scriptures plainly state, "God is holy." Nevertheless it is firmly indicated throughout the Word that God, while being one God, is also of three separate Persons. From the initial statements in Genesis to the climactic closing of the Book of Revelation, we encounter the distinct Personages of Father, Son, and Spirit, often in roles each plays toward humankind such as Judge, Lamb, and Comforter. There is differentiation in unity. At times They seem to speak and act as One: "In the beginning God created the heavens and the earth" (Gen. 1:1). At the same time, reference is made to the presence and action of specific Beings—"the Spirit of God was hovering over the waters" (Gen. 1:2)—during the creation process.

In his letter to the Colossians, Paul assured them that by the One who "is the image of the invisible God, the Firstborn over all creation . . . by Him [the Son] all things were created" (Col. 1:15-16).

Likewise in the creation of mankind there appears to be a consultation and united effort of the Triune God to create the unique bearer of God's image (H. Miller, 24). "Let Us make man in Our image, in Our likeness" (Gen. 1:26). The phrase "in Our image" indicates we are made as a reflection of Him, a reflection of the divine interdependency found in the community of the Godhead.

God's image portrays community. We, as His reflection, bear the same. Thus, according to Kraus, "it is the 'Human Family' that stands at the pinnacle of the creation process, and not the perfected, rational, individual male of Aristotelian vintage" (Kraus, 81). This community inherent in the Godhead has far-reaching implications when we

> ... Christian believers can see some of the striking implications of social Trinity theory. First, the confession that we are created in the image of God begins to resonate with new overtones. In our fellowship and *koinonia,* in such homely endeavors as telling one another the truth or in doing such honest work as will help those in need — 'above all in that love which binds everything together in perfect harmony' — we show not only that we have become members one of another, but also that we as restored community, we-in-the-plural, have become a remarkable image of God.
>
> Cornelius Plantinga
> "The Perfect Family,"
> *Christianity Today,* March 4, 1988, 27

consider the character of God and thus the image of God passed on to persons. The unity of God is found to be in the singular character of that shared community (Moltmann, 96). There is no unity without community. Such sharing within the Triune God reveals the solidarity, wholeness, and mutuality present in the Godhead — the same qualities desired for the church (God's image in the world) as declared by Jesus and the Apostle Paul (John 17, Rom. 12, 1 Cor. 12, etc.).

While each of the Persons in the Godhead is unique, They represent interrelationship par excellence. Moltmann says it this way:

> The three divine persons are not there simply for themselves. They are there in that they are there for one another. They are persons in social relationship. The Father can

be called Father only in relationship with the Son; the Son can be called Son only in relationship with the Father. The Spirit is the breath of the one who speaks. The breath goes out from the Father in the eternal moment in which the Father speaks the Word, which in another relationship is called the Son. . . . Being-a-person *(Personsein)* means "being in relationship."

(Moltmann, 97)

Such interdependence is illustrated richly in the Gospel encounters as the Son came to represent and reveal the Father while the Spirit carries out the fulfillment of claims made by the Son. Scripture records evidence of close connectedness and interdependence between members of the Godhead.

The Father gave the Son, who in turn revealed the Father. "I have revealed You to those whom You gave Me out of the world" (John 17:6a).

The Father gave the Son the persons whom He enlightened, and the Son saw them as the Father's persons. "I have revealed You to those whom You gave Me out of the world. They were Yours; You gave them to Me and they have obeyed Your word. . . . I pray for them. I am not praying for the world, but for those You have given Me, for they are Yours" (John 17:6, 9).

What the Son had to give was given Him by the Father. "Now they know that everything You have given Me comes from You" (John 17:7).

All that the Son had belonged to the Father, and all the Father had belonged to the Son. "All I have is Yours, and all You have is Mine. And glory has come to Me through them" (John 17:10).

The Son summed it up for Philip. "Anyone who has seen Me has seen the Father" (John 14:9).

26

Jesus' work was the Father's work—the Father doing it through Him. He finished the Father's agenda. "Don't you believe that I am in the Father, and that the Father is in Me? The words I say to you are not just My own. Rather, it is the Father, living in Me, who is doing His work" (John 14:10). He finished the Father's agenda. "For the very work that the Father has given Me to finish, and which I am doing, testifies that the Father has sent Me" (John 5:36). "My food . . . is to do the will of Him who sent Me and to finish His work" (John 4:34).

Jesus was dependent upon the Father for the words He spoke to teach. "These words you hear are not My own; they belong to the Father who sent Me" (John 14:24).

He initiated nothing on His own but spoke only what the Father said. "What I have heard from Him I tell the world" (John 8:26). "I do nothing on My own but speak just what the Father has taught Me" (John 8:28). "I am telling you what I have seen in the Father's presence" (John 8:38).

Jesus was dependent upon the Father's modeling. "The Son can do nothing by Himself; He can do only what He sees His Father doing" (John 5:19). "By myself I can do nothing; I judge only as I hear" (John 5:30).

Jesus' goal was to please the Father. "I seek not to please Myself but Him who sent Me" (John 5:30). "I always do what pleases Him" (John 8:29).

Each gave glory to the other. "Father. . . . Glorify Your Son, that Your Son may glorify You" (John 17:1).

Likewise the Spirit joins in this shared ministry. Jesus sends the Spirit to join in ministering to believers (the Father's persons) He left behind. "I will send Him [Counselor] to you" (John 16:7).

The Spirit also is no ad libber. "He [Spirit of truth] will not speak on His own; He will speak only what He hears" (John 16:13).

The Spirit glorifies Jesus. "He will bring glory to Me by taking from what is Mine and making it known to you" (John 16:14).

Note the interactive involvement in the Spirit's arrival as recorded in John 14:26. The Father sends the Spirit. The Spirit is sent "in the name of Jesus" as from Him. The Spirit reminds of Jesus' teachings, not His own.

> What is therefore remarkable is that the social Trinity, shorn of certain angularities and excesses, is probably the most biblically faithful and theologically redolent theory now available.
>
> Cornelius Plantinga
> "The Perfect Family,"
> *Christianity Today,* March 4, 1988, 24

The self-sufficiency and personal independence that characterize our present evaluation of success is totally foreign to the Godhead who exist in interdependent community. A part of the glory of God is this interconnectedness and exaltation of the other.

The individualism which marked the Corinthian church angered and pained the Apostle Paul because it was not reflective of the God whose likeness they represented. The "image" was distorted. Western European and American churches (even evangelicalism) have often espoused an independent individualism that is reflective of culture—not a mirror image of God. (See Chapter 3 on Individualism.)

It is insightful for our understanding of the Scriptures to picture a God who functions in this kind of social relationship. This scriptural display of God in relationship creates a paradigm for our living and ministering as His people who resemble Him in community. For in the high priestly prayer of Jesus, He asks for us to experience the same kind of unique unity as He experiences with the Father (John 17:21). Our "human community is to be the image of the Triune God on earth" (Moltmann, 98). We as persons gathered together are to mirror the divine self with its unique selfless mutuality and care. God's Spirit is placed in our midst to enable this to happen. Such a view of a Triune God

operating in interdependence to exalt the work of each other and to present a solidarity of personhood affects our concept of authority and leadership. It impacts our achievement of task and our valuing of persons in groups. What does it say for our hierarchical systems and domination/subjugation paradigms within the church? The early church with the disciples newly grasping the realities of what Jesus prayed for and gave them gives evidence of this kind of interdependence in action. Observe Peter at Pentecost serving as spokesperson, but with the eleven "standing with him." See the Twelve in Acts 6, gathering the disciples and with one voice declaring, "It would not be right for us. . . . [you] choose" (Acts 6:2-3). As author S.D. Gaede suggests, because God's nature is relational in essence, the ones He created are relational by design (Gaede, 131).

COMMUNITY IN THE IMAGE OF GOD

God created us as persons. Personhood is only known in relation to others. In relationship we discover the distinctives of our personhood. Our identity as relational beings is carved out of interpersonal relating. God knew and experienced community. He made His creatures capable of the same. The creature must be separate, but with a drive to relate. It's through encounter that the self exists "in the image and likeness of God" (Anderson, 74). Adam was created with the capacity and necessity for relating to God. The Divine made a creature with whom He could interact. Like an artist stepping back to admire his work, God surveyed what He had made and, "it was good" (Gen. 1:31). The creature was what God wanted.

He entrusted Adam with responsibility—"Rule over the world of creation. Tenderly care for it and nurture its being. Enjoy the tree fruit of the garden. Relish the gifts of My creativity." God interacted with the person He had made. He set boundaries and launched the creature into the fabulous scene of His making.

But a God who knew community, who recognized the fulfillment of person knowing person, sensitively became aware that the creature was not fully enjoying life as God had in mind. "It is not good," He assessed. "The creature is alone" (Gen. 2:18). The Hebrew concept means "acting independently" or being separate. Adam was not meant to be self-sufficient! The *image* is not

one of aloneness. "Quite clearly the *image* is not totally present in the form of individual humanity but more completely as co-humanity" (R. Anderson, 73). And God drew forth His creative powers to remedy the situation. A helper, an equal one, would complete the community design that God had in mind. But it must be one to fulfill the relational potential of this apex of His creation. And the great Creator allowed the created one to exercise his creativity. As the animals spent time with Adam, he became aware of their uniquenesses and he named each as he saw fit. They became whatever he determined. He put them in categories. He separated the species. He observed their personalities and came up with names for each work of art presented. As Anderson observes, "He searched for a *Thou* for which he could become the corresponding *I*" (R. Anderson, 84). But none of them would suffice for community as God intended. None was designed "in the image of God."

The Creator God must fashion one of like flesh, yet differentiated. In loving response He made her and presented the work of His hands to the creature. The hunger the Creator had put into the heart of the creature was met. As Adam observed the qualities of this new masterpiece, he recognized the likeness to himself and exulted by naming her accordingly, "Woman — a like part of me — bones like my bones and flesh like my flesh" (Gen. 2:23). And God had created two who together as male and female reflected His own differentiated being. Now Adam would know community with co-humanity and with God as a "we."

The record of Adam from the beginning until now reflects God's design that we enjoy Him in relationship and that we know community with one another. It is our destiny, built into every human creation reflective of the image of God. Our God hunger can be muffled, but it can never be drowned out. Our relational need to know and be loved by others was etched into the very image of God within us. The experience of unity comes from relating while differentially separate. Community is never optional — it is a necessity for being what God designed us to be. The pattern in the garden is not happenstance. Community with the Creator is primary, but being in community with others of like kind was required for the Creator to be satisfied that the created being had become what He desired. God has made the

two inseparable. The aged John summarized: "Whoever loves God must also love his [her] brother" (1 John 4:21). "Connection with the King causes interconnectedness between all those connected with the King. . . . Jesus' relation to God as His father becomes the paradigm for universal interconnectedness" (Lee and Cowan, 148). God is relational. He cultivates that hunger for another in us.

Whatever system God touches has the marks of relationship on it whether humankind, the nation Israel, salvation, revelation, or the church. And this relational imprint bears both dimensions—a being in relationship with God and in relationship with others. The image of God is one of persons in encounter.

The garden scenes of unmarred relationships are fertile ground for thought. What must it have been like to know no shame in who you are—to relate purely and totally openly to another. What would it be like to hear God walking in the garden and race to embrace that rich time of communion when the Creator related to His reflected image and there was no fear, no guilt, no separation. This was community in paradise as God intended. The creature was dependent upon God, and the man and the woman were interdependent upon one another. There was no "aloneness" of self-centered independence, self-sufficiency. It was at this point the Tempter struck. He offers the image-bearers the possibility of being self-centeredly independent. The results would be disastrous to the relational encounters. The image would become flawed and clouded. The garden community would be only a fast fading memory.

THE SHADOW OF COMMUNITY AS SEEN IN THE FALL

Independence, self-centeredness, separation, death resulted because the image-bearers chose to believe the ephemeral promise of the serpent. His enticing words broke up their community—"You will be like God" (Gen. 3:5). Though made in God's likeness, the man and woman chose to change their relationship from one of dependency to independence. The penalty was resoundingly announced and enacted. For the fallen ones who had been together in relationship, the judgment was "separation" that would touch every part of their existence. There was the introduction of physical death—the separation of the inner

31

person from the body. There was spiritual death—the separation of the image-bearers from God. Those who welcomed the Creator's coming now hid from Him. When the two guilty ones "heard the sound of the Lord God as He was walking in the garden in the cool of the day . . . they hid from the Lord God among the trees of the garden" (Gen. 3:8). The tender intimacy of relationship with God was gone. It was replaced by fear as the two acted out the separation they felt and hid among the trees that were the Creator's gift to them.

The image-bearers were separated from each other. They knew shame. Interestingly counselor John Bradshaw defines shame as:

> a being wound. . . . Guilt says I've DONE something wrong; shame says there IS something wrong with me. . . . Guilt says what I DID was not good; shame says I AM no good.
> *(Bradshaw On: The Family,* 2)

Bradshaw goes on to call shame a kind of soul murder *(Bradshaw On: The Family,* 2).

Another calls shame:

> a sickness of the soul. . . . Shame is a wound felt from the inside, dividing us both from ourselves and from one another.
> (Gershen Kaufman in *Shame: The Power of Caring,*
> *Bradshaw On: The Family,* 2)

Adam and Eve hid themselves from one another with fig leaves, a visible sign of their alienation. Creation, the object of God's care and cultivation, was impacted and subjected to judgment. The symphonic agreement between humankind and the earth became dissonance (H. Miller, 28–29).

Harmonious relationships were in discord. The chaotic changes reveal dramatic reversals:

> Imagine Adam's horror as he looked around after God's curse. The animals he had named now ran from him! He was ashamed before his wife! And he was afraid of his God!"
> (H. Miller, 29)

In many ways, community too goes into hiding. The image was not totally destroyed but it was fatally fractured. Adam passed on this tarnished reflection to his children. "[Adam] had a son in his own likeness, in his own image; and he named him Seth" (Gen. 5:3). The children bore Adam's damaged image. But the shadow of restored relationship hovers over the devastating curse of judgment. There is the promise of an Offspring who would crush the serpent's head (Gen. 3:15). Bonhoeffer speaks about the restoration of community as inherent in the image stamped in their humankind.

> Since this community is destroyed by moral failure, clearly it has moral character originally, and is part of the divine image in man in the narrator's view. Divine and human community are in some way part of the original moral and spiritual life of man and that means part also of his future life (restored in Christ). . . . This points us to the church.
>
> (Dietrich Bonhoeffer)

After the Fall there could have been a cessation of community with humankind doomed eternally to hunger for relationships that could never be experienced. But isolation and alienation were never part of God's plan.

God would not let His intention of community be destroyed. The image was still there and God was still God.

> . . . the bearers of God's image possessed two unique relationships: the personal relationship between man and God and the personal relationship between man and man (Adam and Eve). These two types of intimate relationships were the content of the image of God before the fall. The personalness of man is the foundation of the image of God, for it makes him capable of relationships. But the building itself is this pair of personal relationships toward God and toward man."
>
> (H. Miller, 38)

The major impact of the Fall occurred in the creature's role as God's image-bearer. As the image-bearer fulfilled the created design of God, these two relationships of relating to God and to one another functioned well. But when the image-bearer fell, both personal relationships were disrupted.

> However, this disruption did not totally destroy either man's relationship with God or his relationship with man. Eve praised God at Cain's birth (4:1); Cain and Abel offered sacrifices to him (4:3-4); and Cain was in "the presence of the Lord" (4:16) when he received his sentence. A relationship between man and God still exists, but we no longer see the intimate encounter with God "walking in the Garden." Instead, the relationship is often characterized by fear instead of joyous intimacy. . . .
> Man's relationship with man suffered in an analogous way. Adam and Eve still lived as husband and wife after the fall; Cain took a wife; and Cain and Abel certainly played together as children. But Cain's smug answer to the Lord's question about Abel, "Am I my brother's keeper?" (4:9) betrayed an attitude of indifference toward his brother rather than a spirit of intimacy with him.
>
> (H. Miller, 39)

Thusly does Miller summarize the self-centered and negative aspects of the existing relationships after the Fall. The image was there—but it had been negativized. The Old Testament is a record of God's continued pursuit of relationship with His creature in this negativized state. The call of the Lord God that rang amongst the trees continues, "[Adam,] where are you?" (Gen. 3:9)

COVENANT COMMUNITY: OLD TESTAMENT FOUNDATIONS

G. Ernest Wright observes that according to the Old Testament the formation of community is God's central act (Wright, 19).

A major way God cultivated this relationship with the creatures He had designed was in the making of covenants. These promise-making acts involved one party binding himself in an act of commitment to another party or parties. Conditions of the treaty were spelled out in the covenant itself.

God covenanted with Abraham as father of the community.

34

While the covenant promise was personalized to Abraham, reference was always made of the covenant's relevance to the people who would issue from his life—a people seen through the eyes of faith as existing already. Witness God's cultivation of relationship, His initiating contact, and His magnanimous giving.

> I will make you into a great nation and I will bless you; I will make your name great, and you will be a blessing. I will bless those who bless you, and whoever curses you I will curse; and all peoples on earth will be blessed through you (Gen. 12:2-3).

> Abram, I am your shield, your very great reward. . . . Look up at the heavens and count the stars—if indeed you can count them. . . . So shall your offspring be (Gen. 15:1, 5).

> This is My covenant with you: You will be the father of many nations. . . . I will establish My covenant as an everlasting covenant between Me and you and your descendants after you for the generations to come, to be your God and the God of your descendants after you. The whole land of Canaan, where you are now an alien, I will give as an everlasting possession to you and your descendants after you; and I will be their God (Gen. 17:4, 7-8).

This promise was reiterated from one generation to the next through the patriarchs.

The founding of the community of Israel was based on the redemptive act of God. It was at Sinai (after having been delivered by their God) that the covenant was renewed with the whole nation that had come out of bondage.

> You yourselves have seen what I did. . . . Now if you obey Me fully and keep My covenant, then out of all nations you will be My treasured possession. Although the whole earth is Mine, you will be for Me a kingdom of priests and a holy nation (Ex. 19:4-6).

God opened up to the Israelites a special relationship, not only with Himself, but with each other. They would together become His priests, His holy nation. Each person would find his or her identity in being related to the community. Some refer to this as "corporate personality" (Kraus, 80). The individuality of a person was not obliterated because each was personally a "child of Israel." But participation in the covenant came as a member of corporate Israel. This created the concept of "individual-in-community." The awareness of the individual's personal responsibility to God did not foster greater individualism but actually increased understanding of the nature of the kind of community where the Spirit bonds persons together into one (Kraus, 86). The meaning of one's personal significance is tied to the fact that one is a part of the corporate unit.

Paul's first letter to the church at Corinth suggests the same idea. "Now the body is not made up of one part but of many. . . . if the whole body were an eye, where would the sense of hearing be? . . . If they were all one part, where would the body be?" (1 Cor. 12:14, 17, 19)

Jesus valued the individual and challenged personal commitment to God and community of believers. Again "relating to God" gives a person identity within the community. "There is no more possibility of personal identity in Christ apart from the brother than there is of loving Christ without loving the brother (1 John 4:20)" (Kraus, 92). Our awareness of who we are as a new person in Christ Jesus is shaped by the identification we have with the body of Christ.

The community shapes us and we build the community. Each of us is responsible and each is representative. Paul warns: "Each one should be careful how he builds" (1 Cor. 3:10). There is no inkling of detached individuals having separated existence apart from others in the community any more than an eye can exist on its own without the body. The body defines who the eye is. It is distinct and individual, but it is nothing without the body.

CONTRAST: SELF-SUFFICIENT INDIVIDUALISM
In contrast to this biblical role of community is individualism. Individualism is the self-sufficiency and independent separation of an autonomous person. The person focused on individualism claims rights and self-fulfillment for the individual. Individuality

(being a unique person), on the other hand, is self-awareness and personhood that are found in taking personal responsibility within a sense of existing in community. In other words, others are impacted by what I do, and I am responsible for that impact. Individuality values the uniqueness of God's created person but always with the thought in mind of what this one contributes to and draws from the corporate body. The image-bearer is always individual-in-community.

Such a concept is foreign to many in the church today because our culture is enamored with individualism, rights, and self. This is the essence of sin.

> Mankind's sin is not the assertion of individuality in community, but the assertion of individual independence and self-sufficiency from God and his fellows.
>
> (Kraus, 85)

Thus Adam wanted to be "like God," Cain denied responsibility for his brother, Achan took silver and gold belonging to God alone, the Babel dwellers determined to make a name for themselves. This self-gratification is individualism (Kraus, 85).

ISRAEL'S INTERDEPENDENCY
God's desire for His covenant people was that they acknowledge a primary dependency upon Him alone. But He also mandated that they acknowledge an interdependency as individuals-in-community. The record of Scripture reveals how He structured Israel to call forth both dimensions. He did this by setting up distinctive requirements for His covenant community.

> Old Testament Israelites were to show mercy by canceling debts made with a "brother." "Every creditor shall cancel the loan he has made to his fellow Israelite. He shall not require payment from his fellow Israelite or brother, because the Lord's time for canceling debts has been proclaimed" (Deut. 15:2).

> The Israelites were to care for their covenant relations. "If there is a poor man among your brothers in any of the

37

towns of the land that the Lord your God is giving you, do
not be hardhearted or tightfisted toward your poor brother"
(Deut. 15:7-8).

Each was to return land and give up slaves when these
involved covenant persons. "If a fellow Hebrew, a man or a
woman, sells himself to you and serves you six years, in the
seventh year you must let him go free. And when you release him, do not send him away empty-handed. Supply him
liberally from your flock, your threshing floor and your
winepress" (Deut. 15:12-14).

While Christians are under a new covenant, this same community awareness is present in the New Testament to be
accorded to fellow believers. "Let us do good to all people,
especially to those who belong to the family of believers"
(Gal. 6:10, NEV).

This deep sense of connectedness is part of what it means to
be a part of the Hebrew race. It runs through generations. We
previously observed that the covenant was made with Abraham
and thus with all his descendants. The covenant went so far as to
include effects of that covenant relationship affecting all other
peoples who interact with the covenant keeping group. With such
widespread connections it is not surprising to find the whole tribe
or people affected by the experience of one of their number.
Thus when Abraham was blessed, Lot also experienced the blessing. Jacob's blessing spilled over onto Laban. Likewise Achan
with his covetousness caused the defeat of the whole people in
the attack on Ai. God sees them collectively. "Israel has
sinned. . . . That is why the Israelites cannot stand against their
enemies" (Josh. 7:10-11). Achan is Israel. To be an Israelite
means you are not an individual with a separate destiny, but an
individual with a corporate destiny (Lee and Cowan, 147–148).
And the Israelite came to love that connectedness with community. In a time of solitary exile the psalmist recalls with longing, "how I used to go with the multitude, leading the procession
to the house of God, with shouts of joy and thanksgiving among
the festive throng" (Ps. 42:4). Facing the treachery of Doeg the

Edomite, David encourages himself with these words: "I will praise You forever for what You have done; in Your name I will hope, for Your name is good. I will praise You in the presence of Your saints" (Ps. 52:9). To be in community with covenant people who join in worship of the God of the covenant was the greatest blessing an Israelite could experience.

Individual fulfillment, Kraus suggests, comes through allying oneself with the life and purposes of the covenant group. In contrast, an individual's worst fate would be to experience being cut off from God's people (Kraus, 81). Judgment of the severest nature was to be severed from the group—to be sent outside the camp.

Paul Miller adds other dimensions of community among the covenant group.

> Judaism had fostered an intense sense of interrelatedness and community. It developed what might be called a "corporate personality." A man was so intensely related to his brother that it was his duty to avenge his brother (II Sam. 14:7). He accepted punishment for his brother's sin (II Sam. 21:1-14). Innocent persons were punished if the head of a household sinned, as seen in the case of Achan (Joshua 7:24). Because a man was regarded as so nearly identical with his brother, levirate marriage was practiced (Deut. 25:5). A parent exercised the right of absolute disposal of a child, all illustrated by Abraham and Isaac (Gen. 22:1), or Jephthah and his daughter (Judg. 11:29), or Reuben offering his sons as hostages (Gen. 42:37).
>
> (P. Miller, 34–35)

Israel's commitment was bifocal. Ruth in aligning herself with Naomi declared, "Your people will be my people and your God my God" (Ruth 1:16). To commit to one, meant commitment to the other. The Jews were called to solidarity with God and with one another. To this day, the majority of Jews remain faithful to this fundamentally communal responsibility for one another.

This corporate sense of identity where the individual identifies with the community is often illustrated in prayer as individuals intercede with and for the community. Moses was not involved in the golden calf transgression nor even present at the scene. He gave evidence of despising what was done. Yet, he spoke not of *them* but of *us* in his contact with God. Note the individual-in-community identification. "O Lord, if I have found favor in Your eyes . . . then let the Lord go with us. Although this is a stiffnecked people, forgive our wickedness and our sin, and take us as Your inheritance" (Ex. 34:9). It is significant to note that Moses made this request in the face of God's suggested option of wiping out the people and beginning again with Moses to build a great nation (Ex. 32:10). His magnificent stance of refusing to bail out of community and instead aligning himself with Israel for the sake of the community is a prelude to the drama at Calvary centuries later where Jesus' commitment to the Father and to us kept Him from responding to the challenge, "save yourself" (Luke 23:37).

Nehemiah had a comfortable position in a foreign court, but his corporate identity caused him to relate to those suffering judgment in his homeland.

> Let Your ear be attentive and Your eyes open to hear the prayer Your servant is praying before You day and night for Your servants, the people of Israel. I confess the sins we Israelites, including myself and my father's house, have committed against You. We have acted very wickedly toward You. We have not obeyed the commands, decrees and laws You gave Your servant Moses (Neh. 1:6-7).

Daniel, righteous prophet, also speaks in terms of community as he addressed God. "We have sinned and done wrong. We have been wicked and have rebelled; we have turned away from Your commands and laws" (Dan. 9:5). Daniel himself has been depicted as keeping the commands and is affirmed by the angelic messenger as one "highly esteemed" (Dan. 10:11). Yet he remains also as "individual-in-community."

The above three illustrations reveal how far the concept of community had come from the early pages of Genesis where the cry was more often, "It's not my fault." This sense of corporate responsibility is difficult, if not impossible to find in the current evangelical scene. Our concept of community must be reshaped

40

by our theology and not by our culture. The fact that the divine perspective seems so far from what we experience today is evidence of how distorted the image has become. What evidences can you cite of this sense of commitment to and identification with others who share the same loyalties you do? Family evidences of sensing individuality but within a committed community? Church experience of assuming corporate responsibility for one person's actions?

God's commitment to the creation of a sense of corporate responsibility bears fruit in these Old Testament responses. In a larger sense the covenant community signals hope in that it gives supportive evidence that God is still trying to cultivate relationship with His image-bearers even after the Fall. There are flashes of the "before-the-Fall" purity in relationships with others unmarred by autonomous self-centeredness.

The last book of the Old Testament, Malachi, contains an ever recurring theme—God's faithfulness to His character and His openness to renewed relationship. " 'I the Lord do not change. So you, O descendants of Jacob, are not destroyed. . . . Return to Me, and I will return to you,' says the Lord Almighty" (Mal. 3:6-7). The Old Testament closes with the promise of One who would minister healing in a broken community. "See, I will send you the prophet Elijah before that great and dreadful day of the Lord comes. He will turn the hearts of the fathers to their children, and the hearts of the children to their fathers" (Mal. 4:5-6). The record ends on a ray of hope for renewed community—with our Maker and with one another.

2

NEWNESS OF COMMUNITY: THE NEW TESTAMENT COMMUNITY

A new command I give you: Love one another.
John 13:34

T he first Testament reveals God's grand design for community—a relationship built with Him and among those who bear His image. This divine schema is majestic in its outlines for it reflects the interdependence of the Godhead who in concert create a being to reflect in limited measure an image of the divine relationship. The pure reflection of this image results in harmonious dependency, intimacy, and open trust.

The introduction of self-sufficient individualism disrupts this interdependence. Relationship with God is not terminated but it experiences estrangement. The divine image reflected in Adam and Eve is marred by alienation, self-centeredness, and mistrust. The innocence is gone. So is the garden community.

Through generations of covenant keeping and law making, God maintained continuing relationship with the image-bearer, cultivating a modified corporate bond—a sense of community— between the chosen ones. But by the time of the Incarnation there were few who knew God intimately, some who knew of God conceptually or religiously, and many who struggled just to survive, looking for temporal rescue from an impersonal God who was oblivious to their everyday existence. It was the "religiosa" who kept God out of the reach of the ordinary individual. The code of commandments became arcane and absurdly complex. Neighbor relations with Samaritans settled comfortably into prejudice. Women and children were devalued and oppressed. Slavery was expedient. The diseased and the poor were an inconvenient drain on society. Social and religious lines were clearly drawn and unquestioned. Community was formed primarily to protect the standing of the individual. In a dry and burdened land the garden community seemed an illusory mirage.

When the time had fully come, God sent His Son born as an image-bearer. While the first Adam bore His image, the second Adam was "the exact representation of His being"—He was the radiance of God's glory, glory as the only begotten of the Father. The Father sent a Person into our world that we might again know authentic relationship. The Son came that we might know life. Life is knowing God—being intimately acquainted with Him. This Sent One didn't just talk about relating to God. He personified it. He didn't allow truth to remain cold and conceptual. He lived it. When Martha in grief recited the cold objective truth, "I know [my brother] will rise again in the resurrection at the last day," Jesus turned the truth into personal reality—"I am the resurrection and the life" (John 11:24-25). Anyone who knew Jesus well knew that truth relationally. He, as a person, was that truth. One cannot have relationship with a concept. But one can relate to a person. Because God is love, wisdom, holiness, and power, we can relate in ways not possible if we view God as only knowing, explaining, illustrating, defining, or revealing these qualities. Because He personifies these things, we not only can understand them—we intimately embrace them in relating to Him. As we "know" Him, we also "know" them. Community comes from interpersonal encounter. In Jesus we have communion with the Father and the Spirit. What all the words of the law and the first Testament could not convey, God communicated in the personal relationship of the Son.

Interpersonal relations among humankind were changed too. As Kraus notes, the incarnation did not result in a new book of theology or a new code of ethics. It resulted in a new community. Not a new principle or idea, but a new order (Kraus, 70).

NEWNESS IN COMMUNITY

Jesus, in His coming, transformed our relationship with the Father. He revealed a personal waiting Father, a Father who knows what you need before you ask Him (Matt. 6:8), a Father who forgives (Matt. 6:14), a Father who cares for common birds and clothes the grass of the field (Matt. 6:26-30), a Father who gives good gifts to His children (Matt. 7:11), and on and on. He showed His followers the Father's love. "As the Father has loved Me, so have I loved you" (John 15:9). This called them to trust the Father (John 14:1). It was an intimate, personal relationship that He portrayed. Those closest to Him responded to this model. They came to know the Father, to love and trust Him because they came to know Jesus in a personal, relational way. They loved Him and He was God in the flesh. God welcomed them into the community of restored sons and daughters He was seeking to create.

Jesus also transformed relations among human beings. There is no relational system He did not touch. "Jesus' direct and profound experience of God as his father . . . and Jesus' simultaneous recognition that the consequences of that relationship inundate all other relationships everywhere and all the time" created conditions for major transformation in personal encounters. The parenthood of God transforms our relationships, reconstructing our human systems (Lee and Cowan, 146, 150).

It is impossible to divorce the proclamation of the Gospel from its impact on personal alliances. The natural family is engulfed by the eternal family. Responding to the subtle pressure of His mother and brothers who would take charge of Him, Jesus establishes new connections. "Here are My mother and My brothers! Whoever does God's will is My brother and sister and mother" (Mark 3:34-35). Neighborliness is redefined. Need, not value systems, now determines "neighbor." As Lee and Cowan profoundly observe, "Need puts us in each other's back yard!" (Lee and Cowan, 149) The specialness normally reserved for our friends is now to be lavished on our enemies. Domination and hierarchical systems are out. To be leader, one must serve (Mark 10:41-45). Patriarchal rule is renounced (Matt. 23:8-10). We are brothers and sisters, family to each other (Lee and Cowan, 150–151).

The husband-wife relationship is compared to a new paradigm,

Christ and the church (Eph. 5:22-32). The father-child association is laced with mutual respect and understanding (Eph. 6:1-4). Slaves and masters are cautioned to condition their responses as though they were "before the face of God." The disdained and the guilty are perceived through nonjudgmental filters. The natural boundaries of nationality, gender, age, economic status must no longer be divisive. Being in community with God means revolutionary rethinking in the arena of mutuality. "So there is no piece of the relational web, whether minisystem or megasystem, that is untouched by Jesus' experience of what God's relationship with us creates among us" (Lee and Cowan, 149). "For all of you who were baptized into Christ have clothed yourselves with Christ. There is neither Jew nor Greek, slave nor free, male nor female, for you are all one in Christ Jesus" (Gal. 3:26-27). A relational revolution was taking place.

A GOSPEL OF COMMUNITY
As has already been noted, Jesus came proclaiming a Gospel that has at its very essence relationships. Leonardo Boff in his hope-filled book, *Ecclesiogenesis: The Base Communities Reinvent the Church,* states it boldly.

> Jesus' whole preaching may be seen as an effort to awaken the strength of these community aspects. In the horizontal dimension Jesus called human beings to mutual respect, generosity, a communion of sisters and brothers, and simplicity in relationships. Vertically he sought to open the human being to a sincere filial relationship with God, to the artlessness of simple prayer, and to generous love for God.
> (Boff, 7)

A cursory glance at the content of Jesus' teaching reveals numerous examples of this. Striking in its newness of perspective, the Sermon on the Mount addresses anger between brothers, "anyone who is angry with his brother will be subject to judgment" (Matt. 5:22) and responses toward enemies, "Love your enemies and pray for those who persecute you, that you may be sons of your Father in heaven" (Matt. 5:44-45). Note that sonship and horizontal actions are connected in this command. Forgiveness on the horizontal plane is linked with forgiveness in the vertical. "If you forgive men when they sin against you, your heavenly Father will also forgive you. But if you do not forgive men their sins, your Father will not forgive your sins" (Matt. 6:14-15). Judging others is condemned. "In the same way you judge others, you will be judged" (Matt. 7:2). Jesus taught that our worship is impacted by our relationships. "If you are offering your gift at the altar and there remember that your brother has something against you, leave your gift there in front of the altar. First go and be reconciled to your brother; then come and offer your gift" (Matt. 5:23-24). The Gospel places high priority on acceptance regardless of social standing. "Whoever welcomes this little child in My name welcomes Me; and whoever welcomes Me welcomes the one who sent Me" (Luke 9:48). Domination was not a part of the Gospel. "You know that the rulers of the Gentiles lord it over them, and their high officials exercise authority over them. Not so with you. Instead, whoever wants to become great among you must be your servant" (Matt. 20:25-26).

Observe the content of the parables. They reflect either our relational life with God or our relational life together among ourselves (Lee and Cowan, 149). These two focuses were at the heart of Jesus' teaching.

Perhaps one of the most profound insights into the Gospel as relationship is its connection with the Law. Jesus revealed the underlying relational truth of the Law when He summarized the Law in the two greatest commandments. " 'Love the Lord your God with all your heart and with all your soul and with all your mind.' This is the first and greatest commandment. And the second is like it: 'Love your neighbor as yourself.' All the Law and the Prophets hang on these two commandments" (Matt. 22:37-40). Loving God — restoring that lost vertical relationship — is the essence of everything God intended when He gave the Law. Everything else in the Law elaborates these two commands. "The Law tells us what the repaired image of God should look like, and it summarizes that repaired image in terms of loving relationships with God and men (H. Miller, 40). The Law which Jesus fulfilled is summarized in relationships — vertical and horizontal. Community is never an option. Jesus recognized that the very heart of God's revelation of Himself in the Old Testament was this mandate for community. His most severe criticism was directed toward the religious keepers of the law who forfeited relationships to preserve their religious "purity." It was unconscionable to put rules above persons. God revealed Himself to persons for the sake of relationship, not to set up rules to keep them afar off. "Why does He eat with tax collectors and 'sinners'?" (Mark 2:16) was the Pharisees' question. Jesus' answer, "Woe to you, teachers of the law and Pharisees, you hypocrites! You give a tenth of your spices—mint, dill and cumin. But you have neglected the more important matters of the law—justice, mercy and faithfulness" (Matt. 23:23). So the Savior prioritizes our encounters with one another.

To love a neighbor was to love the world of persons God had made, the image-bearers. Jesus communicates the specifics of this in His teaching. The meaning of what it means to love God was the subject of much of His proclamation. But Jesus added a new commandment for those who are a part of the new community. "Love one another. As I have loved you, so you must love one another. All men will know that you are My disciples if you love one another" (John 13:34-35). This specific emphasis on cultivating community in the manner of Jesus with those who are His is what will reflect His image in the world.

Such dual emphasis on communion with God and special care for the community of believers laces through the rest of the New Testament. Where we find one, the other is not far behind. There is regular interchange between these two focuses. The epistles abound with Paul's recognition of the presence of these two elements. "We always thank God . . . because we have heard of *your faith in Christ Jesus* and of the *love* you have *for all the saints*" (Col. 1:3-4). To the Ephesians, "For this reason, ever since I heard about *your faith in the Lord Jesus* and *your love for all the saints,* I have not stopped giving thanks for you" (Eph. 1:15-16). "We ought always to thank God for you, brothers, and rightly so, because *your faith is growing* more and more, and the *love* every one of you has *for each other is increasing*" (2 Thes. 1:3). "In view of God's mercy . . . offer your bodies as living sacrifices, *holy and pleasing to God*—which is your spiritual worship. . . . Just as each of us has one body with many members, and these members do not all have the same function, so in Christ we who are many form one body, and *each member belongs to all the others"* (Rom. 12:1, 4-5). "Let us be thankful and so worship God acceptably with reverence and awe. . . . *Keep on loving each other* as brothers" (Heb. 12:28–13:2, the chapter break not being in the original letter). Note the dual sacrifices of Hebrews 13:15-16, "Through Jesus . . . let us continually offer to God a sacrifice of praise – the fruit of *lips that confess His name.* And do not forget *to do good* and *to share with others,* for with such sacrifices God is pleased." Often the two community emphases are bound into one as in Hebrews 6:10, "God . . . will not forget your *work and the love you have shown Him* as you have *helped His people* and continue to help them."

The first epistle of John is classic in its revelation of the connection between the dual relationships. Apparently John faced a Gnostic spiritualizing which caused believers to devalue relationships with one another. *Gnostic* comes from the word *gnosis* or *knowledge.* Gnostic teaching put value on spiritual "knowing" with everything material viewed as evil. By making the relationship with God into a spiritual knowledge with little or no accent on how we treat one another, we deny the Creator's desire that we reflect His image. John says it is impossible to separate one part of the image from the other. Loving God is primary to entering life in the body, but loving others is a necessity for those who enter. "Anyone who claims to be in the light but hates his brother is still in the darkness" (1 John 2:9).

Likewise, "We know that we have passed from death to life, because we love our brothers" (1 John 3:14). Note the twofold emphasis in 1 John 3:23, "And this is His command: *to believe in the name of His Son,* Jesus Christ, and *to love one another* as He commanded us." "We should not think of love as the cause of relatedness. We are already related whether we like it or not. What love does is redeem our relatedness. Nor, for that matter, does the parenthood of God cause us to be related. Rather, it transforms the total texture of our relatedness – or, to put it differently, it reconstructs our human systems" (Lee and Cowan, 150).

John recognizes that to transform and redeem this relatedness, love must be expressed in more than abstract terms. It must be actualized. "Dear children, let us not love with words or tongue but with actions and in truth" (1 John 3:18). Such practical orthopraxy is "how we know that we belong to the truth" (1 John 3:19). This is not a "love in principle" but a love in everyday action. It is not a love based on convenience or comfortableness or on the lovableness of the "brother." John's argument reaches its climax in 5:1, "Everyone who believes that Jesus is the Christ is born of God, and everyone who loves the Father loves His child as well." Miller suggests that it never occurred to John or any of the other apostles that it was possible to be in relationship with God and not to be in community with the family of God. "We are created to bear God's image before the world, in both its horizontal and vertical facets" (H. Miller, 94–95). The Gospel in its treatment of relatedness seems radical when compared with our present-day pseudo-fellowship.

Banks dynamically reiterates the community awareness of the Gospel by writing, "The gospel is not a purely personal matter. It has a social dimension. It is a communal affair. To embrace the gospel, then, is to enter into community. One cannot have the one without the other" (Banks, 33).

> He spent most of His time — reserved most of His instruction for the twelve.
>
> Their fellowship during those three years involved a growing commitment to Christ and a growing commitment to one another. Devotion to Christ was not enough. . . .
>
> They had to learn to live together, to love one another, to serve one another, to work in harmony.
>
> Richard C. Halverson
> *Somehow Inside of Eternity,* 73

A PARADIGM OF COMMUNITY

Jesus not only proclaimed community. He constructed it. "Jesus did not select the Twelve as founders of future churches. *Jesus established the Twelve as a community; as messianic, eschatological church.* The apostles are not to be understood first and foremost as individuals, but precisely as the *Twelve,* as messianic community gathered around Jesus and his Spirit" (Boff, 28).

Ralph T. Morton has written a book for the Iona Fellowship on this very theme. *The Twelve Together* is so named because Morton saw their life together as the basis of their training. The

disciples must be seen as a body not merely a collection of individuals. The impact of being together with one another and with
Him was that they came to view themselves as a body—His
body—the church (Morton, *The Twelve Together,* 10).

So important is the creation of this community in the eyes of
Morton that he claims the story of the Gospels is not the unfolding history of the experience of Jesus, but a history of the formation of the corporate identity of the disciples as they found life
with Jesus (Morton, *The Twelve Together,* 11). The Gospels show
truth and life as seen through the eyes of the community in which
He invested His life and energy. Who He was is revealed to
them. How He taught and lived is experienced by them. The
major energy of His ministry is invested in them. Howard Snyder
puts this in shocking perspective. Judging from the Gospel
records, he says, "Jesus Christ actually gave more time to preparing a community of disciples than to proclaiming the good news"
(Snyder, *The Problem of Wineskins,* 74).

Some of the disciples' most profound lessons evolved out of
their being in community with one another. Christ's command to
"wash one another's feet" (John 13:14) has more impact when
one realizes that the disciples sometimes saw each other as com-
petitors for position with Jesus. They knew each other's flaws
and blind spots because of having lived together. It would be far
easier to serve a stranger, one you didn't know so much about.
The intensity of this kind of living and learning is well stated in
the book *Dangerous Memories:* "To care for each other and accept each other's care in this spirit of deeply paschal mutuality is
to place the relational events of everyday community life in the
ultimate context of love. It is to become one body. It is to reenact
in present relationships the dangerous memory of Jesus' love"
(Lee and Cowan, 122).

The celebration of the supper that took place as setting for the
foot-washing was traditionally a family meal. The symbolic significance of sharing this family memorial meal away from their
households and with this new family of faith must have added
depth to such teachings as "those who do the will of God—these
are my family," and "no one who has left home or brothers or
sisters or mother or father or children or fields for Me and the
gospel will fail to receive a hundred times as much in this present

age" (Mark 10:30). Family, in the Old Testament sense, is not only the place of belonging and the source of accountability, but also a source of protection. Children were a joy and a form of social security for old age. Fields were the sacred inheritance promised by God and highly valued. So it is highly significant that Jesus speaks of the new family of faith which far surpasses in importance the biological family. In this new family, Christ, instead of patriarch, is head. Treasured inheritance of land to support them is left behind, but what is given is a supportive community as "new land" to provide for their needs. And it was theirs in abundance — a hundredfold (Lohfink, 41–42).

As the community of disciples plays a part in Jesus' ministry, it becomes His body in action. And the major part is played not by the disciples as individuals but by these men as a corporate unit (Morton, *The Twelve Together,* 24). All of this is in keeping with the primary and distinguishing feature of their role — their life together with Him. He was not training them to be individuals. At some points he was actually preparing them to play roles much different from what the individual wanted.

This does not mean that their God-given individuality was eliminated. Being in community enabled them to learn how much they needed the others and what they could contribute to the building up of the whole. Jesus was setting up a model for the church, a model that taught them dependency on one another, a model they would operate under in the Acts. A.B. Bruce comments on this pattern.

> It gives one a pleasant surprise to think of Simon the zealot and Matthew the publican, men coming from so opposite quarters, meeting together in close fellowship in the little band of twelve. In the persons of these two disciples extremes meet — the tax-gatherer and the tax-hater; the unpatriotic Jew, who degraded himself by becoming a servant of the alien ruler; and the Jewish patriot, who chafed under the foreign yoke, and sighed for emancipation. This union of opposites was not accidental, but was designed by Jesus as a prophecy of the future.
>
> (Bruce, 35–36)

By calling them into community Jesus gave the disciples opportunity to remold old habit patterns and establish new ones. They experienced Him in relationship. The Gospels pulsate with personal interactiveness. He ate with them, sailed with them, walked with them, went home with them, reasoned with them, cared for them, challenged them, worked with them, believed in them, shared his desires and goals with them. He recognized that their life together with Him would be the basis of their witness when He was gone.

"When the Counselor comes . . . He will testify about Me; but you also must testify, for you have been with Me from the beginning" (John 15:26-27). Luke is careful to point out that his work came directly from those "who from the first were eyewitnesses and servants of the word" (Luke 1:2). Peter assures Cornelius, "We are witnesses of everything he did in the country of the Jews and in Jerusalem" (Acts 10:39). The Law was written, read, and interpreted. The Gospel was lived, modeled, and proclaimed in a community context.

As the Twelve came to know Him and to embrace His values of mutuality among one another, they also embraced His model of relating to the Father. He talked about knowing the Father and it was evident that He did. When He used the word "know" it was in the Hebrew sense of personal contact, loving, intimate interaction. Such knowing could never be solely a function of the mind—it was communion. That was the way they knew Him. And in knowing Him, they knew the Father. In knowing Him, they also came to know each other in such a personal, corporate way that they would be called His body.

One of the appealing aspects about Jesus is His careful attention to individuals. He seldom saw persons en masse. Each was valuable and worthy of His ministry. However, it is also characteristic of Jesus that He was regularly involved in establishing community "precisely for those who were denied community at that time, or who were judged inferior in respect to religion" (Lohfink, 88). Thus we find Jesus open to women, to tax collectors and sinners, to the poor and the abused, to the lowly tradesmen of His day. These persons would become, in community, the devoted subjects in the new kingdom, the genesis of the church.

A NEW COMMUNITY OF WITNESS – THE CHURCH

Thus it was to the community of witnesses and not to individuals as such that the messianic mission was given. The community is central to representing the incarnation of Christ. "According to Luke, the disciples were actually instructed to withhold verbal witness to the resurrection until the new community of the Spirit was formed as the authenticating context for their message (Luke 24:48-49)" (Kraus, 23). It was in the forming of this community that meaning came to their mission and message. The community of believers actually became the means of establishing the validity and authority of an individual's witness.

They portrayed in actuality what believers verbally described. Thus they became a "community of interpretation," embodying in relationships the meaning of the Gospel announcement. By their very lifestyle they interpreted scriptural meaning (Kraus, 71). Even today Scripture is interpreted primarily (by unbelievers and believers) by how the Gospel is lived more than by principles of interpretation. Acts records that Peter was "standing in the midst" of the disciples when he interpreted the Gospel for Pentecost celebrants (Acts 15:28). Thus it was community, under the direction of the Spirit, that offered the context for discernment and obedience as the first-century church worked out the Gospel in relationships (Kraus, 72).

A study of Acts reveals that community was fundamental to, not optional for, early Christians' experience. In passages where the apostles deal with responsiveness to God, in the second breath, there is emphasis on the corresponding relationship to His family. The writer of Ephesians commends for "faith in the Lord Jesus and love toward all the saints" (Eph. 1:15). Each epistle echoes this dual emphasis of relationship with God coupled with living out the Gospel with brothers and sisters in the faith. Hebrews speaks of offering a "sacrifice of praise" to God and a "sacrifice" of "doing good and sharing with others." Both of these are listed as pleasing God (Heb. 13:15-16).

Banks notes this dual connection in Paul's writings.

For Paul the gospel bound men and women to one another as well as to God. Acceptance by Christ necessitated acceptance of those whom he had already welcomed (Rom. 15:7);

reconciliation with God entailed reconciliation with others that exhibited the character of the gospel preaching (Phil. 4:2-3); union in the Spirit involved union with one another, for the Spirit was primarily a shared, not individual experience. The gospel is not a purely personal matter. It has a social dimension. It is a communal affair.

(Banks, 33)

The concept of togetherness that was fostered in the early church is highly significant. It is graphically depicted in the "one another" passages found in the epistles. Believers are admonished to numerous responses that will develop such togetherness. They are called to such behaviors as:

giving honor to one another (Rom. 12:10);
living harmoniously with one another (Rom. 12:16);
admonishing one another (Rom. 15:14);
waiting for each other (1 Cor. 11:33);
demonstrating equal care for one another (1 Cor. 12:25);
serving one another (Gal. 5:13);
bearing burdens of each other (Gal. 6:2);
giving comfort to one another (1 Thes. 5:11);
building up each other (1 Thes. 5:11);
maintaining peace with each other (1 Thes. 5:13);
doing good to one another (1 Thes. 5:15);
lovingly bearing with each other (Eph. 4:2);
being subject to each other (Eph. 5:21);
forgiving one another (Col. 3:13);
confessing to and praying for each other (James 5:16);
exhibiting hospitality to each other (1 Peter 4:9).

This partial listing reveals the call to the whole community to participate in this kind of living. As a community they were called to this kind of collective edification. It was not individualistic and internal as much as it was outward expression in a local community. This is New Testament style "edification" *(oikodome-oikodomein)* (Lohfink, 100). And such "upbuilding" was equally enjoined in everyday living as in the liturgical setting as each shared a hymn or lesson or revelation so that all might be enriched to grow (Lohfink, 103). Such community mindedness and community motivated action is almost a foreign idea for our modern self-centered conduct.

The corporate responsibility painted across the canvas of the New Testament is shocking to us moderns who have grown up in a culture that stresses individual responsibility. The biblical conception of everyone who belongs to a community sharing in responsibility for all aspects of that community is counter to our "leader-responsible-for-all" mentality.

For example, all are responsible for the conduct of the community. The behavior of community members is revealed to be of such a nature that the whole community will be impacted by the conduct of a few. In like manner, all in the community share in the responsibility of dealing with that behavior (1 Cor. 5:1-5; Gal. 6:1; James 5:19-20). Discipline and nurture of community members is the concern of all within the community. Infractions of godly living were never private affairs. The entire local church was debilitated. Sin was a community concern. The corrector must also be open to correction. Mutual admonition produced health in the life of the church (Rom. 15:14). Domination by hierarchical tiers of authority, as evident in the world system, found no place in God's "new order." To be a member was to be responsible. Fractures in unity brought the church into action. Conflicts were to be resolved absolutely, not just driven underground or ignored as incidental. Bondedness was too important to be threatened by negative individual differences. Continual growth of all was too vital an issue to be isolated to a limited few who led—all must "instruct one another" (1 Cor. 14:31; Col. 3:16; Eph. 4:15), and thus take responsibility for contributing particular insights given to one for the benefit of the whole. Special abilities are never for self-indulgence but for community enrichment (1 Cor. 14).

> Whenever individualism tended to break down the community, Paul seems to have reminded his readers that God had called them into a "fellowship" (1 Cor. 10:16). Where the "strong" within the community wanted to ignore the "weak" Paul reminded them that God had called them into a Christian community (Rom. 14:1-15:13).
>
> James Thompson
> *Our Life Together*, 15

Leadership responsibilities became a corporate affair. Such is the radical unfolding of God's family living as unveiled in the theology of the New Testament (Lohfink, 103–106; Banks, *Paul's Idea of Community,* 139–141).

While realizing the reality of human inadequacy and failure when it comes to relationships, nevertheless, the Apostle Paul continually places before the community a vision of what one day would be reality and which the present community must emulate in their common life together (Banks, 188). Community was and is kingdom living in the making. We are never closer to the heart of God than when we respond corporately to Him and His Word as His corporate people who reflect His glory. He chooses to be glorified in His church and in His Son (Eph. 3:21). The people of God amplify the voice of God in declaring the Gospel as good news for all (Peterson, 98).

Community consciousness and development is inherent in both the Old and New Testaments. It flows from the lips and actions of Jesus, it is basic to the theology that pours from the pen of Paul, it is portrayed in the teaching of the apostles. It pulses in the Gospels and is the heartbeat of the early church. It does not replace or supersede man's relationship Godward, but it is absolute necessity for one who would be God-related.

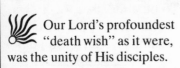
Our Lord's profoundest "death wish" as it were, was the unity of His disciples.

Richard C. Halverson
How I Changed My Thinking About the Church, 53

"The authentic religious heritage of Judaism and Christianity is primarily a communal and not an individualistic one. It shows how we are to be *together* in the world, not just how to be good individuals. It reminds us that 'who is my neighbor?' is our most fundamental kind of question." It is the "way we have learned from Christ" (Lee and Cowan, 120–121).

3

THE UNDERMINING
OF COMMUNITY:
INDIVIDUALISM

He cannot have God for his Father who does
not take the church for his mother.
John Calvin

I n what ways do you see your life, your attitudes, your values, your responses, and your theology affected by individualism?

While the concept of community is deeply rooted in biblical soil, we live in the day of the self-made individualist. "Meism" is nurtured as a cardinal virtue. Self-centered individualism is considered an essential right of being a person. This is the principal language of our time.

It is not surprising therefore that we view people and society as "things" to be "used" for our individual satisfaction and growth. It goes without question that the individual predominates over the group. This mentality threads through our approach to all strata of relationship building.

Friendship today is viewed as important for meeting "my personal needs." Dyrness notes that even the vocabulary we use indicates the priority of the isolated individual in *choosing* to develop relationships. "We 'make' friends, we 'work' on our relationships" (Dyrness, 103). The optional nature of such connectedness is obvious. Allan Bloom in his sweeping synopsis of the student world depicts young people today as self-centered in relationships, where the underlying tone is freedom and few obligations. Personal, momentary gratification is not experienced as love and is often not characterized by any sense of moral commitment to one another—it is a relationship with no rigid strings of attachment (Bloom, 123–125).

Marriage is also viewed as a chance to enhance "my growth" and have "my needs cared for." The personal fulfillment requirements now placed upon a marriage are multitudinous. The union is seen as a contract for convenience. The freedom to move into and out of this contract is a matter of individual choice. The option to have children, to stay married, and a host of other free choices common today have created "a new atmosphere for marriage and a new meaning for family life" (Bellah, 110). If a relationship does not fulfill us—whether friendship, group, church, marriage, or other—it can be easily discarded. "I'm not having my needs met" is justification for discarding any relationship. We must move on and not look back. In a "throw-away" world we have the "notion that relationships are 'things' to be selected and rejected at our convenience" (Gaede, 140).

The family itself is seen as the sphere for producing self-reliant, independent individuals who are deemed successful when they deny their need of the relationship. Bellah's interviews for his book *Habits of the Heart* reveal the family as reinforcing the priority of separateness. "The idea we have of ourselves as individuals on our own, who earn everything we get, accept no handouts or gifts, and free ourselves from our families of origin turns out, ironically enough, to be one of the things that holds us together" (Bellah, 62). Even the recent publicity and remedial help for the phenomenon of codependency fosters in its wake a fear that *any* kind of dependency on a relationship is a sign of frailty and a cause for alarm. Self-sufficiency and preservation are promoted and pursued.

The passion for self-fulfillment at any cost has accentuated our need for personal autonomy and separateness. We can decide on our own. Nobody tells us what to do. We can also "drop out" if that is what is required to insure our freedom. This condition has become so prevalent that we have given the category a label, "Midlife Crisis," though the response is not limited to the midlife era exclusively. Individuals leave spouses, children, and responsibilities behind in pursuit of "freedom." In formerly unprecedented moves, the individual exercises his "right" to do whatever he wants, whenever he wants, without concern for the effect of his actions (Miller, 66). In like manner persons today quit jobs, break moral rules, and abdicate responsibilities with no more explanation than the self-focused, "I felt (or didn't feel) like doing it." We live with these "new rules of the game" in operation in our world. Rare is the family untouched by one of these scenarios of autonomy.

"Rights language" is becoming our native tongue. Moral decisions are increasingly made on the basis of rights rather than absolutes and virtues (MacIntyre, 64–67). Dyrness summarizes MacIntyre's views in this way: "What is demanded by the individual—has come to replace virtue language—the good practiced by the person" (Dyrness, 97). It is interesting to note that the concept of personal rights as we know it did not even have a means of expression in Hebrew, Greek, Latin, Arabic, or Old English before the Middle Ages, or Japanese before the mid-nineteenth century. Individual rights were invented to lend support to autonomy (MacIntyre, 67–68). Kraus speaks of this emphasis on the autonomy of the individual as identifying " 'freedom' with 'individual independence.' Likewise, " 'civil rights' means the individual's right to 'life, liberty, and the pursuit of happiness' " (Kraus, 76). The media frequently notes crimes that go unpunished because of the offsetting factor of intrusion on another's personal rights. America is considered a nation with a low ratio of citizens per lawyer as suits to preserve these "rights" proliferate. Rights, autonomy, freedom—each fosters the other. Bloom, in his book, *The Closing of The American Mind,* states it succinctly, "In modern political regimes, where rights precede duties, freedom definitely has primacy over community, family, and even nature" (Bloom, 113). But is "freedom" actually found in self-centered individualism?

Competition is handmaid to individualism. And competition in America is as normative as baseball and apple pie. Many would list competition as having made America what it is today. We have grown up feeling that we are responsible for our success and we must take every opportunity to stay ahead of the competition. Our proverbs reflect this sense of responsibility for our own destiny. "He who hesitates is lost." "Strike while the iron is hot." "The early bird catches the worm." This attitude has invaded Christendom as well. We pride ourselves on being "better Christians" than others. Though we sing "saved by grace," we quickly lapse into a "do-it-yourself" kind of Christian living. It is as though we start with God, but then take great pride in "making it on our own." Success in the world's point of view is the "self-made person." "Our culture thinks that the person who really deserves our respect is the one who started with nothing and made himself important with no one else's help" (Miller, 66). We admire those who are not dependent on others. Independence is not just celebrated on July 4. Our heroes are the

> On Capitol Hill individualism is rampant. There are now 535 political parties in Congress, the same number as members.
>
> John Naisbitt and Patricia Aburdene
> *Megatrends 2000*, 302

solo survivors, the prima donnas, the Lone Rangers, and the self-sufficient entrepreneurs who made it to the top by climbing over others. Our country was founded on such a capitalistic spirit.

Such strong identification with individualism is bound to pervade our groups. In fact, Kraus claims that "the group has become for us a collection of individuals created by individuals for their own individual advantages" (Kraus, 76–77). We are preoccupied with "what can I get" from "joining" with others. Dyrness boldly declares, "In general, Americans do not join groups for what they can contribute, but for what they can get out of them" (Dyrness, 98–99). Any association is to meet *my* needs. It becomes difficult to advance another with what you have to offer when an individualistic, competitive spirit suggests this offering may give her the advantage, power, and status over you. We are enculturated into building our own kingdoms and we take greater pride in personal achievement than in group enterprise where the individual's progress depends on and enhances all. We fear letting another know our weakness because it could be used against us. "Dying to self" is basically un-American.

Current scenarios are a far cry from the community depicted in the biblical vision given by God. In many ways the present individualism is also far removed from the conditions envisioned by those who came to a new land to found new values. In 1630 John Winthrop, first governor of the Massachusetts Bay Colony, enjoined his fellow colonists, "We must delight in each other, make others' conditions our own, rejoice together, mourn together, labor and suffer together, always having before our eyes our community as members of the same body" (Winthrop, 92).

WHAT IS INDIVIDUALISM?

Individualism as pictured above is a distortion of the biblical view of the sacredness of the person. It is a perversion of God's intentions in fashioning us as unique created beings, no two alike. The person, as designed by God, is no threat to the building of community. To be an individual is God-given.

Bellah and his associates depict two crucial distinctions in understanding individualism. The first depiction is a "belief in the inherent dignity, indeed the sacredness, of the individual." The second framework is "a belief that the individual has a primary reality whereas society is a second-order, derived or artificial construct" (Bellah, et al., 334). This latter view basically asserts that individuals with their self-interests come first and have priority. Relationships are formed voluntarily to maximize that self-interest. In plain language, "I will relate to you if it does something for me." The individual is superior and controls the relationship to her own end. Bellah and colleagues warn against this isolated perspective where the individual thinks he can stand alone, not needing others unless he determines so (Bellah, et al., 143). Such self-centeredness makes the individual responsible only to himself and for himself.

Kraus draws a similar distinction calling the first view "individuality" and the second, "individualism." Speaking from an Old Testament framework he sees individuality as calling "attention to the individual as a responsible person in community, while the latter [individualism] exalts the independence of the individual and his private rights. Individuality is affirmed in the form and content of the covenant; individualism is considered a matter of alienation and pride" (Kraus, 84–85). This latter perspective is the essence of sin—being individually independent and self-sufficient from God and from others. Adam wanted to gratify himself and be self-sufficient—to "be as God," as the tempter put it. Sin

61

is never seen as recognizing individual rights within community nor taking individual responsibility before God or others. Old Testament leaders exhibited this kind of self-awareness and responsibility while assuming strong identity with the group and even taking responsibility for group sins (Kraus, 85). Pursuit of personal interests was never the sole consideration. While the individual in covenant relationship could default, the whole group felt the pain and the separation, and worked together to restore and renew the relationship.

Dyrness argues that the "basic content of autonomous individualism is not biblical. We are not made to be individuals . . . we are created in and for relationship" (Dyrness, 101). And it is in relationship that we reflect His image as He is in relationship in the Godhead.

The common themes which occur throughout the works discussed above are: self-fulfillment, autonomy, rights, freedom, self-centeredness. These are the facets of negative individualism and the factors that mitigate against community.

Individualism puts self at the center of a person's world — everything revolves around the nurturing, exalting, and gratifying of that self. "I'm looking out for number one" is the phrase which reflects this facet. Personal success at the cost of all else, satisfaction of needs and drives, standing up for my rights, getting my due — these are the expressions of a self-driven culture.

Autonomy refers to self-directing freedom and moral independence. Inherent in autonomy is the idea of self-sufficiency and personal responsibility. But individualism distorts this self-assumed responsibility to the point of abdicating any responsibility for others. "Am I my brother's keeper?" Autonomy sees the self as superior to and isolated from others. Autonomy exalts freedom, emphasizing freedom from conformity to anything outside self. It abhors restrictions and self-denial and prides itself in "being one's own person." In its distortion it denies relatedness to others and operates as if no one else exists, taking no responsibility for the "fall out" of actions and decisions made by the single-focused self. "That's not my problem" is the expression of one who has removed himself emotionally from the group and cares only for what concerns him.

Though it aims for freedom, self-fulfillment, and self-sufficiency, individualism has not brought all it promised. It is not the idealized state once portrayed as the end of all being. "The American individualism so characteristic of the contemporary United States generates a pervasive loneliness and anxiety" (Lee and Cowan, 63). Yankelovich in researching American society found that "a me-first, satisfy-all-my-desires attitude leads to relationships that are superficial, transitory, and ultimately unsatisfying." One of his surveys showed that "70 percent of Americans now recognize that while they have many acquaintances they have few close friends — and they experience this as a serious void in their lives. Moreover, two out of five (41 percent) state they have fewer close friends than they did in the recent past" (Yankelovich, 248). Could this be an echo of the need for community that God put within the heart of those who were created "in His image"?

M. Scott Peck states the reality with which we are faced:

We can never be completely whole in and of ourselves.
. . . There is a point beyond which our sense of self-determination not only becomes inaccurate and prideful but increasingly self-defeating. . . . We are inevitably social creatures who desperately need each other not merely for sustenance, not merely for company, but for any meaning to our lives whatsoever.

(Peck, 54–55)

While the Bible clearly speaks against self-centered, self-sufficient individualism, it is not against individuality. Self-gratification and autonomy as defined by our culture are not fostered by God. Evidence is strong in Scripture that we are created in and for relationship. Those who claim religious status with a competitive spirit, as the Corinthians did, are identified as carnal and immature. Self-sufficiency — claiming not to need God or others — is at the heart of infidelity and sin. Pride in achievement is decried. Knowing God is nurtured and expressed through ongoing community. Because of the strength of our cultural ties it is easy for believers to fall into an individualistic lifestyle. "We tend to fall into a 'me and Jesus' mentality that ignores the centrality of relationships and ministries among Christians" (Miller, 64).

Our individuality, on the other hand, is not created or achieved by us but is a gift from God (Dyrness, 104). The Bible is full of encouragements to grow and to value persons as individuals, uniquely created as one of a kind. The Gospels pulsate with Jesus' individualized treatment of persons like the Samaritan woman or Zacchaeus, both of whom were made to know their personal importance when they encountered the Messiah.

Coming to know Him meant being introduced into community. None remained isolated individuals. God creatively recognizes both individual and community by introducing the concept of the individual in community. Kraus sees this as unique to Yahweh and His covenant relationship (Kraus, 79). In balance, both the individual's relationship to God and the corporate relationship to God are seen as fulfilling His plan. The individual is not lost or engulfed by his solidarity with the group as envisioned by Communism. The person's individuality is preserved in the midst of the group. It is the group that brings self-awareness and a sense of identity to the individual. I am of the group but uniquely my own person. "A communist society is collective: it sees itself as made up of many individuals who are essentially interchangeable units. . . . The church, however, is not *collective* by nature, but is *corporate*. The parts are not identical but are 'members . . . of the body' of Christ (1 Cor. 12:12-30). Each 'organ' is unique and retains its individuality, but all function together as one body. The individual is not lost in the corporate identity of the church, but is freed to function as who he really is, for as each individual functions in the body, he will bear the vertical and horizontal relationships of the image of God" (Miller, 67). When the people of God function together, it is as a living organism. When they come together, Christ has promised to be there among them in a way that He is not present for the individual alone. He dwells in us individually but when we come together corporately we reflect the image of God (Miller, 67). We reflect the corporate interaction of the Godhead. We operate as the body of Christ. What we have together is greater than the sum of the individual parts. No one loses individuality in this coming together, but rather one discovers and esteems individual uniquenesses as they are revealed in the web of relationships. The apostle explained this pictorially in 1 Corinthians 12. The ear is uniquely for hearing because no other organ is designed for that purpose, but the ear alone would be useless because the other functions would be missing. It is the fact of being bound together in one body that creates the true value of the individual parts. Competition, autonomy, and claims to self-sufficiency are unthinkable when seen in this perspective. "To read individualistic religion into Scripture is an anachronism" (Kraus, 97). While "individually members of" the body of Christ (1 Cor. 12:27), we are also "all baptized into one body" (1 Cor. 12:13).

INDIVIDUALISM'S PENETRATION OF EVANGELICALISM

When the blatant concepts of individualism are examined in the light of biblical standards they are seen to be clearly opposed to the character formation desired by God. However, in subtle ways individualism has become acceptable and normative for evangelical Christianity. Lukes defines religious individualism in its purest form as "the view that the individual believer does not need intermediaries, that he has the primary responsibility for his own spiritual destiny, that he has the right and the duty to come to his own relationship with his God in his own way and by his own effort" (Lukes, 94). While much of this statement strikes a responsive chord in the soul of evangelicals, our theology and praxis, colored by our cultural context, tend to diminish the emphasis on individual in community and foster attitudes of aloneness and personal interpretation that acts apart from others.

> Gradually, the idea of a covenant community gave way to a vision of collected individuals. Faith was not so much a mutual conviction regarding creedal statements and a consequent common experience, but an individual experience — more to the point, a decision which each person could understand in his own way.
>
> Michael Scott Horton
> *Made in America*, 166–167

Barton W. Stone was a frontier preacher who lived 1772–1844 in Kentucky. Stone's rugged individualism led him to reject traditional ideas about the importance and role of the institutional church. His views led him to leave the Presbyterian church. Stone epitomized the way many evangelicals in America viewed the church. In true frontier individualism the cry became, "Every man for himself, and God for us all!" Such rugged individualism pervaded not only politics, but also the realm of faith. "Is this not what life is all about, one man facing up to his responsibility on his own two feet and not trying to hide in the crowd or permit another man to mediate between himself and God? Just as the ideal American of an earlier day stood alone in taming the frontier and in modern times achieves dignity and worth through individual endeavor in, say, industry or sports, so the American Christian must face God alone and come to terms with Him on his own" (Woodbridge, et al., 164). Martin E. Marty contradicts this attitude with biblical religion's emphasis on community, not solitariness. "Little religious value is associated in historic Christianity with the idea of the individual off by himself or herself, competing against all others, often in the name of God" (Marty, 39).

Centuries earlier Luther, in reaction to abuses of the Catholic Church, launched a rebellion whose energizing force was an emphasis upon "inner light," the priesthood of the believer, and justification by faith alone. Calvin added to this individualistic bent "ruthless self-examination" and concentration on an individual's personal achievement. The true believer became egocentric and perfectionistic (Lukes, 95). Such emphases resulted in a preoccupation with individual progress and personal sanctification. All of this separated a believer from others and isolated growth to the individual sphere. It also nurtured an attitude of private rather than community concern. Much of our theological thinking today, particularly in the reformed tradition, is based on the presupposition of an autonomous individual person who is prior to, and thus superior to, a group of believers. Thus the individual-in-community concept was moved off center to give precedence to the personal development of the individual (Kraus, 106). Social dimensions were considered suspect. To this day the social gospel is tainted for many with "suspect" liberal tendencies.

Conversion is limited to the realm of the soul, a "rational change in belief patterns called faith." The salvation experience is not viewed as incorporating reconciliation with fellow persons.

"Saved individuals will, or should, be more loving, honest, and altruistic, but conversion does not change the fundamental patterns of individual-group relations" (Kraus, 106–107). This kind of thinking, that salvation does not result in a conversion of the whole person, prevents us from seeing human relationships as being "redeemed." "We may expect in the church a new degree of cooperation and mutual caring; and we may hope that the saved individuals will compete fairly and with at least a modicum of compassion in the worldly order. But by theological definition, salvation does not introduce us to a fundamentally new order of relationships in which the private principal is superseded by commonalty as the basic operational assumption. Private gain, even in the religious sphere, remains the primary motivator" (Kraus, 107). And we accept this valuing of the individual over the group instead of embracing God's more equitable order of individual-in-community. Our thinking about groups and relationships will always be colored by what this does for the individual. And that is cultural individualism. In this kind of thinking the church is always secondary to personal gain.

Our "free" church paradigm is premised on voluntary association and commitment of individuals, based on the individual's Christian experience. Again, the individual is the controlling factor. Private personal experience and choice are the operative factors. A private faith is a natural corollary. Faith is a personal matter—of no business to others. If a believer grows, or how he or she matures, is "off limits" to the body of Christ. Prayer, practice of disciplines for growth, change in lifestyle—these are not to be intruded upon by others, nor even inquired after. Wesley's methodical societies were radical in their corporate responsibility and regularized accountability for one another's growth. By today's standards, the early church was meddling and overstepping bounds when it dealt corporately with sin and took seriously every weakness.

Personal piety is a matter of one's own individual choice and is evaluated by internal motives rather than a community. It is natural that this kind of thinking would arise out of a private rational faith apart from community which depended upon the subjective question, "Have you come to know Jesus Christ as your personal Savior?" The individual's word on this was taken to be gospel truth because such a transaction was between an individual and his/her God. This is a far cry from our Puritan roots where calling served others more than self. Even the development of a person's relationship with Christ when it came at the expense of that community was considered to be antisocial and thus anti-Christian. Puritan Thomas Goodwin is quoted as saying, "To be proficient in 'holy duties' is indeed more sweet to a man's own self, but to be proficient in our calling is more profitable to others — to the Church, the commonwealth, or the family — and so may glorify God more" (Horton, 167). "Subjective criteria become the norm for reality and truth in religious profession. Spirituality is defined in terms of personality characteristics, belief patterns, and personal piety" (Kraus, 110). Love today is easier to extol as a theological concept and psychological feeling than as an action and a moral commitment to relationship regardless of how I feel or reason. Evangelicalism has been concerned with the number of these interior decisions more than with the outworking of said faith in community. Groups remain at the discretion of the individual, a voluntary association of individuals who group together for self-fulfillment and the good life (Kraus, 104–111). Prayer remains inherently individualistic, praying for "my needs" and "my development."

That individualistic thinking dominates our perspective is evident when doctrines are considered. For example, the doctrine of Creation is believed to demonstrate that the autonomous individual is prior to the social group when in actuality the "family" stands at the zenith of God's creative efforts. The autonomous, non-sufficient man was the only "not good" aspect of God's creative force and was remedied by the formation of Eve which satisfied both Adam and God. When the doctrine of sin is considered, we automatically think of "my sin," not corporate sins in which we all participate. Salvation is seen as very individualistic. On my own, without the necessary influence of the body of Christ, I see myself making a personal, internal commitment which results in a privatized conversion. Sanctification is most often considered as "what I do to promote my own spiritual growth." Corporate sanctification is abdicated as being too binding and too much beyond our control. Is sanctification possible apart from the body of Christ? Doctrines of the sacraments are usually focused on an individual's relationship to God more so than on the strengthening, affirmation, and meaning these acts bring to the corporate unit of the church. Worship and witness are automatically conceived as personal and individual, whereas Scripture as often pictures these as collective and needing the body for fullest impact.

Divine guidance is pictured as an inner-directed impulse. Redrawn from a corporate dimension there is wisdom from the Spirit that comes through the body for our motivation and direction. Our perspective on eschatology more often than not is visualized as the individual being rescued from this planet and finally receiving the rewards for personal efforts accomplished while in the flesh. While this theme is certainly biblical, there is equal emphasis on the "bride" as a corporate whole presented without spot or wrinkle to the Bridegroom for His delight. Biblical doctrines are enriched by the "individual-in-community" balance.

Individualism naturally impacts the realm of ethics and morality. How I determine right and wrong can become a very individualistic decision. Lukes comments that "ethical individualism can be seen as the philosophical consequence of taking the idea of autonomy seriously and carrying it to its logical conclusion" (Lukes, 101). If I am not impacted by others and allowed to determine my own course of action, based on my own choices of what seems right to me, then feelings are more likely to influence my choice. The "oughts" of outside sources, obligations, and moral standards are set aside as ethics for a society. Free thinking and free behavior become the rule of thumb for the individual. A name often associated with religious individualism is Sören Kierkegaard, the first existentialist who interpreted Christianity as a "personal private inward faith" in opposition to the conformism and worldliness of the Lutheran Church. It was Kierkegaard, ever the champion of the individual, who desired that his tombstone be inscribed with "That Individual" (Lukes, 97). This isolated inner life conception, while righting wrongs of misconceived and misused corporate emphases, led to further offenses in new directions. "The rise of ethical individualism clearly has much to do with the decline of Christianity as an all-pervading basis for moral certainty" (Lukes, 102). When the source of moral values is the individual, biblical absolutes are ignored. And the church that promotes biblical values is seen as one voice among many offering choices to the individual who autonomously makes up her own mind. Interpretation of Scripture, left to the individual, often becomes that which supports the individual's lifestyle. Moral relativism is in vogue today.

How did evangelicalism become so influenced by individualism? As a culture American ideals and values foster individualism as a way of thinking and living. It is almost a symbol of national identification (Lukes, 28).

INDIVIDUALISM AMERICAN STYLE

In the campaign of 1928, Herbert Hoover coined the phrase "rugged individualism" which has since become a source of national pride. But long before the phrase became popular individualism was "at home" in the cultural mores of the United States. Bellah and associates describe it as the core of what it means to be an American (Bellah, et al., 142). Self-realization, individual freedom, privacy, and autonomy have long been embraced by poets, pioneers, politicians, psychologists, entrepreneurs, and ecclesiastical bodies. Our whole system of free enterprise expresses this individualism. Productive justice says that each individual has a right to enjoy what his mind can invent and develop. Lee and Cowan counter that Christians live under a rubric of distributive justice which allows every person the right to receive enough of the world's goods to live a decent life (Lee and Cowan, 81–82).

The Declaration of Independence hallows the inalienable rights of every citizen. The culture of America is particularly fertile ground for the development of individualism. With individualism at the very core of American culture, to even question the virtues of individualism seems almost anti-American. Those who have raised questions about the "be-all" and "end-all" of American individualism have often been accused of socialistic or communistic leanings. "Anything that would violate our right to think for ourselves, judge for ourselves, make our own decisions, or live our lives as we see fit is not only morally wrong, it is sacrilegious" (Bellah, 142). Personal dignity and freedoms are a matter of national pride. All of this, of course, militates with vigor against the building of community. Lee and Cowan ask the question, "Can we redeem our precious individuality by trans-forming it into a radically relational form?" (Lee and Cowan, 61) Can Christians who have been bombarded with cultural mores extolling American individualism be re-created to value the sanctity of the individual within an overarching sphere of community? Personal autonomy is schooled into us from the cradle on. "The ultimate ethical rule is simply that individuals should be able to pursue whatever they find rewarding, constrained only by the requirement that they not interfere with the 'value systems' of others" (Bellah, 6). In other words, "my value systems" are my own and nobody else's business. We grow up thinking of ourselves as independent agents, free of encumbrances. Being a person means you choose for yourself.

Advertising cultivates this image. You determine what is best for you. Personal gratification and success are laudable ends. Classic phrases that have made advertising history reflect this inalienable right of the customer. "Go for the gusto." "Have it your way." "You deserve the best." Watch for this theme of individualism that permeates television ads. Leaf through a major magazine publication and observe the copy that sells products today. What is the bottom-line appeal?

Our heroes are those persons who have "made it on their own." They represent the self-contained who has achieved success by virtue of his own outstanding ability, single-mindedness, and freedom from obligation and encumbrances. We glorify entrepreneurship and achievers who stand out from the crowd. Imagine the Lone Ranger setting up housekeeping and becoming a part of the community. "How can a Marlboro man become a candidate for intentional community?" (Lee and Cowan, 62) We put individuals into the limelight, ignoring the teams that allowed them to succeed. Their feats are attributed to what they did to foster their own success. If they "made it," they did it by their own virtue, ability, and fortitude. "Pulling yourself up by your own bootstraps" is an ethic to be emulated. We inspire our children with *The Little Engine That Could.* Each of these values contains enough admirable aspects to cause them to be desirable. After all, a person should learn to take responsibility for self, be motivated to live above the mediocre, make use of traits and opportunities. Where the redemption is needed is in the exclu-

71

siveness or priority of such values over equally valuable communitarian ideals that focus on a like responsibility and sensitive awareness to others. No one, particularly the one who wants to live a godly lifestyle, stands alone. One of the benefits that feminism has brought to our independent, competitive society is a new emphasis on the relational impact of what were considered individualized decisions and actions.

How do we define what is "good" today? As mentioned, one author perceives that "in general, rights language—what is demanded by the individual—has come to replace virtue language—the good practiced by the person" (Dyrness, 97). "I have my rights" is at the opposite end of the spectrum from "I have responsibility." This first kind of thinking results in treating others and groups as a whole as stepping stones to personal growth. "A major problem with a preoccupation with my individual development is that it provides no intrinsic value 'for you,' except as an environment for my growth" (Dyrness, 98). Groups are used—whether friendships or family—to facilitate individual development. When they cease to provide this in the way the individual desires, they are discarded. To justify our abdication of responsibility, we rationalize with "rights language." Groups often become little more than collections of individuals bent on their own ends. This prompts competition and protectionism or a holding back of commitment. Personal goals cannot be sacrificed for group growth. Community cannot be experienced because it's "each one for himself." John F. Kennedy reminded Americans of what they had lost by challenging, "Ask not what your country can do for you, but, rather, what you can do for your country." Becoming so preoccupied with our own navel gazing, we as a country have lost sight of good being outside ourselves.

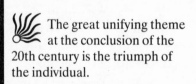

The great unifying theme at the conclusion of the 20th century is the triumph of the individual.

John Naisbitt and Patricia Aburdene
Megatrends 2000, 298

Such distortions reflect the typical imbalance of virtues gone amuck. American history supports these strains from its beginning. We point proudly to the tenets of the Declaration of Independence and our Bill of Rights. Yet today the stress points of our nation reflect the tendency to accent the individual at the expense of the relational. Benjamin Franklin's "Poor Richardisms" have been ingrained into our national philosophy as moral guides. Many people actually think that his "God helps those who help themselves" is a verse from the Bible. Jefferson's "All men are created equal," sets the tone for spotlighting individualistic rights. We live our individualism with religious passion.

Even before Hoover introduced the phrase "rugged individualism," our leaders have ridden individualism for their own ends. Teddy Roosevelt epitomized this free spirit for many Americans. American individualism encompasses such traditional values as natural rights and free enterprise, giving ethical priority to productive justice which declares that each person has a right to what he or she works for or produces. Is this Christian? Should some be robbed of a decent life while others enjoy excess? Furthermore free enterprise is sustained and encouraged by competition. While competition and "king of the hill" mentality are accepted as "normal" for our society, is this concept really Christian? What does it do for those who lack the ability to compete? To those who fail to win? To those who win? Is this the meaning of "rugged" when placed with individualism?

American individualism includes that precious right of individual freedom — freedom to decide individually — freedom to develop as an individual. With all the potential that this right brings, when it becomes the ruling norm in a society, what are the results? We've already seen the impact on theology when it is viewed individualistically. A separatistic, look-out-for-yourself modus operandi that functions with self-centered concern for one's own growth and benefit is at the heart of the Garden Fall. But when such sin is baptized with nationalism, it suddenly becomes acceptable and is embraced even in the church. J.B. Phillips' paraphrase of Romans 8 calls up short this tacit response, "Don't let the world around you squeeze you into its mold" (Rom. 8:2). Leo Buscaglia targets the fallacy of self-sufficiency which we have come to accept.

Most of us have been raised to believe that strength lies in independence. Society tells us that we must make our own

way. We come to believe that only when we no longer depend upon others can we say we have reached full maturity.
We see *need* as immature and *dependence* as weakness. We
fear commitment in that it may destroy our individuality and
our much coveted freedom. In so feeling, we build self-
imposed barriers to genuine encounter and the deep unions
we so desperately seek.

(Buscaglia, 195)

Not only our pioneers and politicians but also our poets have
enculturated us to think individualism is the highest gain. Ralph
Waldo Emerson's treatise on Self-Reliance shows how immersed
the poets of America were in this tradition. The glory of the
individual self is extolled in his charge to, "Trust thyself: every
heart vibrates to that iron string" (Emerson, 49). Speaking of
being economically responsible for ourselves he writes, "Do not
tell me. . . of my obligation to put all poor men in good situations. Are they *my* poor?" (Emerson, 53) Walt Whitman exulted
in "Song of Myself" the glorious freedom he felt in expressing
who he was in uninhibited fashion, "I celebrate myself, and sing
myself . . ." and again "Afoot and light-hearted I take to the
open road, Healthy, free, the world before me, The long brown
path before me, leading wherever I choose." Thoreau lived out
this individualism at Walden Pond. The fact that Ringer's *Looking Out for #1* was on the bestseller list week after week in 1990
reveals that this theme is still striking a very responsive chord in
the average American's life. James Bryce observes that throughout American history, "individualism, the love of enterprise, and
pride in personal freedom, have been deemed by Americans not
only their choicest, but their peculiar and exclusive possessions"
(Lukes, 31).

INDIVIDUALISM AND SMALL GROUPS
What is the result of this cultural heritage on the development of
community in America? As has already been noted, Americans
tend to use groups for their own personal ends. Since this is a
common phenomenon, we also fear that the group may use us.
George Barna suggests that this kind of thinking results in the
demise of loyalty, memberships, and commitment for the long

haul. He cites the decline in church membership and the emphasis on short-term commitments to book and record clubs as symbolic of this trend. Other interesting signs are a higher percentage of no-shows at events after committing to come, brand
loyalty dropping in most product categories, lessening commitment to remain in an unhappy marriage. Personal interest and
self-preservation are the desirables. "Commitment is viewed negatively because it limits our ability to feel independent and free,
to experience new things, to change our minds on the spur of the
moment and to focus upon self-gratification rather than helping
others" (Barna, 34–35).

But such lack of commitment is also distressing when we are
on the receiving end. As mentioned, Yankelovich, Skelly, and
White in their surveys found that this "me-first, satisfy-all-my-
desires attitude leads to relationships that are superficial, transitory and ultimately unsatisfying" (Yankelovich, 248). Popular author M. Scott Peck looks at the psychological results and notes
that independence requires wholeness but wholeness requires
our needing each other in order to find any meaning to our lives
(Peck, 54–55). We experience the most holistic sense of significance when we give to others what we are and when we need and
receive from them who and what they are. Paul in his apostolic
treatise on gifts stated the same truth centuries before. "If the
whole body were an eye, where would the sense of hearing be?"
(1 Cor. 12:17) Again it is the individual in community (not individual versus community) which most reflects the balance necessary for fulfillment. Insightfully, Deborah Tannen capsulizes this
twofold need.

> We need to get close to each other to have a sense of
> community, to feel we're not alone in the world. But we
> need to keep our distance from each other to preserve our
> independence, so others don't impose on or engulf us. This
> duality reflects the human condition. We are individual and
> social creatures. We need other people to survive, but we
> want to survive as individuals.
>
> (Tannen, *That's Not what I Meant*, 31)

These needs are not sequential but simultaneous. It is not just that we teeter-totter back and forth between meeting one and then the other. "Anything we say to show we're involved with others is in itself a threat to our (and their) individuality. And anything we say to show we're keeping our distance from others is in itself a threat to our (and their) need for involvement. . . . Whatever we do to serve one need necessarily violates the other" is Tannen's assessment (Tannen, *That's Not what I Meant*, 33–34). In group conversations this can be identified as one person expressing closeness to others, as in "I would really like to meet with all of you every week." Followed by, "But I don't want to impose my needs on all of you," which reflects a distancing to keep the threat to our individuality at a tolerable level. On the other hand, comments that show our individuality are often tempered with follow-ups that deny rejection and imply relatedness. "I don't feel the need to meet with members outside of this group, but I do enjoy the times we spend together once a week." These conversational gymnastics are mere reflections of our attempts to remain true to our uniquenesses as individuals and to our relatedness to others in the group.

Individualism impacts a group when rights and needs take precedence over relatedness, when each person remains more committed to his or her personal agenda than to the life of the group. Such lack of commitment is often unspoken, but is read loud and clear by others and spreads quickly to the rest of the group so that each begins protecting his or her own plans and egos. The conversations in this kind of group usually gravitate to an information level and persons "go through the group" to get it over with. In such a group it becomes very difficult to share honestly. It is easier to isolate and deny, to pretend to be satisfied when you aren't, to ignore what's really going on and proceed with organization.

Our individualistic tendencies can cause us to move from group to group, trying to get met the self-centered needs that drive us to get involved. Groups can become perfunctory exercises that we periodically try, but we may never succeed in knowing real community. Many have substituted group membership for the experience of community and their feelings about groups have turned sour or humdrum. We hunger for community— encounters with others that cause us to reach out, to self-dis-

close, to commit, and these occasions bring a feeling of wholeness, of belonging, of valued distinctiveness, and of relatedness to
others.

4

THE TODAY SHOW: RELATIONAL FAMINE

America is one vast, terrifying anti-community.
Charles Reich

U ntil recently, the nostalgic strains of "Cheers" announced one of the network's most popular and long-standing sitcoms. The words that open every show betray the hunger of our world for someone to care.

Sometimes you need to go where everybody knows your name:
And they're always glad you came....

The characters that form the "Cheers" family are a motley bunch—egotistical Sam Malone, naive Rebecca, undisciplined Norm, eccentric Cliff, feisty Carla, slow-witted Woody, and Frazer, the strange, intellectual psychologist. None of them is the kind of person deliberately chosen to be in a church small group. Yet, together, these socially marginal people find acceptance and a place of relationship in a Boston bar.

Charles Swindoll reflects:

The neighborhood bar is possibly the best counterfeit there is to the fellowship Christ wants to give His church. It's an imitation, dispensing liquor instead of grace, escape rather than reality, but it is a permissive, accepting, and inclusive fellowship. It is unshockable. It is democratic. You can tell people secrets and they usually don't tell others or even want to. The bar flourishes not because most people are alcoholics, but because God has put into the human heart the desire to know and be known, to love and be loved. . . .

(Swindoll, 128)

It is no accident that the most popular TV shows of the '90's feature people who have developed pockets of community. The award-winning "Cosby Show" depicts a two-career family with happy cared-for kids, a modern "Father (and Mother) Knows Best" scenario. The highly popular "thirtysomething" revolved around the close network of mutual friends who share life and changes as they traverse the "thirty passage." "The Golden Girls" depicts a community of single seniors—two often lonely groups. Dorothy, Blanche, Rose, and Ma form a womb of care, belonging, and support. They serve as a group sounding board for one another as they encounter life in the 60-plus years. Even "LA Law" portrays the office members as concerned about each other's lives and legal assignments. The show's opening always features the partners together in their weekly staff meeting, a type of community with shared vision gathered

 Finding Friends — For a Fee

"Wanted: a buddy." That's not the kind of classified ad you expect to find in the local paper. But now a San Jose, Calif., couple has started a company that hopes to do for friendship what computer dating services did for courtship. Buddy Brokers . . . aims to find pals for professionals who can't do it on their own. . . .

For a monthly fee of $49 married couples and clients of the same sex are matched according to likes and interests . . .

Newsweek, February 12, 1990, 40

around a boardroom table. Such visual stimuli strike a satisfying chord within us. Ideally we want a family like Bill Cosby's, we want committed friends like the "thirtysomething" gang, we hope for caring, involved companions who will stick with us in golden years. And while work may be individualistically focused, we'd like to think we belong to a team who cares about us apart from our production quotas, who sees us as persons living holistic lives. We want someone to know us and to be glad that we exist. Though culturally as a nation we embrace individualism and set our course to pursue personal success, internally our hearts hunger for community. Reality is harsh. Relationships heal hurts and help us face reality. The media we choose for relaxation and healing reflects this priority of relating.

The climate has changed. The years of rugged individualism fostered a climate where persons did not desire nor trust intimacy (Peck, 28). The parents of today's Baby Boomers (those born between 1946 and 1964) collected casual acquaintances by the droves (the once-a-year-Christmas-card-contact variety) but had few, if any, intimate friendships in which they could be real. This generation and its parents grew up with values that made a priority of privacy and guarded statements. "What would the neighbors think?" expressed the fear of being exposed and vulnerable. In the true style of individualism it was dangerous to get too close, to admit need, or to be totally honest outside the family framework. The film, *Dead Poet's Society*, depicts this era and the tragic consequences of this lifestyle and orientation.

Succeeding generations, beginning with the second half of the Baby Boomer wave and on into the '60s, looked at these image-protecting values and rejected them. "Being real — getting in touch with who we are" became their theme. They became the expressive generation. This inward focus manifested itself in sensitivity groups, disdaining of traditions, living free, and being personally fulfilled. Such shared values brought persons together in more honest and intimate interactions. They marched, staged sit-ins, broke rules, and exposed themselves psychologically, philosophically, and bodily. The sheer force of their numbers reshaped society. Today we live with the results. These cultural changes have fostered the need for the intentional building of community among persons who yearn for community but probably have not experienced it. We long for a place of personal fellowship and belonging in an impersonal world. We thirst for a caring community in a world that can't take time to care.

While it is true that we expect and desire more of every relationship today, compared to what was experienced in the past, the natural networks of community no longer provide the elements of care and personal support to sustain us in an impersonal, high pressure world. We'll examine further three of these networks: *Family Structure, Neighborhood and Friendship Ecosystem,* and *Work Place.*

FAMILY STRUCTURE

With divorce now impacting almost one in every two marriages, the most natural housing of caring community is being shaken. Of the two persons who seemingly care the most for a child, one is likely to leave before that child turns eighteen. "Trends indicate that of all the children born in 1990, six out of ten will live in a single-parent household for some period of time before they reach the age of 18" (Barna, 67–68). Newsweek announced that 70 percent of adults in the U.S. now believe that couples who fail to get along in marriages where there are young children should not feel obligated to stay together just for the sake of the children *(Newsweek,* Barna, 18). Such reinterpretation of commitment is certain to affect the security and values of persons left in the relationship.

Allan Bloom reflects, "Of course, many families are unhappy. But that is irrelevant. The important lesson that the family taught was the existence of the only unbreakable bond, for better or for worse, between human beings" (Bloom, 119). Few persons know the security of a stable family network where commitment is made and kept regardless of circumstances. The generation that is shuffled back and forth between Dad's family and Mom's family questions if there is a place of belonging, if persons can be trusted to care, and if getting close is going to mean being hurt. Can relationships be trusted? For these folks, a small group is a place to learn caring and to develop commitment.

Another family phenomena is that of survival replacing relationships. Major energy goes into the securing of income to make possible the continued existence of the family. This leaves little energy left over to meet the needs of the family and to cultivate relationships.

Children are often left to their own devices, creating a new breed called "latchkey children," so called because of the door key they wear around their necks. "Estimates of the number of children who care for themselves during some part of the day range as high as seven to fifteen million" (Louv, 84). Surprisingly, a Census Bureau survey revealed that the highest percentage of these children come from white higher-income households where the mother is educated and in a white-collar occupation (Louv, 84). Barr Films, located in Pasadena, California has on the market a "do-it-yourself" video for children called "Home Alone: You're in Charge" (Louv, 92–93).

As each person becomes more responsible for self and for fulfilling her own needs, relationships become more a "catch-as-catch-can" experience. Children themselves are busy as never before. Full schedules have become status symbols. A local stationery store advertises a "Day Runner For Kids!" With the aid of two cartoon mice, Winston and Butler, children learn to organize their lives by filling their Day Runner calendars to schedule in time for activities, schoolwork, and play. The supplier asserts that such "full-color books will keep six- to twelve-year-olds happily busy." Today's family doesn't allow for the "killing of time together." "One programming message sent commercially, politically, and personally is that everyday parenting is somehow not enough, that quiet time spent with a child is somehow not as valuable as the time spent with the child by an expert (a soccer coach, a violin teacher). This mythology also suggests that a child's freeflowing dream time is less valuable than a planned activity . . ." (Louv, 109). Life is programmed, productive and performance-based rather than relational. It takes time and effort to build intimacy. And time is something we don't have. Neither do we have much intimacy.

That bastion of relationship building, the family meal, is disappearing. The popularity of fast foods and "pull from the freezer, pop in the microwave" time-saver meals enable us to "keep on schedule" while adding one more item to our accomplishments. Sitting down to relax over a meal with conversational sharing and developing relationships has been replaced with TV viewing over the "TV tray." By each doing his own thing, individual priorities may be fulfilled but not necessarily community priorities. Vacations tend to be shorter and are less likely to incorporate all the household members. Most homes now provide more than one television set so family members can watch separate programs in different parts of the house (Barna, 70). We are an information generation who finds it increasingly difficult to communicate with one another. We are shaped more by the media than by persons.

The use of machines such as TVs, computers, VCRs, Walkmans, boom boxes, and others, occupy much of the family's relational time. Richard Louv in his provocative book, *Childhood's Future,* reflects on this substitution. "I came to believe . . . that much of the reason so many of us today spend so much time in the company of machines is because the true company of people is becoming harder to come by" (Louv, 127). Social worker Judy Frank targets the same need. "What we hear over and over from the kids is, 'I want someone to play it with me.' We see kids who are hungry for personal interaction, somebody to really sit and play with them. Playing with a machine, no matter how brilliant its responses, still leaves a child essentially alone" (Sussman). On the home front we are cultivating persons who are starved for personal relationships, someone to listen, to care, to help them process issues, to deliver the human touch. Somewhere that need must be met. Perhaps the rise of cults in recent years is due in part to the fact that they provide a sense of belonging and support in an atmosphere of community.

NEIGHBORHOOD/FRIENDSHIP ECOSYSTEM
As a consequence of the changes in family relationships, persons are seeking personal and relational gratification from sources outside of the home. The stress points occurring within the family force us to seek elsewhere for understanding, affirmation, and help. We long for friendships that will meet those needs. Descriptions of Baby Boomers portray them as searching for the elusive gold ring of friendship in the midst of their frantic search for success and fulfillment trapped by a scarcity of time to develop those relationships. Boomers usually live far from former support systems, face demanding jobs and hectic schedules. It's diffi-

cult to juggle the needs of personal success, short-term commitment, and pursuit of new dreams in such a way as to provide
the juggler with all good things. Often boomers look for quick
and useful friendships to provide them with temporary satisfaction for the need of closeness. One researcher labels them "a
generation of individuals, held together by a string of loose relationship" (Downs, 31).

Both neighborhoods and circles of friends are seen as transitory for modern Americans. Knowing that on the average one in
five Americans move every year, why pay the price to get to know
someone you will soon be leaving? Pilgrims on the move tend not
to put down deep roots. Pilgrims must be ready to move on, a
factor that breeds autonomy. People you know in the "now" are
not likely to be people you hang around with in the future. This
realization causes a "temporariness" in our relations. Charles
Swindoll shared the confession of the wife of an executive (who
had moved three times within seven years). "To decrease the
pain of saying 'good-bye' to our neighbors, we no longer say
'hello' " (Swindoll, 20).

Overpopulation has produced interesting emotions. On the
one hand, the constant stimulation of too many people produces
in us a need for solitude when we have a choice. We shrink from
having to interact with "one more person." We stare straight
ahead at the closed elevator door while people crush in upon us.
The television, which we can shut off at will, seems like a friend-
lier companion than a live person who requires involvement and
may demand more than we feel we can give. Many persons will
join a large church or a large "small group" to fulfill both the
need for community and to protect themselves from others. The
"fence" is the neighborhood symbol of individualism by which we
keep others out of our lives.

On the other hand there is a loneliness in the depersonalization forced upon us by the bigness of our society. We are given
numbers to represent us. Our mail comes to Occupant. To our
employer we are often known by our position. We find we are
not credible unless we present the required forms of identification. We are warmed when someone remembers our name. Glob-
alization and our awareness of the magnitude of persons living
on this planet cause our sense of significance to shrink. "The

time required to double the world's population has dropped from 1,000,000 years to 200 years, to 80 years until now. At present accelerated rate of population growth, the earth's population will double in 35 years" (Luft, 151). The meaningfulness of "the person" is diminishing.

We experience what one author calls "functional relationships." These relationships exist totally as a means to an end—a way for us to get something we need. We have no relationship with the grocery clerk, gas station attendant, toll booth operator, or bank teller than as a means to help us achieve our ends. They could be machines. We become used to "using people," to interacting without the "personal," to expect nothing more than results. Each "nonperson" has no purpose but to be instrumental in satisfying our need. We therefore don't "get involved" in their lives as persons. We are isolated from the fact that the service station attendant's marriage is breaking up, or the bank teller just lost her mother to cancer. TV coverage of personal tragedies serves only to arouse interest in us. We cannot care for so many people so we compensate by viewing them in anonymity. If we don't know, we cannot care, and thus we are not responsible. This lack of knowing and bonding has opened the door for increase in vandalism and crime in neighborhoods. The Neighborhood Watch program is an attempt to help neighbors get to know one another and thus to assume responsibility for "watching" what happens to a "real person's" property. It attempts to construct community based on mutual concern so that mutual benefits may occur. It uses community to guard individuality. In protecting our privacy we have lost our bond of community. In "moving ahead" we have lost our sense of connectedness. In keeping our distance we have lost the warmth of intimacy. The network of neighbor and friend seldom provides the longed for gratification for community, a hunger that is part of the image of God within us. Small group leaders must accept the fact that the church family often is seen in the same way as the neighborhood/friend system—quick and expedient, and easily left behind when another group more pertinent comes along.

In what ways have you experienced depersonalization and overwhelming isolationism in your world of neighborhood and friends?

WORK PLACE

A former source of community for many was the work scene. It was there they found a place to belong and persons who came to know and care for them over the years. Fueled by competition and the high priority of production, today's workday community is endangered. It is hard to foster the growth of another when you know that such development may cause that individual to get the job advancement you're after. Students face the same issues when class grading is done on the curve. One pre-med classroom reported students giving each other fraudulent exam papers so as to increase their own chances of getting into med school with the right answers.

With an eye to their own personal success, workers want to relate to those above them, those who can grant them favors and build influence. The number of persons vying for a limited number of jobs causes competition which makes us protective and isolated.

Bellah summarizes the stark reality which underlies our actions. The predominant ethos of American individualism is the determination to press ahead with the act of letting go of all criteria other than radical private validation (Bellah, 79).

For hundreds of thousands of workers, work is their identity. It is the reason for their value and they realize that for them to succeed, they must do nothing that shows weakness or need or would compromise their personal advancement. Caring for others can get in the way of objectivity in decision-making.

Workers also reflect the fact that the company has little or no commitment to them as persons. They function as a cog in the machine. Each knows that if a person becomes nonproductive, sick, or old, that one is disposable. It is with shock that longtime higher management employees have received their walking papers because of mergers and streamlining for increased productivity. Those who had worked with them simply close in and fill up the gap without missing a step.

We cannot afford to become involved. The bottom line is performance. The result is anxiety and insecurity and higher demands with little commitment to persons. What other factors in today's business scene tend to undermine the building of community?

THE FRAGMENTED LIFE

Not only does the work that we do seem a meaningless part of a whole that we seldom see, life itself seems fragmented into isolated parts and roles. Nobody knows you whole. Some see you as parent, others as worker, and still others as church member. Each of these has its own separate world. Therefore you can put on and take off various roles depending on which sphere you are in. Because of mobility and the numbers of persons living today, it is possible to take up existence in a setting where no one has known you in the past. Children live far from parents. Those you went to school with have long been left behind. Relocation in business or change in marriage status means totally beginning again. There is little if any sense of continuity with the past. Indeed many adults see these times as "starting over," cutting ties with the past and ties with former community. Life is a loose string of acquaintances, a disconnected series of roles that do not overlap. Social roles today tend to be so splintered that most persons are known in only one role, which can lead to increased freedom but also to increased insecurity and loneliness.

In what ways does your life appear as disconnected parts where the elements of one segment are unknown to the others?

RAPID CHANGE

Another factor motivating persons today to search for community is the insecurity and anxiety caused by accelerated change. Already mentioned is the accelerated rate of population growth which causes a doubling of the earth's population in the brief span of 35 years and increased ease of mobility which allows us to relocate on a temporary or permanent basis in entirely new settings. Millions are whisked into workplace settings miles from their homes, retreating back in the evenings or on weekends. Only a few years are now required for the innovative cycle between the origination of an idea and its application, a process that used to take as much as a millennium. We are bombarded with information which continually changes our lifestyle and thinking. In only four and a half centuries the increase in publication of new books has gone from 1,000 a year to 1,000 a day. Scientific literature is currently being produced at the rate of some 20 million pages per year (Luft, 151). Innovations caused by the computer alone affect each person every day. We are dwarfed by the amount of change that engulfs us and requires us to readjust. We have become "change junkies." We must have constant change. It is a "fix" to dull our feelings. The constant state of flux in which we live gives birth to a sense of rootlessness and insignificance. What can we substitute for the personal relationships found in community? Machines lack emotion and care. Things are designed for obsolescence. Time spins by, another ever-present reminder that we are the victims of relentless change. What moorings can we clutch to bring some security and control?

BABY BOOMERS AND BUSTERS — GENERATIONS IN THE LIMELIGHT

As a group, Baby Boomers (those born between 1946 and 1964) have had a distinct impact on the social and economic culture of the twentieth century and will likely continue to impact the perspectives and values of America until the late twenty-first century. The magnitude of their numbers has demanded that business, politics, and society in general pay attention to them. They have demonstrated they have the buying power and ideological clout to impact the nation.

Nearly one third of all Americans now living were born in the years 1946 to 1964. Statisticians and prophets were surprised by this unforeseen groundswell of births that began after the end of World War II and continued for almost two decades. As this huge section of society went to school, communities rushed to build new facilities. When the wave hit college, new institutions sprang up to meet the increased demand. The entrance of so many into the job market created a crisis in unemployment. The arrival of Boomers at middle age has created a flurry of activity to produce more comfortable middle-aged perks for this ample and affluent consumer block. Already plans are in the making for increased health services and needs for when the Boomers retire. They influence the nation as the wave rolls by.

But it isn't simply the sheer numbers that mark the Baby Boom generation. Ideologically they think of themselves as uniquely different from previous generations and expect that others will treat them as different. They are unique and they know it. Competition among them is keen. Boomers grew up knowing there were many ready to take the place of the less-than-the-best. They lived life with a purpose, placing higher expectations on themselves and refusing to compromise the ideals they embraced. Boomers refused to serve in a war with which they didn't agree. Traditional commitments were discarded if they failed to meet the needs of the Boomer. Why continue to vote the party or live in the marriage or stay with the company if your needs aren't recognized and fulfilled? Institutional loyalty was passé. There was always another choice. In fact, choice impacts our view of group membership and small group offerings.

James Fowler sees our present era as characterized by "over-choice." We are offered an unprecedented range of choices from cars to cereal brands, from athletic shoe styles to recreational opportunities, from kinds of small groups to issues with which we're involved. But such a plethora of choices and individualized control has left our nation with what Fowler characterizes as "homeless minds and hearts." The soul and mind are "no longer attached or connected to particular places, communities, or traditions that provide standards and guidelines for the exercise of choice. . . . We are exposed to too many models of reality, too many perspectives on values and meanings. How shall we commit ourselves to *one* in the midst of the many that appeal to us?" (Fowler, 8) Where is focused commitment? Where are lasting values? We live in "the vertigo of relativity" (Fowler, 8). Another possibility is always on the horizon so one can always move on to another cause, another partner, another conviction, another group.

The Baby Boom generation questioned other traditional values. Absolute values appeared as relative values. Keeping promises was reinterpreted for every situation. Such formative principles as blind loyalty, the Protestant work ethic, duty and respect for authority, and long-term involvement were seen as relics — values of a former generation. Life must be meaningful and Boomers embraced whatever satisfied their present needs. Experience was more important than the possessions that the previous generation hoarded. Fun and enjoying life was what made it all worthwhile. All of this has impact on Boomers' involvement in small groups.

Boomers grew up with TV. With a flip of the dial they changed channels and learned to be in control. They also learned to live with constant change without being threatened by it. Boomers are risk takers and as they come into an age where they will take over more and more major leadership positions we can expect them to act in the role of change agents. They are not used to being bored or putting up with the status quo. Too many other options present themselves. The church or small group ministry made up of Boomers better be prepared for radical change.

What implications do you see growing out of each of these Boomer values?	
Boomer Values	**How Groups Are Affected**
Short-term involvement Not motivated by duty, blind loyalty "I am my own authority" Say what they think — confrontation vs. politeness Look for what helps them Have high expectations Refuse to do what is meaningless to them Want practical action, not theory	

The constant change and fast-paced living in a highly competitive world is not as comfortable as it used to be for the Boomer. Now entering middle age, the Boomer is portrayed by *American Demographics* as experiencing nostalgia for the roots of a former culture. The "Country" look remembers with warmth small town America where store clerks really care about you and where homeowners do not lock their doors, where persons live together in real community and feel close to the land. The evidence of this strange stirring in the hearts of Baby Boomers is the widespread success of "Country" magazines in an industry that is otherwise depressed. Perhaps all the mobility of this generation has created a craving for the feeling of community. There is no widespread exodus to rural areas in the real world. But there is a hankering for the peaceful, secure relationships of a time gone by, a whispering of something meaningful being missed by our present lifestyle ("Buying Your Roots: The Baby Boom Goes Shopping for Community." *American Demographics,* Vol. 13, No. 1, January 1991. Ithaca, NY: Dow Jones & Company Inc., 32–33).

Having a voice that was heard was something the Baby Boom crowd took for granted. Discussion and having a part in decision-making is natural to this vocal generation. They want to be consulted about any plan in which they are expected to participate.

Boomers are intensely conscious of and concerned about having their needs met. Madison Avenue capitalizes on this passion in its product design whether that be "healthy fast food in microwave packaging that requires only four to six minutes from carton to plate," 24 hour service, or a pair of Levi's with a "skosh more room for the mature figure." The church that plans to attract Baby Boomers will probably reach them through some need-meeting agency such as divorce recovery workshop, film series, athletic team, grief support group, or community project such as a job reentry seminar.

Supportive groups that work at meeting individual needs and building friendships will be entry doors for this generation. Personal relationships are desirable but difficult on many counts. High mobility and intense competition undermine attempts at lasting friendships. Baby Boomers read lots of books on intimacy but tend not to experience it. Many resort to what some authors label "cocooning," retreating from a crowded and hostile environment to their condos and technologically-loaded family rooms. These retreats bring loneliness and a heightened sense of the need for personal contact. Prowling a crowded mall with thousands of fellow shoppers does not alleviate the ache for a personal friend to share more than an escalator ride with. Small groups in the church offer a safe place to meet and get to know people who can become friends and support systems in an age when both seem to be far away or even nonexistent. AT&T's "Reach out and touch someone" just isn't sufficient.

Baby Busters is the generation born after 1964, sometimes called Baby Boomlet because of their relationship to Boomers but much smaller numbers. Busters grew up in smaller families, attended smaller classrooms, and found life to be far less competitive than their predecessors. With fewer persons in the running, success came much easier than for the previous generation. As the "favored few," Busters were given the best and that "best" was replaced with the newer model as soon as it came out. It is not surprising that they felt they were entitled to everything. And they grew to expect that all things would be handed to them. This expectation that their needs would be cared for by others has prompted a hesitation to assume responsibility, a slowness about growing up. Busters seem to live in constant flux and indecision. They drift from one major to another, from one casual relationship to the next, from one pursuit to some new fad. Life is lived for the present moment with little thought for tomorrow. "Buy now, pay later" is in sync with Buster values. In many ways these young adults are a lonely crowd without the strong moorings of absolute values, without purpose — feeling strongly about neither the pursuit of a cause or a reaction against the social climate of their ancestors. It is as though they are anesthetized by the multitude of crises and issues and immobilized by their indecision. Many simply don't understand the radical passion and competitiveness of the Boomers. Busters are able to live with their own contradictions and inconsistencies without questioning them. Anderson cites as expressions of the current eclectic style, men wearing business suits with ponytails, and earrings for men, or women wearing suits and sneakers to the office. "Rather than trying to integrate all aspects of life and philosophy, they select their convictions *a la carte*. Life is like a cafeteria line where one can select a meal that includes caviar and pizza, Sausage McMuffin and shrimp scampi, apple pie and mustard sauce" (Anderson, 107–108).

Many Busters are children of divorce. They have learned to live in isolation, felt devalued and have grown up in the shadow of the noisy but influential Boomers. Groups for Busters will present challenges in modeling values never experienced. Commitment, community, and conviction are virgin concepts let alone actualized experiences. Such groups will probably have to exist with "light" involvement, functioning with paradoxical statements, with slow maturation, and fluctuating responsibility. The leadership must be able to live with these blurred issues as Busters discover caring relationships that enable them to face an uncertain future and purposes that give perspective and value to life.

The conditions fostered by our present society and lifestyle set up an opportune time for the building of Christian community. In an impersonal world, we need a community that cares. In the midst of loneliness, we need friends. Facing stress-filled situations of transition and demand, far from extended family, we need the church family for support. As we sense our insignificance in impacting a world that is overrun with people and information, we must band together with others of like vision and faith. It is a great time for the Gospel of community to be proclaimed and actualized.

Scan the front page of a newspaper or the table of contents found in a current issue of a news magazine. What additional societal factors mentioned there affect the need for or shape of community today?

PART II
TRUE COMMUNITY

5

THE REAL THING: TRUE COMMUNITY

I am cast upon a horrible, desolate island, void of all hope
of recovery. I am singled out and separated, as it were,
from all the world, to be miserable. I am divided from mankind,
a solitary; one banished from human society.
I have no soul to speak to or to relieve me.
Daniel Defoe, Robinson Crusoe

Shipwrecked and cast upon the shore of a tropical island, Robinson Crusoe had food in abundance, an un-
limited stay in an island paradise where the climate
was ideal, and the natives were peaceful. He was supplied with
tools for working, weapons for defense, and seeds to plant. His
situation seemed pleasant if not ideal. He was the lone survivor
of the disaster. Yet he was morose and dispirited. He felt his
aloneness and cursed his solitary life. He was devoid of human
contact and that colored his perception of his situation.

Most of us who are crammed into crowded elevators, stalled
on crowded freeways, and overwhelmed by the sea of humanity
that engulfs us in the mall have a hard time identifying with
Crusoe's scenario. We are "grouped" or "peopled" to death. But
even in the midst of our groups we often remain solitary individuals. We hunger for communication and intimacy. But we fear it
may rob us of our individualism, and in our society individualism
is a cardinal right.

We also find it difficult to trust. A large percentage of Baby
Boomers and Baby Busters have experienced a divorce within
their home. This experience taught them to trust no one but

themselves. As a culture we seem to long passionately for intimacy (witness the large number of popular works now addressing this subject) while living in a climate of mistrust in our actual relationships. Our Depression era parents enjoined us to "trust no one but the family," but the collapse of the family has left us with no one to trust. Trust is a core component of community. So we settle for being in a group where we can experience some relatedness while also retaining conditional limitations of trust. If the group doesn't go as we hoped, we can always drop out without having invested too much.

This utilitarian view of groups is fostered by a lifestyle that is used to choices. It is normal today to feel that we have the option of choosing what is best for us, quickly discarding any choice that does not measure up. To us the question of relating is a choice. But thinking "Christianly," community is not optional. A prior bonding with God supersedes our utilitarian evaluation. We need community to be the kind of people God intended us to be. True commitment to community is not made on the basis of performance or feelings. Commitment involves "hanging in there" to work out unresolved issues and stick with persons whose personalities are not like ours. In our utilitarian lifestyle, this kind of commitment seems foreign, resulting in very little awareness of the existence of true community. Community is forged out of time and commitment.

DEVELOPMENT OF TRUE COMMUNITY
True community is more than being together. A person does not develop trust in others simply by being in a group where members study together, pray together, and share a common group leader. Trust involves relatedness. Relatedness is more than presence although that is the beginning. To relate one must know, and to know one must work at being open to trust. Relatedness has a price tag that not only includes time but also energy and concern. Devotion to community requires caring enough to exert effort. It may also require the sacrifice of effort spent elsewhere. Community building requires the unrelenting conviction that it is one of the most important things we can do to experience fulfillment. We will never be whole or satisfied without the experience of community.

Trust requires time. Our instant-minded culture may be frustrated with the impossibility of quick community. We find ourselves settling for a quick "community fitness exercise," squeezing our required relational quota into a weekly regimen of a two-hour group workout, a type of relational aerobics. We must not fall into the trap of promising the real thing in a time frame that is geared to allow no more than the development of pseudo-community in group togetherness. Repeated experiences of this nature cause members to think that is all there is. Sometimes community happens in greater depth than at other times, but you learn not to expect what can't be created. If true community with its risks and depth is the goal, "it is asking too much of human nature to expect people to work toward a level of real trust and mutual sharing and then start the same process anew the following year—and each following year" (Wolff-Salin, 129). Our fear of cliques has inadvertently fostered a weakened view of community. Some persons, having gone through this pattern for years, rebel at putting more energy into new group programs that may still not provide true satisfaction.

True community is also shaped by reality and sacrifice. In Mary Wolff-Salin's phraseology, there is pain in proximity (Wolff-Salin, 37). And true community is not the place of bliss and harmony that some would envision as the ideal. The bubble bursts for the one who believes that true Christianity is the absence of conflict and difference. In reality, both interest and ongoing vitality in relationships are born out of the freedom to share who one really is. This necessitates sharing the positive as well as the negative. Honesty will inevitably lead to conflict. True community provides the security and boundaries to work through conflict in the climate of committed love. When it is evident that members care enough about the others to work through honest differences, their awareness of the reality of community is enhanced.

The role of the church is to proclaim and enable true community. As Christians we cannot be satisfied with the provision and quality of small groups as persons experience them in the world. The church of all places is a place of learning what true community is as God conceived it. Believers cannot settle for group times that are only as good as the local Alcoholics Anonymous meeting. Our getting together must be depicted as more. We will have to educate and exert effort to give persons today a deeper concept of relatedness than that which most have been exposed to in groups. No matter that they have not experienced it previously. The church's prophetic role is to offer the unique opportunity for an unsurpassable quality of community that is uniquely Christian. Where else can persons know that kind of unshakable commitment? Where else can they experience that kind of trust that grows out of faith not in people but in the *God who dwells in the people He has claimed?* The church cannot simply put people in groups to accomplish ecclesiastical ends. Community with others in His family is our heritage. Such community is a setting for discovering biblical insights impossible to "know" in a secular group setting. Christians must internalize and proffer a vision of community that the image of God in each of us responds to. There ought to be a sense in these body of Christ networks that we have "come home." We have found the "family" for which we have longed. This is the scene in which our images of Christ find opportunity to be lived out.

For community to exist there must be a "setting aside" of individualism that centers only on its self and its advancement. Some would see community developing as each person accumulates increased skills and advanced experience. In another sense, community building grows out of "giving up." It is constructed out of the tearing down of barriers which we erect to protect and magnify ourselves. Community requires the sacrifice of these barriers.

The first barriers to community are our preconceived expectations, created out of our fear of the unknown. To fill the void of the "not-yet-experienced," we grasp expectations that are usually false. While these projections become security for us, we soon slip into the role of tyrants as we try to make this group experience conform to our expectations, and as we seek to force others into our preconceived molds. We are often trapped into fulfilling role expectations we have placed upon ourselves. When fitting the expectations is the goal, it becomes difficult — if not impossible — to really hear or experience anything outside the preconceived notion.

The second barriers to community are our predetermined expectations based on limited, brief, and distorted experiences, i.e., labeling or prejudice. These too must be brought to our consciousness and given up for community to develop. As long as we continue to see others through the pigeon holes of "hot shot," "nervous Nellie," or "stickler for details," we keep them at a distance and lock them into behavior patterns. All we see reinforces our evaluation and keeps us from openness to blending. Christians have their own sets of labels that prevent bonding— "super spiritual," "liberal thinker," "charismatic," etc.

Third, community requires us to give up our rigidities that make us think *we* alone know the right way, have the correct solution, or have experienced the truth. Feeling this superiority, we begin to view ourselves as the "saviors," "fixers," and "healers" of others' maladies. If they have a problem, we can solve it. If they have a pain, we can make it better. If they disagree, we can convert them to better thinking (our way). Such intention is motivated by a need to eliminate "your pain so I feel better," to change "your ideas so mine aren't threatened," to take care of "your problem so I can become savior." In true community, persons care and come alongside, realizing that their presence or "thereness" brings greater strength than quick solutions. We often puzzle over Christ's role of "witness" when He could eliminate the discomfort. "When you pass through the waters, I will be with you" (Isa. 43:2); "Even though I walk through the valley of the shadow of death, I will fear no evil, for You are with me" (Ps. 23:4); "Go and make disciples. . . . And surely I am with you always" (Matt. 28:19-20). *True community involves being present with another.*

Being in community means I must be willing to give up my self-centered need to control and manipulate. This is not absence of planning; rather it is openness to being influenced by others and willingness to sacrifice my need to always be in control so that others may go through what is necessary for *them* to build interdependence with one another. This may mean that I will "fail" or both members and leader will come face-to-face with their own inadequacies and shortcomings. Leaders can *enable,* but not *control* group attitudes, progress, and insights. Closely aligned with this sacrifice is that of the need for approval. Letting members and groups take responsibility for their own actions may not be popular. For those of us who are born rescuers this is a painful sacrifice for the sake of evolving community (Peck, 94–103).

True community is built on the sacrifices of old resentments and angers, on facing insecurities and fears, and in giving up preoccupations. But the resulting relational openness and commitment is never seen as the "sum of sacrifices." It is a whole new dimension of relational intimacy never imagined. Perhaps the concept is best illuminated by Donald G. Barnhouse's illustration of Peter's suggestive, "We have left everything to follow You!" And Jesus' reply: "No one who has left home or brothers . . . will fail to receive a hundred times as much" (Mark 10:28-30). As a boy Barnhouse loved to play marbles while the older boys played ball. There came a day, however, when the team needed a second baseman and they asked him, "Hey, Kid, can you field a ball?" Thereafter he played ball. Barnhouse adds, "I didn't give up marbles, they gave me up!" In like manner, the taste of community is like the exhilaration of a new world. Our old expectations and prejudices of being in control and "fixing things" for others give us up. There is a mutuality and a life-giving found in giving up, in brokenness, in dying to self. "Unless a kernel of wheat falls to the ground and dies, it remains only a single seed. But if it dies, it produces many seeds" (John 12:24). "Whoever wants to become great among you must be your servant" (Matt. 20:26). "Whoever wants to save his life will lose it, but whoever loses his life for Me will save it" (Luke 9:24). Community is not cheaply bought. Such a view explains how Dietrich Bonhoeffer could speak of a people who love the *idea* of community more than the *experience* of community.

In fact we find it easier to escape into numerous substitute states than to embrace the building of community. It is inevitable that the development of community will require a dying to self, and we avoid this with any alternative that presents itself.

In the early stages of a group we avoid the honesty of community-building by taking flight into politeness, denying who we really are. This produces a form of pseudocommunity where differences are treated as nonexistent and "peace at all costs" is the rule of the day. Avoidance of facing and working through issues cannot long survive in the guise of good manners if we come together often. And so we frequently move to scapegoating—

placing our undealt-with frustrations and distresses on the shoulders of one who can be blamed for those uncomfortable feelings. This may be a leader or a group member — but they are targeted as the focus of our irritation over our dissatisfactions with the group and our inability to be all that we expected to be in this gathering. If not scapegoating, then subgrouping and other forms of organization are chosen to serve as outlets for our pent-up frustrations over not achieving what we hunger for. "Let's divide into two groups and come up with some answers" tries to escape having to work through feelings and insights in the process of community building. "But it will take so much longer" reveals our ignorance of the value of processing and accentuates the more objective accomplishment of "getting an answer." "Let's vote on it" is another trap door that releases groups to "move on" without dealing with differences.

Sometimes we miss community building opportunities by ignoring the pain of others or of ourselves. By denying the pain, we can move on and cover the agenda. Community is often forged out of exploring painful areas. In the name of expediency, we trade "our forethought for a mess of pottage."

When we fruitlessly attempt to "change" others or fix their conditions, we often forfeit community-building experiences that cause us to come alongside and hear and accept. Conformity is the *opposite* of community. Community embraces a variety of viewpoints, abilities, and experiences. It is energized by uniqueness and acceptance.

Liaisons and resulting exclusions are another means of resisting community building. Pairing, whether romantic or otherwise, can interfere with a group's development as a whole. Whenever some are excluded or ignored as nonexistent, community is undermined. Facing these alliances directly may help to relieve their exclusivity. "We all want to know the benefits of your insights" or "I'm guessing we're all curious about the joke you two seem to be sharing. Why don't you let us all in so none of us feels excluded."

Dependency gets us off the hook of community building by forcing a leader or strong members to carry more than their share (Peck, 107–118). This excuses some from responsibility and destroys the mutuality so necessary to community. "It's not my responsibility," becomes easy avoidance. Those who are strong can be "fed" by others needing them. The cultivation of dependency is often done "in the name of kindness" when in actuality it is a *codependency* where the weak have learned to manipulate the strong. However it is exercised, dependency must not be allowed to replace the interdependency of community. To do so is to head for disaster in the end—uncommitted, uninvolved, ungrateful members and overworked, overprotective, over-controlling leaders who have become victims of the group and often end up bitter and disillusioned. Many Christians embrace this posture under the guise of "caring for another who is weak." Our responsibility is always under the lordship of Christ as the only head to promote the health of the body—our own healthy evaluation of ourselves and the equipping of others in the body. Biblically speaking, strengths are given for the good of the body, for the strengthening of the church, for the common good. The only dependency for believers is upon God Himself. Our relationship to one another is more like a rabbinical story quoted by M. Scott Peck.

A rabbi was lost in the woods. . . . For three months he searched and searched but could not find his way out. Finally, one day in his searching he encountered a group from his synagogue who had also become lost in the forest. Overjoyed, they exclaimed, "Rabbi, how wonderful we have found you. Now you can lead us out of the woods!" "I am sorry, I cannot do that," the rabbi replied, "for I am as lost as you. What I can do, because I have more experience being lost is to tell you a thousand ways you cannot get out of the woods. With this poor help, working with each other, perhaps we shall be able to find our way out together."

(Peck, 116–117)

Community construction requires constant commitment to interdependence and a gentle open attempt to keep this value before the group. Otherwise we soon settle for less and then feel empty and dissatisfied without knowing why. Community is like a pearl of great price—when recognized for its value, it is worth pursuing at any cost.

To taste this sense of genuine community is to hunger for it even more. Peck describes this community as a place where one feels safe, a feeling that grows out of experiencing acceptance. This security is possible because members feel free to expose wounds and weaknesses to each other and to be affected by the wounds and the joys of others (Peck, 67–70). Acceptance may be even more difficult in a system where Christians evaluate according to rules and regulations. It is easy in such a system to feel rejected on the basis of actions, and this rejection is taken as rejection of the person—not the act. Differences too are valued in true community. "Instead of being ignored, denied, hidden, or changed, human differences are celebrated as gifts" (Peck, 62).

Such community is reminiscent of that of the Trinity where the unique role and ministry of each member is seen as being enriching and magnified by the others. Lee and Cowan see community characterized by mutuality— not only understanding and respect for differences, but also ability to share appropriately one's needs, feelings, knowledge, and beliefs. This appropriate disclosure and accurate empathetic understanding constitute necessities for authentic intentional community (Lee and Cowan, 124–125). True community consists of an increasing commitment to be open and congruent in sharing, to understand and accept another in a climate of caring, and to cultivate an awareness and motivation for growth in each other with increasing recognition of the value of each individual within the group.

> What I am at any given moment in the process of my becoming a person, will be determined by my relationships with those who love me or refuse to love me, with those I love or refuse to love.
>
> John Powell
> *Why I Am Afraid to Tell You Who I Am?* 43

Two major threats to community are exclusivity and transference. In exclusivity, one or more group members are isolated from the others. Competition is exclusive—it receives some and eliminates others. It judges and bans as non-acceptable. For one to feel "in," another must feel "out."

Transference threatens mutuality—hearing and understanding another. All of us have a history of relationships. Present interactions remind us of past reactions and patterns. Effects of these former relationships are carried into our present life with others. A similarity can trigger old feelings or patterns. It becomes easy to misinterpret happenings and the responses of persons so that they appear to be repetitious of previous occasions. This can become a significant barrier to hearing and understanding another. Persons get locked into predetermined roles and motivations. Leadership seems easy to target as the culprit here. An unpleasant experience with an authority figure in the past can cause us to transfer the same feelings to a present participant without seeing the differences in the present situation. We interpret responses personally and react to issues and comments with intense feelings and defensiveness. Communication is short-circuited and community is damaged. Unfinished emotional business inevitably is transferred to close relationships. Like ghosts from the past they haunt our interpretations and bring hurt and division (Lee and Cowan, 135–138).

You feel the leader is trying to control the plans to go a predetermined way and you find yourself being disagreeable on minor issues, rebelling against a controlling parent. Your suggestion is ignored by the group in favor of another's plan, and you experience the same feelings and self-doubt you had when growing up with a favored sibling. You leave feeling hurt and angry, amazed at the intensity of your response but too ashamed to bring it up since no one seemed to notice your angry silence. A conflict arises in your group and you shrink back from it in fear. Remembering what happened in your home whenever conflict arose, you flee from the conversation and refuse to discuss issues. Feelings are like reverberating echoes of responses in the past. They naturally occur. How can we prevent such feelings from the past from destroying present relationships? Cultivating an *awareness* of patterns and personal conflicts that trigger confusing here-and-now events with there-and-then people is a first step in changing responses. Ask questions such as: What kind of authority actions tend to alarm me? What kind of person makes me angry or scared? What situations arouse unusual intensity of feeling within me? Then *identify* differences in the present scene.

"Anyone's history of woundedness from significant relationships of the past will inevitably be painfully touched from time to time if she or he risks drawing close to others in intentional community" (Lee and Cowan, 139). Groups are not responsible for these feelings. Individuals who are committed to community building will work at taking responsibility for resolving this past unfinished emotional business so as to be able to form community in present relationships without being bound by past formations. Questions about feelings help. Are you feeling suffocated by this list of commitments we've agreed upon? You aren't feeling freed by knowing what we expect? Do you fear we will limit you personally by these guidelines? What would help you feel more comfortable with these commitments? True community requires healing and investment in new communal patterns. Supportive community gives opportunity to move on in relational growth while imitating the positive learned patterns of past relational behaviors.

WHY SMALL GROUPS?
Why do persons join groups? What motivates a person to limit individualistic tendencies for the sake of community? Biblically as described earlier, we need community to fulfill our pull in the direction of reflecting the image of God. This awareness of and interdependency with others is part of our creation format. We will never be whole apart from giving ourselves away to others and receiving from them their uniqueness. For believers, to be in Christ is to be in relationship with others in His body.

Group dynamicists see psychological needs driving us to form groups. One theory FIRO (Fundamental Interpersonal Relations Orientation) (Schutz, 1958) measures three basic drives which groups seem to satisfy. The first is inclusion. We have an inherent need to be a part of a group and accepted by others. Second, we have both the need to influence or dominate others, and to be influenced or dominated by others. This need is categorized as control or power. This need does not imply negative power usage but can be exercised in organizing and initiating activities, in assuming responsibility, and in attempting to persuade others. As persons feel a need for this kind of influencing they may join groups to implement such a need and in so doing care for others. The third FIRO need is that of openness or affection. We want to like others and to be liked by them. Groups enable us to express this positive desire (Forsyth, 55). These three are measured in both the need to express the behavior and the need to receive the behavior from others. *Inclusion:* we like to be with others and we like others to invite or include us when they do things. *Power:* we like to take responsibility for doing things and we enjoy having others take charge of doing what needs to be done. *Affection:* we work at building close relationships with others and we enjoy people demonstrating friendliness toward us.

Other studies (Festinger, 1950, 1954; Schachter, 1959) suggest that persons join groups to validate their opinions, attitudes, and beliefs. Groups help shape our perspectives and give reassur-

---

1. Think about a small group of 3 to 5 persons you are or have been involved with. What are/were the costs? Rewards?

2. On a scale of 1 to 5 (1 = low, 5 = high) rate yourself on the following:

   a. my need to demonstrate affection to others in the group
   b. my need to receive affection from others
   c. my need to be included when members gather informally in "after group sessions," parties, informal social events such as going out for a cup of coffee
   d. my openness to include other members in my leisure time activities
   e. my need to be in charge of situations in the group
   f. my willingness to allow others to be in charge of situations in the group

How do you think one of the group members would rate *you* on the above?

3. What verbal and nonverbal acts do you use:

   a. to show affection to the group
   b. when you receive affection from others in the group
   c. to make sure you are included in "after group" sessions, parties, informal social events
   d. to include other members in your leisure activities
   e. to take charge of situations
   f. to motivate others to take charge of situations

Adapted from Kathleen S. Verderber and Rudolph F. Verderber
Inter-Act, 4th ed., 198

---

ance. They clarify information cognitively and confirm our validity as persons. For instance, when facing an unknown situation where we lack security in our assessment of or ability to handle a dilemma, we tend to seek out others who will give us the value of comparison. We, therefore, tend to seek others who provide reassuring information of a similar nature and who assure us that we (and our situations) are normal. When there is a clash between understanding accurately or being reassured personally, we generally will choose reassurance over accuracy (Forsyth, 58). Thus, groups enable people to feel OK about themselves, giving social approval that each is a valuable human being—even if it is because an individual thinks like others in the group. This explains in part why some street gangs have such a hold on their members in spite of the inaccuracy of their ways of thinking. The gang validates the importance of the person.

Persons also join groups because it is in the group they find the personal support needed to cope with life. As mentioned above, groups give us affirmation of our worth and value and provide information and advice when we need counsel. In expressing value statements about our abilities or personal traits, groups can sustain our fragile self-esteem. Emotionally, groups provide opportunities for self-disclosure and expression of feelings—we find an audience who cares. This not only relieves stress but gives us relief from the loneliness of carrying burdens alone. Emotional distortions are lessened and our well-being is enhanced because group support buffers detrimental psychological, mental, and physical behaviors (Forsyth, 58–59).

As declared by the Creator in the Garden, "It is not good for any human to be alone"—self-sufficient, unrelated to others. We are made to be in community. Helping each other find that community is helping to fulfill the will of God. As sung by Barbra Streisand, "People who need people are the luckiest people in the world." And Robinson Crusoe would agree.

6

AND NOW FOR
A CHANGE:
TRANSFORMATION
IN GROUPS

*The important thing is this: to be willing at any moment
to sacrifice who we are for what we can become.*
Charles Du Bois

"Change" is seldom neutral. We talk of "change for the
better" or "change for the worse." We are exhilarated
by the prospect of change or threatened by its demands. Boomers, more than any previous generation have grown
up living with rapid change. For the most part persons initially
resist change because it means leaving what is "comfortable" and
moving to the unknown. But there is no forward motion without
change. The Christian life is expected to be one of transition and
transformation as believers are formed more wholly in the likeness of Christ. At the heart of all life is growth and development,
positive or negative.

Paul the Apostle wrote to the Galatians, "My little children
. . . I am again in the pains of childbirth until Christ is formed in
you" (Gal. 4:19). And to the Corinthians, "We, who with unveiled faces all reflect the Lord's glory, are being transformed
into His likeness with ever-increasing glory" (2 Cor. 3:18). To the
Romans he sent this word, "Be transformed by the renewing of
your mind" (Rom. 12:2). Such texts indicate a process involving
both Spirit power and personal prompting in spiritual formation.
This formation is enabled by focusing on and then reflecting

110

back the image of Jesus. Evidence points to the will and the attitude as being major participants in this formation process. Formation also involves our actions—it requires "walking in the truth." Scripture indicates that regular practice is necessary to produce qualities of likeness. "Solid food (the teaching about righteousness) is for the mature, who by constant use have trained themselves to distinguish good from evil" (Heb. 5:14). Constant use issues in a maturing discernment of right living. Jesus Himself, extolled the hearing and putting into practice of His words. The Parable of the Wise Builder is a direct illustration of acting on known truth. "Everyone who hears these words of Mine and puts them into practice is like a wise man who built his house on the rock" (Matt. 7:24). The rich young ruler was told, "If you want to be perfect (complete, mature), go, sell . . . and give to the poor" (Matt. 19:21). In other words, "Practice the truths you claim to know."

The purpose of a small group is not meetings but maturity. True community leads to growth. "Stuck groups" are usually those who have closed their minds to change. They have chosen to remain within their comfort zones. Group vitality is based on movement and growth, both in the individual and in the corporate sphere. Community generates various expressions of formation. The presence of the Spirit, the gathering of believers in the name of Jesus, and the living, active Word of God combine to produce an amazing climate for growth. When every occasion of Christian community is viewed as an opportunity for Christian formation, groups take on new importance and the structuring of the time together becomes one of purposeful interaction. Group times then become more than just finishing a project, spending time together, or even getting to know each other.

In their journey toward Christlikeness, group members may grow in character, may discover new understandings, may develop skills that enhance their relationship with God and others, may accomplish ministry to the body or to the world. But when seen in the framework of Christian formation, there is a God-centered focus to whatever is done. Then we don't treat others with esteem and care just so they will "feel at home in the group." Their "at homeness" and experiencing genuine love enhance their openness to the formation of Christ within them and within relationships in the group. We don't share openly just because we want people to know us and like us. Such sharing can be a means of personal formation. One person's disclosure may be utilized by the Spirit of God to help someone else gain perspective and encouragement. Refreshment times are more than icebreakers or small-talk time. They become occasions for informal formation and enjoyment of God's unique work in persons of his likeness.

The Latin phrase *coram deo* capsulizes the perspective of formation. *Coram deo* means "in the presence or before the face of God." Everything is done as it were with God being present to enhance and make use of acts and conversations to achieve his purpose. Words, activities, even rituals of a community become filled with his presence and are made more than mere human expressions—they are done to the glory of God. Even the most mundane act (giving a cup of cold water) becomes an investment in the process of formation. With this kind of focus, words are formed differently, actions are carried out that normally would not even have been thought of, and group events (even committee meetings) become occasions for seeing God at work in who we are and what we do. We find God in the ordinary and find that the former ordinary becomes significant and purposeful. When God is in our midst, formation is possible. It happened to Peter in a work group (his fishing team), to Cleopas and companion while having dinner together (in their Emmaus home), to Martha in the midst of grief (at Lazarus' wake), to a Samaritan lady during a routine household duty (getting water from the well). Every group occasion, whether support group, study group, or committee meeting, is an opportunity for our formation when seen as *coram deo.*

Of course the Spirit of God is the Agent of formation. Only the Spirit can form us in His likeness, and that can occur in the midst of any spontaneous happening. However, certain conditions have been shown to facilitate this reforming within a group. These conditions do not cause the actual transformation in themselves, but rather create an environment that helps put us in a place where God can move among us and shape us to reflect more fully His image.

What are some of these conditions which foster a transforming climate where persons grow and are changed in their outlooks and behaviors? What aspects of a small group climate have helped you to change?

EXPECTATION OF TRANSFORMATION

The first is an expectation or readiness for change. The leader who plans with transformation in mind will lead differently. The member who comes expecting to be changed by this group encounter will respond differently, both to information and interpersonal relationships. This openness to God's action in transforming attitudes, changing patterns, and moving us into deeper insight is in essence faith. Such belief in the power and person of a God who works in community to mature us is essential to the Spirit's working God's will in our midst. Nazareth was left barren when it came to experiencing miracles that its Native Son performed elsewhere. The inhabitants chose not to esteem Him as more than a carpenter's son and thus their expectations were limited. On other occasions where transformation was experienced, Jesus enjoined Jairus to "keep the faith" that his daughter would be restored (Mark 5), extolled the centurion's expectation that his servant would be healed (Luke 7:9), and commended the bleeding woman who approached Him with the conviction, "If I can just touch His clothes, I will be healed" (Mark 5:28).

Regrettably, many groups become humdrum and lose direction as time sets in. Persons who have become "old hands" at group meetings fail to expect more than what has already been experienced. It is difficult to maintain the expectation that because God is at work here, every encounter, every happening is an opportunity for life change to occur. We lose the element of openness to change and settle for the comfort of our present situation. Groups where persons are new to each other often see more formation and increased insight because of their openness to change. Leaders who expect transformation lead with a different goal in mind. Teachers who believe persons and groups will be reshaped as a result of insights and processes will teach content in a more focused, life-related way. Members who come expecting to be changed, experience significant growth. Perhaps this is why we so often grow through crises events — we are forced to change and we open ourselves up to God to work newness in our lives. Expect transformation when the people of God gather around the Word of God with the Spirit of God present. Our expectations are never too high when these conditions are present. How can you create a spirit of expectation of change in your group situation? What steps would foster this conviction? What must take place in you if this is to occur?

CLIMATE OF SAFETY AND COHESION

Cultivating a climate of security and belonging is essential to persons opening themselves up to make changes. Threat, being unsure of how you are accepted, and feeling you can't be honest about who you really are, keep a person protective and promote a desire to maintain the status quo. Willingness to let go and to trust are conditions that grow out of knowing and feeling at home with others. Chances for retooling attitudes and revising concepts and habits are increased whenever a strong "we-feeling" is developed within a group. Coaches know this principle works. In promoting transformation it is advantageous that all the members of a group share in the perception that change is needed. A desire for change may begin with one, but that hunger must spread or the individual will simply be written off as a "deviant" from the group's "norm." Groups that are uncomfortable with things as they are and express a desire for more are strong candidates for moving forward, becoming improved groups. Support and recovery groups are often significant in helping persons develop new patterns of coping because members realize others accept and understand them. What can you do to create a sense of belonging in your group? What would say "you belong" to members of the group? What acts create a setting that is secure for risking? What indicates that members don't feel secure?

ATTRACTIVENESS OF INFLUENCER

If I like my group—for whatever reason—I am more likely to change. Strong, positive feelings about a group put a person in a position of being receptive to different and transforming influences. These positive feelings come when members feel the group is important in their lives and is meeting the needs which they bring to the group. Feeling like they are accomplishing something in their group can cause persons to risk making changes so the larger group goal can be realized. Liking and respecting persons in the group means we hear their comments and are open to their ideas. Attractiveness of a group because it meets these or other personal values increases its ability to bring about change. What seems to make your group attractive to you? What makes it attractive to other members? What would increase its attractiveness for the person who seems to be "stuck," comfortable, or afraid to grow?

FOCUSED ON NEED
The more closely transformations are tied in to the goals of the person joining the group, the more likely they are to occur. For example, if a person joins a group to "learn how to study the Bible," they will be more likely to change habit patterns in personal disciplines if those disciplines can be shown to help them achieve that goal. A person who is going through a transition in life and needs a supportive relational structure is likely to respond to suggestions that group has for responding differently to new situations. Persons whose goal is to find friends are good candidates for developing relational skills never before experienced. The desire to complete a project causes some people to put aside personal biases and be open to new learning. A goal helps persons see transformation as necessary and goal-directed living means acting to bring about the desired purpose. Knowing what conditions and motivations group members have is an asset in developing goals for growth in their lives. Attempts to influence will be more effective if they are appropriate to the groups in which they are made. Are you aware of each member's purpose in being in the group? What is your purpose in leading? What would members say is the purpose of the group?

PRESTIGE OF THE PERSUADER
E.F. Hutton is almost synonymous with influence. "When E.F. Hutton speaks, everybody listens," has become a trademark statement. The more respect and prestige a group member has, the greater the likelihood that he or she will influence others. Prestige is accorded persons according to values in the group. Some gang leaders may have prestige in their gangs but are not

accorded the same prestige in the neighborhood. Who are the influential persons in your group?

GROUP VALUES AS INFLUENCERS

How can you break out of ruts? Efforts to move people or parts of a group in a direction deviating from the norms of the group will be most difficult. For example, if the group norm says so-and-so is the leader and nobody else, efforts to develop a shared leadership style without changing the norm, will encounter strong resistance (Tubbs, 26–27). A person trying to move a group to deeper levels of sharing will find it difficult if the group's unwritten standard is safe surface sharing only. In other words, transformation will more likely take place when the values of the group support such a change. This has implications for pulling a leader or member out of a group to give them special training and then expecting them to go back to a group and act in a changed manner. The values of the group must change also, not just one individual. As you think through your group and areas where you would like to see change, are you aware of any group norms or values that would undermine that change?

Change, as any innovator knows, takes time and is often met with resistance. However, without change, there is no growth. The above principles have implications for changing the patterns of training small group leaders. These principles also provoke questions that need to be answered and describe conditions that need to be created to enable transformation in the believer group member and in the group as a whole.

DEVELOPMENTALISM AND TRANSFORMATION

A factor to be reckoned with in this process of change is that persons, by their very nature, are continually moving from one stage to another. Taking into account this development of the person in sequential stages is called developmentalism. This theory says we never just teach content or just "run a group." We always focus on who the persons are and what they have experienced, what they are currently experiencing and what conditions they presently experience. A group leader who expects transformation to take place is always adapting content and methods to reach the group member. Just as it would be foolish to expect a four-year-old to work an algebra equation, so it is unthinkable to expect believers who have had little experience in applying Scripture to their everyday lives, to do this automatically. They need the "constant use" to develop that skill and experience its benefits. Being aware of what members know and are presently experiencing enables the "fitting" of content to life. This sensitivity to persons and their situations is necessary for formation to take place. Try listing for each group member a descriptive phrase or two that capsulizes his or her present developmental conditions. Be aware of physical, mental, relational, emotional, and spiritual stress points of growth they are exposed to right now.

Developmentalism also suggests certain needs and characteristics that are unique to an age level. Certain characteristics appear to be true for most persons in a defined age range and give us insight into the most valuable information and ways to influence change at that period of life. For example, learning theorists have discovered that young adults are coping with establishing their own identity, designing a dream to follow, and selecting standards by which they will operate in following the dream. Mid-lifers also struggle with identity caused by the transition in parental roles as children leave home and require new ways of relating. As work takes on less importance and offers less fulfillment, the midlife individual must face the realization that life is half over and former sources of fulfillment are no longer viable. With these conditions occupying a major portion of their time and thought, these two age levels will respond to different types of group structures and leadership styles, will embrace different expectations, and will recognize different implications from the same content. If you work with a defined age level in your group, what "influencers" of that age have you noticed? How has this made impact on your group structure, your group goals, your leadership style?

In the same way, groups as a whole go through different phases of development and thus should be led differently, structured differently, and focused to meet the kind of insights and experiences needed by members going through that transition. The Scripture is always relevant. But how we package it and draw relationships to life changes so that persons are met with the truth at every point of life. Is it true that a person matures spiritually as she matures in years and experience? No. Maturing developmentally can enhance growth in Christlikeness, but does not automatically produce it. Each stage presents a unique opportunity to challenge persons with the lordship of Christ over that stage. What new issues of His lordship do you see in your present life stage? In the present phase of your group development? What new questions and values must be dealt with at this period of growth?

Developmentalism sees the leader as a guide, not an expert who knows all the answers. The leader's role is to set up situations which will help persons grow — to get them involved in the process. Everything that is done in the group is seen as affecting growth. The arrangement of chairs for participants impacts growth. How effectively persons are made to feel a sense of belonging affects growth. What they are expected to do within the group affects growth. How information is presented affects growth.

What awareness do you have of developmentalism in your group? What characteristics that affect your group seem to be similar? What individual characteristics have you seen that seem to influence your group? What one change in your group would enhance members' growth and transformation?

PART III
GROUP
DEVELOPMENT

7

GENESIS OF A GROUP

When is a group a group?

Which of the following would you label as groups?
- A crowd of people gawking at an accident
- A connection of shortwave operators
- A police battalion
- Several fans in line discussing their hopes of getting a ticket to a crowded sports event
- A traffic school class

While each of these collections may be referred to as a group, in the sense of the word *group* being used here, none of them qualifies as a group. Compare the qualifications that are similar in each of the definitions of *group* below. Underline words that are the same.

A group consists of a small collection of people who interact with each other, usually face to face, over time in order to reach goals.

(Adler and Rodman, 224)

A small group is a collection of individuals, from three to

121

fifteen in number, who meet in face-to-face interaction over a period of time, generally with an assigned or assumed leader, who possess at least one common characteristic, and who meet with a purpose in mind.

(Barker and Wahlers, 8)

A Christian small group is an intentional face-to-face encounter of no more than twelve people who meet on a regular basis with the purpose of growing in the knowledge and likeness of Jesus Christ.

(Hestenes and Gorman)

A group isn't a group without interaction. Students in a lecture or believers in a congregation can feel very much alone even though surrounded by other persons if they are expected to passively listen and don't exchange dialog with the leader or others. Simply occupying the same area at the same time does not turn persons into groups. For "face-to-face" encounters, groups are limited in size—usually no more than twelve with eight as the optimum number. The common characteristic that unites persons may be assigned, self-realized, or assumed but it must always be there. It may range from having a common cause or goal to having gone through similar experiences. Groups tend to be intentional—not just spontaneous gatherings—and they must occur regularly. A group must meet at least once a month.

Think of some groups you've encountered. Which of them measured up to these criteria for small groups? If you have experienced a "group" that never seemed to become a group, were any of the above factors missing?

The shared purpose that group members have usually determines the kind of group being formed. Notice how these broad categories suggest definite purposes: Contact/friendship groups, Evangelism groups, Nurture/discipleship groups, Study groups, Support groups, Recovery groups, Equipping groups, Prayer groups, Mission/project groups, Worship groups, Committees. Some groups are categorized by the persons targeted: Singles groups, Seniors groups, Intergenerational groups.

Think of groups in your present awareness. In which of the above categories do they fall? Do most of the groups in which you have been a member fall into the same category? Which kind of group have you yet to experience?

GROUP NEEDS

Groups need a reason for being. The *purpose* is a key element in the survival of a group. Without a purpose, groups flounder and eventually die. Every group needs a task growing out of that purpose for its existence. That task may range from completion of a project to the development of friendly relationships with others in the group. Tasks may be multiple in number such as developing a sense of togetherness while learning how to minister to a group of refugees recently arrived in your city.

A second need found in groups is that of individual members. This need may be in sync with the group purpose or at times, it may be in competition with it. For example, the need to be safe and secure may cause a member to hold back what he/she has to offer when the group climate seems risky. Because a person so strongly wants to belong, that individual may refuse to critique the group's actions which could help them avoid problems later. One woman knew that the presentation planned by the males in her group would come across as authoritative and controlling, but she refused to interject her insight for fear she would be labeled as "too sensitive." All of us come to group encounters with histories, wounds, and sensitive areas where we doubt and fear. Each of us consciously or unconsciously operates out of needs for feeling valued and understood, for feeling loved and accepted, for feeling we can achieve something worthwhile. Until trust is built (and even after that is achieved), persons in groups can be expected to operate on the basis of these individual motivators to feel whole and significant. Unusual behavior or intense emotions portrayed by individuals usually means they are working from some subconscious agenda that is inherent in who they are as individuals. For example, always having to be right may indicate that a person is unsure and needs to validate his identity by being in control. Initially a group goal is made up of a composite of personal or individual goals owned by members of the same group (L. Barker, et al., 69). That makes it imperative that every member place his/her desires for the group on the table so those expectations have a part in shaping the group goal.

What is an individual need of yours that you bring to a group you are currently in?

Finally, besides task and individual needs, every group is concerned with the need to stay healthy and be built together as persons. This need is called Group Maintenance. When an individual pursues accomplishment this need is often set aside. But when one must not only achieve, but achieve with a collection of others, this relationship process is vital. It seems difficult to balance these two goals of task accomplishment and group maintenance. Often a project is pushed through by a leader or strong subgroup only to find that the group is left with anger, apathy, and little enthusiasm for the results. Committees are notorious for concentrating on "business" and covering the agenda while ignoring interpersonal relationships, misunderstandings, and members' self-esteem. On the other hand, some groups focus so strongly on interpersonal relationships that they neglect to achieve a set goal that could risk conflict and strong feelings within the group. Group relationship and group efficiency appear to feed each other. Both are needed. Wheeless, Wheeless, and Dickson-Markman (1982) found a positive correlation between group solidarity, satisfaction, quality of interaction, and goal attainment. Working together, members become aware of one another's competency and thus are drawn closer together which in itself increases the possibility of their successful performance (L. Barker, et al., 199). When groups seem to have a hard time achieving their goals, examine the amount of time spent on the task compared to time building interpersonal relationships. Adjust the focus appropriately to spend more time on relating. This will be difficult to do because when a project gets bogged down we tend to push harder, not pull off and build caring among people. What we are talking about is developing an increased awareness of others through listening skills and through sharing personal agendas.

Groups constantly face the dilemma of sacrificing productivity for member relations or vice versa. Berkowitz (1954) and Thelen (1954) both found that groups had greater long-term efficiency if they spent more time initially in building interpersonal relationships (L. Barker, et al., 198). In getting to know each other and each other's agendas, persons build foundations for problem solving and goal reaching. This says something about how we might structure clear task groups such as Bible studies, skill development sessions, and committee meetings.

MORALE AND PRODUCTIVITY

High morale breeds high productivity. Groups whose purpose is clearly problem solving need a different leadership style from those whose purpose is building a support system for sharers. Napier and Gershenfeld have listed generalizations that can serve as guidelines in targeting efficiency and morale.

1. Morale will be higher in groups in which there is more access to participation among those involved—the more open the participation, the higher the morale.

2. Efficiency tends to be lowest among groups that are the most open. Since more wrong ideas need to be sifted out, more extraneous material is generated and more time is "wasted" listening to individuals even when a point has been made.

3. Groups that are most efficient tend to be those in which all members have access to a central leadership figure who can act as an expediter and clarifier as well as keep the group on the right track in working through the problem.

4. Positions that individuals take can have a definite influence on leadership in the group as well as on potential conflict among group members. In the process of performing communication functions—such as deciding on goals, giving directions, summarizing, and being self-assured—groups can predict potential leaders who may be chosen for positive and/or negative qualities (Schultz, 1986).

5. Groups with centralized leadership . . . tend to organize more rapidly, be more stable in performance, and show greater efficiency. However, morale also tends to drop

and this, in the long run, could influence stability and even productivity (Glazer and Glazer, 1961; Hearn, 1957).

6. Leaders in groups without strong identities (low cohesion) do best to direct and run things, but in groups that have high cohesion, leaders are more effective when they take group members' needs into account and work in a more collaborative way (Schriesheim, 1980).

(from Napier and Gershenfeld,
Groups: Theory and Experience, 42–43)

Personality may serve as a factor in these groups as some persons want to get the job done, being task-centered, while others gravitate toward cultivating warm interpersonal relationships. Leadership teams often eliminate imbalance by offering both of these emphases in the personalities making up the team. Blanchard and Hershey recommend the solo leader's cultivating awareness of and skills in various leadership styles to help balance these complementary focuses. In forming a group it is helpful to keep in mind that three needs will be present and vying for attention: task achievement or group needs, individual personal needs, and maintenance of relationship needs.

In thinking through a group you are presently in, what individual needs have surfaced? Which persons seem to express the need for productivity within the group? Which persons exhibit interest in maintaining good group relations?

PERSONAL NEEDS AND GROUP STRUCTURES
Personal needs of members also have an effect on how groups are structured. Luft cites the importance of matching authoritarian and egalitarian structures with certain personalities for the effectiveness of a group process.

Individuals searching for safety or security are likely to feel better in a more authoritarian group, and their performance seems to improve. The person for whom self-esteem is important, however, seems to prefer groups in which the structure and leadership are more egalitarian.

(Luft, 17)

Because these personal needs come with members into group structures, they have an effect on achievement of the task and satisfaction over group relations, both of which determine effectiveness of a group. Thus knowing the personalities of members can be helpful in designing group structure and leadership style.

Of course every person feels a need to gain a measure of safety in a strange and uncomfortable situation. When persons join a group there is a natural anxiety that comes from concern about how others perceive them and about how they perceive others in the group. "Anxiety, to one degree or another, is the prevailing and dominating emotion at the start of any group setting" (Napier and Gershenfeld, *Groups: Theory and Experience,* 7). There is also present a vacillation between belonging and withdrawing—a paradoxical tension that is born out of being an individual and a group member at the same time. This creates insecurity as members are torn between interacting and protecting. We feel the need to share "this is me," and then pull back wondering what others think about us. In reality, others are primarily preoccupied with their own needs and figuring out ways of coping with tensions they feel.

One way we gain a sense of security is by ordering—looking for ways of comparing and finding similarities in the great amount of new data that confronts us upon the forming of a group. By this means we keep from being overwhelmed. For example, we will begin to align ourselves with persons in a group who fit our idea of what a good group member is like—those who are most like us and thus least threatening because they don't cause conflict with our own values and desires. We identify with these individuals and thus feel safer in a tense situation. Later we may realize how inaccurate and incomplete our assessments were. But at this point such "ordering" gives us a sense of mooring and control in an uncharted territory. It becomes evident that needs constantly arise in the act of group formation. While group members may be talking objectively and calmly, in actuality they are actively working to bring a sense of well-being and harmony to an unsettling scene (Napier and Gershenfeld, *Groups: Theory and Experience,* 18–19). This is bound to affect behavior and is one reason individuals may appear to be entirely different persons inside a group than when outside it.

A SYSTEMS PERSPECTIVE

The previous multiple motivations suggest the importance of viewing group behavior in a systems perspective. Complex behaviors do not result from a single cause. Rather, an individual's behavior grows out of a blending of interdependent forces relating to one another and multiple causes joining together. For example, a member's personality combined with a certain group size and group leadership style when set in the midst of a group's interpersonal relationship conditions may cause a person to act in a way never before observed. A complex network of needs and esteem requirements may influence group participants to interact in unusual ways. Changing the leader may not eliminate negative reaction because that is only one factor in a system of causations.

Most of us have seen the spiral children's books which divide an animal into three parts: head, torso, and legs. By flipping different parts of the page the creative child comes up with the strange combinations of mixed breeds. Consider the same by picking one element from each of the categories on page 127 and consider how one element in the system affects all others in that combination. Vary the combination by one factor and project the change in results.

Add to this the other factors such as group experience, longevity of group, norms established, etc., and the complexity of a group's or individual's behavior becomes real.

The very presence of other persons has an impact on individuals that is not present when that one works alone. The presence of others can provide a source of support and comfort when one faces an anxious situation. On the other hand, it may create defensiveness and protectiveness within us. Knowing that others are there and will observe with resulting reward or condemnation influences our behavior in groups. Others provide guidelines about what is acceptable and what is unacceptable behavior as they model what is appropriate. The presence of others may inspire us to new heights of productivity or may distract us from our task achievement. Groups by their very social structure trigger reactions within us (L. Barker, et al., 44–48).

Can you think of a group whose simple presence helped you deal with anxiety?

Personality Factor	Member Need	Leadership Style
Extrovert	Establish identity	Authoritative-
Introvert	Feel accepted	Confident
Sensing (Learns	Be seen as	Empowering/
information from	knowledgeable	Coaching
sight, sound,	Feel secure	Delegating
feeling, etc.)	and wanted	Mutually Shared
Intuitive (Learns	Please others	Supportive
information by	Growth in	Authoritarian
drawing meaning	relating	in charge
from what is		
seen, heard, etc.)		
Thinking oriented		
Feeling oriented		

Group Format	Size	Your Choice
Bible study	Four	Personality _____
Sharing	Twelve	Need _____
Project	Fifteen	Leadership _____
Worship	Five	Format _____
Support	Eight	Size _____
Committee of		
Experts		

When was the presence of others a motivating factor, causing you to do your best work?

How has knowing others would think highly of you, valuing your ability, challenged you to do more than if you were alone?

But presence of people is not the only factor impacting how groups form. Natural environment plays a largely unconscious part. Three major factors are space, seating arrangement, and size.

SPACE
Space communicates silently. One has only to observe persons crowded into an elevator or seated closely on public transportation to become aware of how people react when the relationship does not fit the distance dimensions. Anthropologist Edward Hall identified four distance zones in human interaction. *Intimate distance* moves from 0 to 18 inches while *personal distance* ranges

from 18 inches to 4 feet. *Social distance* varies from 4 to 12 feet. *Public distance* extends from 12 to 25 feet (Hall, *The Silent Language,* 1959). Women have been observed to use shorter conversational distances than men (Heshka and Nelson, 1972; Willis, 1966). Children interact in shorter distances than adults (Meisels and Guardo, 1969). And persons in Latin American countries tend to choose smaller interactional distances than persons in Anglo-Saxon nations (Hall, *The Silent Language,* 1959). Too close proximity is more tolerable at our sides than when directly in front of us (Blumberg, et al., 10).

SEATING

Seating has an effect on interaction and appears to be impacted by a person's status or attitude in terms of leadership. Persons who are in or desire leadership positions gravitate toward the ends of rectangular seating arrangements. Others in the situation generally viewed those sitting in these positions as leadership whether in actuality or as viable candidates. This silent assessment explains why persons in organizations are sensitive about placement and spatial distances in offices and desk size (Blumberg, et al., 12).

The task to be performed will often dictate where persons sit. Casual conversations select corner-to-corner or face-to-face arrangements. Competing persons often sit opposite and often at a distance from opponents (Tubbs, 101–102). The arrangement most advantageous to interaction is the circle. Motivation to speak is higher when one faces others and can see them clearly. Because of that factor more interaction takes place across a circle than side by side. One of the more difficult interaction positions is three on a couch. Being out of the circle or seated at a corner in a rectangle usually means the person in that position will remain outside the interaction. In a small room persons feel comfortable sitting further apart than in a large room which will cause them to sit closer together. High background noise whether loud music or multiple conversations drives persons to decrease the amount of distance between them. This principle explains the presence of loud music in bars and how certain sales situations occur amid music and multiple conversations in one large room (Blumberg, et al., 12).

These are a few factors to consider when structuring for inter-action among persons in groups. Such factors are usually in our awareness at the forming of a group but lapse into unconscious-ness as time goes on. Nevertheless, seating plays a part in the roles and interaction group members exhibit. It also affects where the leadership sits and the way that leadership comes across. A leader who sits along the side of a rectangular table silently expresses a desire for a more democratic style than the leader who leads from the more authoritative end of the rectan-gle position. Most persons in a group feel uncomfortable if the leader is not seated in a leadership position. Try sitting in a corner position and watch the uncomfortableness of the group. The corner seat is usually a silent member. Likewise in a circle arrangement the leader pushed back from the group creates a leader-oriented discussion pattern of interaction where most if not all conversation is directed to and from the leader. Seating of participants becomes the quiet controller of the interaction that takes place in the group.

Examine the following living room design and then respond to the questions.

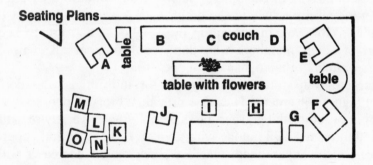

Where would the leader likely sit?

If you chose to be a low participant, where would you elect to sit?

An active participant would probably sit where?

Which persons are likely to find difficulty in interacting with each other because of where they are seated?

What minor rearrangements would you make to facilitate bet-ter interaction?

Crowding has a physical and a psychological side. Females tend to feel more comfortable in smaller rooms which promote intimate conversation among them while males prefer larger rooms. Moving persons closer together for conversing or turning up the heat in a room both create the sense of crowding and cause persons to respond negatively to one another (Napier and Gershenfeld, *Groups: Theory and Experience,* 42).

SIZE

Size has been shown to be a factor affecting leadership, the participation and reaction of members, effectiveness of the group, satisfaction of members, and ability to reach group consensus (Wilson and Hanna, 186). Size is best determined by the objective of the group. Those desiring to stimulate individual thinking and questioning require a small group while objectives that incorporate broad exposure with many points of view will be best achieved in a larger group (Brilhart/Galanes, 46). Most researchers agree that for optimum discussion and involvement *five* is an ideal number (Luft, 23; Tubbs, 105). The upper limit in which a small group can function has been noted as twenty (Palazzolo, 37). An example of such a group would be an intergenerational group where the group is broken into subgroups of families. However, in any group over eight there is great likelihood of silent members who don't contribute at all. This of course affects other dynamics of the group.

Larger groups provide anonymity for individuals who don't want high involvement. They also provide a broader pool to draw from in accomplishing group tasks with a greater variety of skills and abilities available along with greater knowledge and experience. On the other hand, member participation decreases with increasing size, the conversation centering on the talkative few who tend to speak to each other instead of to the whole group. The central person (usually the leader) tends to do more and more of the speaking. "Speeches" made by participants usually increase in length. Some evidence suggests that the total amount of talking lessens as size grows. Lessening participation is closely tied to lower satisfaction with a group (Brilhart/Galanes, 45). Larger groups—of ten or more require an inordinate amount of time to handle organizational procedures just to keep the group functioning. This means less time spent on the task (Tubbs, 105).

Persons who want to join a closed group will often plead, "It's just one more." But the number of potential relationships multiplies astronomically with each member added. In a four-person group the possible initiating interactions total twenty-eight while in an eight-person group the number jumps to 1,056 (Brilhart, 57).

"Each group member is under increasing pressure to maintain appropriate relationships with an increasing number of group members. There are more relationships to maintain and increasingly less time in which to do so" (Palazzolo, 167). Such pressures cause increased evidence of tension release (jokes, etc.) while the actual showing of tension decreases dramatically, going underground. Suggestion making and information sharing grows while opinion seeking and opinion giving fades (Hare, Bales, and Borgatta, 493–512). With increase of size comes a more formal, mechanical style of offering information such as the typical round robin method. Members seem less sensitive to exploring another's point of view and give evidence of trying to control others, pushing them to conclusions and reaching decisions regardless of whether all are in agreement. Because there is less "check in," there is likely to be more resentment and less feeling of ownership. People are more likely to withdraw.

As groups grow larger, they tend to subdivide into smaller unit groups. It is possible to have several subgroups functioning, sometimes at cross-purposes, at the same time. The forming of these blocks can slow down progress and drain energy from the group. Their side conversations may annoy the others in the group. When subdividing, *even sized* groups tend to divide into equal parts which can increase conflict, disagreement, and a struggle for power while *odd sized* groups are more likely to reach decisions sooner aided by their unequal division (Palazzolo, 168).

The larger a group becomes the greater the amount of inequality of member participation. A few will participate heavily while others may not be involved at all. Any group over eight will often have silent members. The talkative few usually address each other rather than the other members. Talkers are usually considered to have a lot of influence whether saying something significant or not.

From your experience how many persons do you think will dominate the conversation when the group numbers twenty

How many would dominate a group of ten? When eight persons comprise the group? In a group of five? A group of three?

When the group size is twenty, five or less will dominate. With eight or ten persons, three. With five the number is likely two, and with three, probably no one (Napier and Gershenfeld, 39–40). Again from your experience, how many do you think will take part in the participation of the above sized groups?

With increasing size comes less time for each member to participate. This is complicated by the need to hear from every member so as to feel that all are involved and contributing. The larger the group the more requirements are placed on the leader. What are some of these requirements as you have experienced them in larger groups?

The larger groups become the more the leadership tends to take over and the more members in the group desire and accept that takeover of the important group functions (Wilson and Hanna, 187). At the same time, the influence of a leader seems to be lessened as the size of the group grows. Hare discovered that leaders tend to be more influential in smaller sized groups while Hemphill found members from increasing sized groups require leaders to exercise more effective control (Hare, 1952, 261–267; Hemphill, 11–22).

In beginning a group, space factors, seating of members, and the size of the group are hidden but significant shapers of group process and accomplishment. Think of a time when one of these factors impacted a group scene of which you were a part. What took place? What steps would have improved the dynamics of the group's function? Space? Seating? Size?

Another major factor that sets the scene for a positive group experience is the presence of a shared agreement variously known as a covenant, contract, or group agreement.

SHARED AGREEMENT

The old saying, "What you don't know can't hurt you," proves untrue in life and in small groups. Hidden agendas undermine a group and keep it from functioning effectively. Some expectations are unconscious and remain so unless group members are encouraged to explore them. A "contract discussion" allows for that exploration.

A group's contract is basically a shared agreement of the purposes this group is set on accomplishing and the responsibilities required of each member if that purpose is to be achieved. Such a statement of expectations lets everyone know what he/she is getting into. Many prefer the term *covenant* because this word expresses our commitment to one another as those under God's love.

A group's covenant can be determined by the leaders and then shared in such a way that allows others to buy into that depiction of purpose and responsibility. For example,

> This group is for those who want to actively share in the study of Scripture together always culminating in the specific practical application of truth to their everyday lives. Members will study a chapter ahead of time and be present to contribute their ideas and personal implications to the group time. We will meet every week for twelve weeks with members contributing refreshments on a rotational basis.

In describing what is expected the leaders realize that this group isn't for everyone—but only for those who want these ingredients in this purpose. Before committing to such a group, each potential group member needs to be made aware of what that commitment means. Too many times persons join a group thinking it will be one thing when there was no intention of going that direction. Or they get involved in a group that will ask from them something they are unwilling or unable to give.

Another method of covenanting is to ask interested persons what a group needs to be if it is to be fulfilling to them. Sometimes the reverse is helpful—what is something you don't want in this group?

As each shares hopes and plans the group begins to take shape and persons begin to determine whether or not that shape fits them. Talking about expectations and commitments at the beginning helps to prevent frustration later when the group doesn't fulfill the plans of the joiner. Most persons investigate a car make and model prior to their purchase and check out loan commitments before signing up. Premarital counseling at its best seeks to enable couples to talk through their values and dreams before making commitments, to realistically talk about where they are headed and what each expects of the other. A small group covenant is similar to each of these practices.

Some groups even place their agreements in writing so there is no confusion and so the agreed-upon items can be referred to later as group-owned. When the group agrees to responsibilities ahead of time the leader is not seen as foisting upon the group the leader's hidden plans. Almost anything can be discussed in a group covenant discussion but it is better not to overburden members with too many details. Allow them, however, to make decisions wherever possible about what the group will do, how it will develop, and what priorities are in place. Some personalities can live with greater "fuzziness" than others. Some items you may want to include in your covenant discussion are:

- what you hope to achieve—your purpose
- what you will do as a group—your task(s)
- what the leader can be expected to do
- what members are required to do
- time commitment
- place
- refreshments
- baby-sitting
- special requirements (abilities, events outside meeting times, age, sex, marital status)

Em Griffin suggests these commitments:

1. *Attendance:* I need everyone in the group in order to grow. One person's absence will affect the whole group. . . . For the time I am here I will concentrate on what I am feeling at the moment and on my response to others in the group. . . . I will stay in the here and now.

2. *Affirmation:* There is nothing you have done or will do that will make me stop loving you. I may not agree with

your actions, but I will love you unconditionally. It is more blessed to care than to cure. This is not a therapy group. I will avoid the tendency to fix people.

3. *Confidentiality:* What's said here stays here! A permissive atmosphere flourishes when others are trustworthy. I will never repeat what another has said unless given specific permission.

4. *Openness:* I will strive to reveal who I am—my hopes, hurts, backgrounds, joys, and struggles—as well as I am able.

5. *Honesty:* I will try to mirror back what I see others saying and doing. This way I will help you understand something you may want to change but were unaware of. You can help me in the same way. This may strain our relationship, but I will have confidence in your ability to hear the truth in love.

6. *Sensitivity:* I will try to put myself in your shoes and understand what it is like to be you. I will try to hear you, see you, and feel where you are, to draw you out of the pit of discouragement or withdrawal. But I recognize that you have the individual right to remain silent.

7. *Accountability:* I am responsible for my own growth. I won't blame others for my feelings. None of us are trapped into behaviors that are unchangeable. I am accountable to myself, others, and God to become what God has designed me to be in His loving creation. I will help you become what you can be.

8. *Prayer:* During the course of this group, I will pray for the other members and bask in the confidence that they are praying for me.

(Griffin, 35–37)

Joining together in committing oneself to these kinds of goals not only brings a sense of security and direction but also sets before the group the possibility of transformation. Groups will never reach their highest potential until persons are willing to sublimate personal needs not in harmony with the group's objectives. Shared values that reinforce the group's purpose and shared commitment to responsibilities that will build the group's health are a powerful dual contribution to member satisfaction and growth. Spelling it out at the beginning is imperative for the survival and progress of a group.

Covenants, because they are shared ventures, require the support of all parties. They insure that one party doesn't have greater responsibility than the other so the group doesn't become the leader's group with the leader responsible for "enforcing," "doing the caring," and "getting the task done." It helps to develop a member-owned group with leader and members aware of their mutual responsibilities.

Covenants may be discussed and revised at any time. If persons renege on commitments, the group can rethink its decisions. For example, "It seems to be hard for all of us to be here at the time we decided to begin our group. What would you like to do: adjust the time, recommit ourselves to what we decided, discuss issues that prevent our being present on time, or what?" Such open, responsible discussion helps to eliminate frustration, anger, and gunnysacking that comes out later over some other issue. It prevents blame and judgmentalism and promotes sensitivity and harmony.

Beginnings are important. They establish foundations for what is to come. Being aware of and consciously designing with the above issues in mind can mean the difference between a healthy, fulfilling group and a frustrating experience of involvement with others in a group setting.

8

DROPPING THE MASK: SELF-DISCLOSURE

In order to see I have to be willing to be seen.
If a man takes off his sunglasses I can hear him better.
Hugh Prather

God's revelation of Himself is at the core of the Gospel. Jesus' coming with this mission is summed up in John 17: "I have revealed You to those whom You gave Me out of the world" (John 17:6). At the same time, He refused to disclose Himself to all. "Many people saw the miraculous signs He was doing and believed in His name. But Jesus would not entrust Himself to them, for He knew all" (John 2:23-24). Self-disclosure, trust, and intimacy are all bound together. Each of us has a need to know another and to be known by another. But because rejection is a real possibility, fear and discretion prompt a conflicting need to conceal and protect. Self-disclosure with accompanying feedback is absolutely necessary for the forming of relationships, but revealing who you are isn't easy and feedback may portray an "inaccurate" you.

TO DISCLOSE OR NOT TO DISCLOSE
Smith and Berg in their excellent work on *Paradoxes of Group Life* pinpoint the issues. Before disclosing who we are, we often feel the need to know another so we can disclose in a climate of safety. But how can we know about others unless someone is

willing to reveal himself first? (Smith and Berg, 111) And so we proceed cautiously, offering each item of personal information as a test to determine the safety of revealing ourselves further. As each bit of information is safely received, more is revealed. And so it often happens in a newly begun group that the self-disclosure becomes greater with each person's sharing so that those who "took the plunge" at first may end up feeling that they didn't share deeply enough.

Of course, to be acceptable, we only show our good side with great reserve. This results in "politeness" and an air of unreality or boredom with stilted and often open spaces between conversations. This game of showing only the *acceptable me* usually results in ambivalent feelings—positive feelings over being accepted and having navigated successfully through the cultural mores of the group—but also a disturbing realization that the *me* that has been accepted is a sham. Because I know there are parts of me that others would find difficult to accept, I find unacceptable the acceptance I have gained. As John Powell has capsulized so poignantly, "I am afraid to tell you who I really am, for if I tell you who I really am you may not accept me and that is the only me I have" (Powell, 12). The dilemma we face is not only in what do I share with you about who I am, but also in the fact that I will never know if you will accept me as I am until I attempt to disclose the real me. Assurance that I will be accepted is never enough—I can only find such acceptance as I trust and self-disclose my realities (Smith and Berg, 111–113).

All of this is going on inside persons as they form a group and are asked to share. No one usually overtly refers to the stressful pull of paradoxical needs, but it is there. Persons will seek to relieve some of the tension with humorous comments such as, "Well, I suppose I should tell you the good things so you'll want me in this group." Or to balance the guilt we feel about such a biased picture, "Now don't ask my wife (husband) about me because she'll probably tell you the opposite." Or, "Of course I do have one or two faults, but you'll find that out soon enough."

TO TRUST OR NOT TO TRUST

The dynamics of disclosure are closely connected with the dynamics of trust and this area is also marked by paradoxical feelings. Groups depend upon the development of trust for their being, but before we can trust we want to know how others will respond to us. To discover this we must be willing to expose and trust. Cultivating such a climate when others are fearful of trust is a challenge to the beginning group leader. In beginning groups it is hard to get an honest reading on the group because no one wants to be branded as a negative thinker. Persons often hide their true feelings and seek to blend into a "we all feel the same way about everything" climate, a pseudocommunity. They may exhibit a politeness and patience they don't feel because they don't feel safe voicing their actual feelings. Negative feedback must be presented if a person is to experience a climate of trust, because reality tells us that no one is received positively all the time. Yet we fear the negative because it may imply rejection. Trust says it is safe to share both negatively and positively, and the person is accepted with the realization that both negative and positive traits comprise that individual (Smith and Berg, 115).

TO RISK OR NOT TO RISK

Another realm of paradox is that of intimacy. We feel freer to share risky thoughts and feelings once we have discovered a commonality with others. This discovery promotes intimacy. But the only way we can find the acceptance of commonality is to risk sharing what we truly think and feel, and then discover that others connect with us. We accept ourselves as we are accepted by others, but we can accept others only as we accept ourselves. "That's what *I* was thinking," is an affirmation of our disclosure by another. But in order to receive that affirmation of acceptance we must accept our own value enough to venture forth with a statement of risk.

Often in a group forming trust, you will hear qualifying statements prefacing remarks. These qualifiers include: "I may be off base, but I think . . ." "I may not totally understand the issue but it seems to me . . ." "I'm probably biased, but I. . . ." Such hesitations are not so much indicative of humility or tactful understanding as they are of self-doubt and fear of nonacceptance. Later in the saga of the group these conditional statements will disappear as persons find they are accepted and can state things as they see and experience them without fear of rejection.

BECOMING AN INDIVIDUAL IN THE GROUP

All of this underscores the absolute necessity of building a base of connectedness and commonality between individuals before collectively relating to the group and the group purpose. Some persons feel that the common goal or interest of the group is enough to build acceptance. In actuality, persons must first work at connecting with each other before connecting with the group. We become a team only after we have discovered who we are as individuals in relation to others in the group. Then we can either supply or deny our individual traits and needs for the sake of others. This phenomenon may help to explain why committees take so long and often fail to become one. We do not allow for the "wasted time" needed to connect with one another as persons.

An example of this occurred when a publishing house sought to gain direction for future materials by bringing together several high-powered Christian education pastors known for their contributions to the field. Since the publisher was paying for this day of insight, the group was immediately plunged into its task, eliminating the trivia of getting to know the other participants. The substantive issue was, "What do *you* as an *expert* see as the major trend impacting Christian education in the next decade?" However, with such a "billing," each person felt the pressure to live up to the expectations placed upon him or her and experienced some intimidation at the expertise assumed in the other "experts." As a result, the expertise shared was neither helpful nor memorable because members did not listen to what was said, being preoccupied with what they would reveal about their *expertise* when their turn came. The anxiety of fulfilling the group purpose took precedence over building a sense of relationship and trust where members could have developed some form of solidarity and agreement upon significant concerns. While they undoubtedly shared common experiences and could have enriched one another and the outcome of the group, they failed to find this connectedness and remained a collection of individuals instead of becoming a group.

Both listening and speaking are required for a sense of intimacy to develop. *Listening* becomes a means to understand others *and* to understand yourself. *Speaking* becomes both a means of connecting with others *and* connecting with yourself. Responding to the admonition to "don't talk, just think," one child questioned, "How do I know what I think until I hear what I have to say?" One of the greatest assets a group leader can give a group is the opportunity to speak (connect) and listen (understand) (Smith and Berg, 120–125).

LEVEL OF RISK
In developing a sense of intimacy and trust through self-disclosure, there are numerous factors that will impact what a leader does. One of these is how members feel about the level of risk involved. Why is it some things seem of higher risk than others? Each person has his or her own personal ranking. Read the list below and indicate how appropriate you feel each item is for disclosure. Use the following scale.

L = low risk, appropriate to disclose this item to almost anyone.
M = moderate risk, appropriate for persons in established friendships or fairly well known.
H = high risk, disclosed to only a few most intimate friends.
X = disclose to no one.

___ 1. Style of music you prefer or dislike
___ 2. Things you feel angry about
___ 3. Your personal political views
___ 4. What you and your spouse (closest friend) fight about
___ 5. Your personal view of God
___ 6. The nature of your present relationship with God
___ 7. Area where you question God's ways or Word
___ 8. Your educational background and feelings about it
___ 9. Weaknesses of yours that disturb you
___ 10. Personal achievements and characteristics that bring you pride
___ 11. Details of your secret ambition
___ 12. An area of self-doubt
___ 13. Unfulfilled dreams and desires of your life
___ 14. What you do to relax
___ 15. Parts of your body you are most pleased with
___ 16. Features in your looks you would most like to change
___ 17. Parts of your personality you would like to change
___ 18. A person you resent highly and why
___ 19. What you enjoy most about the opposite sex
___ 20. What you would most like to cover up if your life were revealed

If you qualified any response, why did you choose the qualifier you used? In addition to the personal assignments of risk we make to certain topics, there are generally agreed-upon items which project more risk than others.

Risk Factor #1 — Time
Time is a variable when it comes to disclosing. Typically the past is the safest time frame to disclose. Our histories contain events which seem less risky to share because there is nothing we can do about them. Sharing of future plans, however, contains more risk since we lock ourselves into having to follow through on what we said we will do. The greatest risk of all is contained in disclosure of present acts because they are open to evaluation, to affecting relationships, and to being changed by others right now. For example, watch how the risk factor goes up in the following: "I tried to impress persons in high school by covering up my feelings and coming across as confident." *(Past)* "I'm going to ask my boss for a raise next week and tell him all the reasons I deserve it." *(Future)* "I'm trying to impress you right now with a recital of my abilities because I know you are impressed with confident, self-sufficient persons." *(Present)* The time frame of the disclosure affects the risk.

Risk Factor #2 — Focus
The focus also colors the risk. In general, disclosing feelings is more risky than sharing facts. "Most persons list speaking to a group as more stress producing than any other activity." *(Fact)* "I feel very nervous and fearful right now in telling you how I feel because I am afraid you won't think I'm a good Christian." *(Feelings plus Fact)* Feelings are seen to be more personally owned than facts. Feelings often reveal the real us while facts are non-judgmental. For example: "I came from a single parent home *(Fact)* and I hated it for what I felt I missed." *(Feeling)*

Other Risk Factors
Being asked to disclose an evaluation of yourself or others takes on a higher risk than non-evaluative statements. "Let's share with Bill how he could be a better leader," or "In groups of threes, discuss your evaluation of our group." Another high risk

144

factor in the previous statements is disclosure given about someone present as opposed to giving information about someone not present.

The number of receivers increases the risk factor in any disclosure. The larger the group, the safer must be the topic chosen. Thus what the person is asked to share can be balanced by the "to whom" the sharing is addressed. *High-heat content* ("Share how you were hurt by someone you cared about") can be offset by *Low-threat structure* (one to one) or a *High-threat structure* (in front of the whole group) can be tempered by *Low-threat content* ("Where do you enjoy going on vacation?"). When several of the above factors of risk are mixed so some are safe and some are threatening to disclose, the participant has to weigh the pluses and minuses and decide on the level of risk. For example, a secure person who is new to the group is asked to share with the whole group what gifts and abilities he or she brings to the group from past experience. Which factors would encourage risk taking and which would inhibit it in this situation?

An excellent summary table of felt risks in a disclosure situation is found on page 144 (*Bridges Not Walls,* Stewart, 214).

JOHARI WINDOW
The Johari Window is a model that describes awareness in interpersonal relationships. Named for its two creators, Joseph Luft and Harrington V. Ingham, it is pronounced as though combining *Joe* and *Harry.* The model consists of four quadrants called *Open, Blind, Hidden,* and *Unknown.*

The *Open* area, Quadrant 1, consists of behaviors, feelings, and motivations that are known to the self and known to others. Such openness reveals common knowledge of which both sender and receiver are aware.

Quadrant 2, the *Blind* area, includes behaviors, feelings, and motivations that are known to others but not to the self. We commonly refer to such lack of self-awareness on the part of a person as a "blind spot." What may be very evident to those around us is closed to us. While we may become aware of "blind spots" as others reveal them to us and are believed, there will doubtless always be a blind area which we reveal to others but are not aware of ourselves.

A SUMMARY OF FELT RISKS IN DISCLOSURE

DIMENSIONS	LOW RISK	MEDIUM RISK	HIGH RISK
A. Content			
A1. Time	Past events	Future	Present events
A2. Topic	Ideas, general concepts		Feels, own concepts
A3. Evaluativeness	No evaluation components	Evaluation implied	Evaluation direct
A4. Cast	People who are not present		People who are present
B. Sender			
B1. Assumptions about the world	Basically friendly	Mixed bag	Basically hostile
B2. Task definition	Problem-solving	Mixture of politics and problem-solving	Power struggle
B3. Personal security	High self-acceptance; low defensiveness	Defensive depending on the content area	Low self-acceptance; high defensiveness
B4. Job security	High, very certain of position	Moderate security	Low, very tenuous
C. Receive (As Perceived by Sender)			
C1. Personal security	High self-acceptance; low defensiveness	Defensive depending on the content area	Low self-acceptance; high defensiveness
C2. Commitment to relationship	High commitment	Some testing	Low commitment
C3. Power orientation	Collaboration with sender	Mixed orientation	Controlling the sender
C4. Receiver's competence	Very likely to handle new information well	Sometimes well, sometimes badly	Very unlikely to handle new information well
D. Climate (As Felt by Sender)			
D1. Norms	Support disclosure		Discourage disclosure
D2. History	Disclosure, went well		Few disclosures: bad experiences when happened
D3. Taboos/policies	Few areas prohibited		Many areas prohibited
D4. Trust	High trust		Low trust

J. Stewart, *Bridges Not Walls* (1986). Used with permission of McGraw-Hill, Inc.

The Johari window

Known to Self   Not Known to Self

Known to Others

Not Known
to Others

Luft, Joseph, *Group Processes,* 3rd edition, Mountain View, CA: Mayfield Publishing Co., 1984, p. 60.

The *Hidden*, Quadrant 3, incorporates the behaviors, feelings, and motivations which are known to ourselves but which are hidden from others. Each individual's responses are colored by an awareness of thoughts, motives, agendas, and experiences known to the sender but unknown by others in the relationship. Relationship building consists of revealing the hidden area and bringing it into the *Open* quadrant. Such action usually results in a reciprocal action being taken by others, thus developing a basis for trust and growth in relationship.

Quadrant 4 houses the behaviors, feelings, and motivations which are known neither to self nor to others. These four quadrants represent the whole person in relationship to other persons. The size of the quadrants increases and decreases accordingly as the relationship changes. For instance, as disclosure takes place the *Hidden* quadrant decreases while the *Open* quadrant increases. As Quadrant 2 becomes known to an individual because of feedback from others, the *Open* quadrant grows and the *Blind* quadrant decreases. Each encounter with others moves quadrant lines within the window but the window continues to contain all four quadrants. The following diagrams illustrate the shifting of boundaries as a relationship is developed.

Luft, Joseph, *Group Processes,* 3rd edition, Mountain View, CA: Mayfield Publishing Co., 1984, p. 62.

Note that a change in one of the quadrants will affect the other quadrants. The larger the first quadrant, the better the communication. When Quadrant 1 is small, threat is high and communication is usually poor. As trust develops among members, awareness of *Hidden*, *Open*, and *Blind* facets of the relationship increases along with a desire to move into the *Open* quadrant items from *Hidden* and *Blind* quadrants (Luft, 59–69).

Dropping the Mask

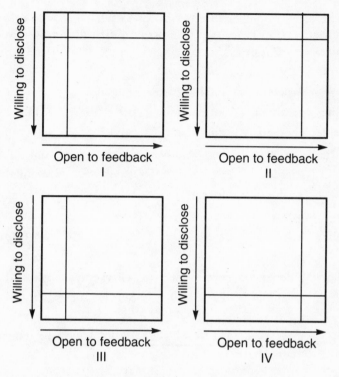

Adler, Ronald & George Rodman, *Understanding Human Communication,* p. 175.

Beebe and Masterson in their third edition of *Communicating in Small Groups* present an enlightening exercise that illustrates the Johari awarenesses.

1. Form groups of three to five people.
2. Check five or six adjectives from the list on page 148 that best describe your personality as you see it.
3. Select three or four adjectives that describe the personality of each person in your group and write them on separate sheets of paper. Distribute these lists to the appropriate group members.
4. Fill in square number one ("known to self and known to others") with adjectives from the list that both you and at least one other member of your group have selected to describe your personality.
5. Fill in square number two ("not known to self but known to others") with those adjectives others in your group used to describe you but you did not use to describe yourself.

6. Fill in square number three ("known to self but not to others")
with adjectives you have used to describe your self but no one else
used to describe you.

able	dependable	intelligent	patient	sensible
accepting	dignified	introverted	powerful	sentimental
adaptable	energetic	kind	proud	shy
bold	extroverted	knowledgeable	quiet	silly
brave	friendly	logical	reflective	spontaneous
calm	giving	loving	relaxed	sympathetic
caring	happy	mature	religious	tense
cheerful	helpful	modest	responsive	trustworthy
clever	idealistic	nervous	searching	warm
complex	independent	observant	self-assertive	wise
confident	ingenious	organized	self-conscious	witty

	known to self	not known to self
known to others	1	2
not known to others	3	unknown

From *Communicating in Small Groups: Principles and Practices,* 3rd ed., by Steven A.
Beebe and John T. Masterson. Copyright © 1990, 1986 by Scott, Foresman and Company. Reprinted by permission of HarperCollins Publishers.

FACTORS AFFECTING DISCLOSURE

Because disclosure is so important and impacts relationships in such a major way, what will facilitate it in a small group? Physical factors such as seating can enhance or undermine sharing. Gaze is important for disclosure. When we do not want to disclose (in crowded elevators, on the bus with strangers, or in a class where we do not know the answer and don't want to be called on), we look intently ahead or stare into space, anywhere but directly into the face of another. Conversely, a group where participants can see one another's faces close enough to read nonverbal responses, means members will be encouraged to disclose themselves to one another.

SHARING QUESTIONS

Creating opportunities for group members to disclose and give feedback will strengthen group bonds and facilitate accomplishment of group tasks. Often groups begin their times together with sharing questions. Each of these is designed to help persons reveal safe information and find those who are like and unlike them. Sharing questions should be used for at least ten weeks in a beginning group and reintroduced whenever members sense a distancing from one another or seem to remain at a shallow level of interaction. Simply being together in a group does not guarantee that members will be building personal relationships. Sharing questions and relational games can free persons to bond.

Developing appropriate sharing questions requires a knowledge of your group and an awareness of group principles. In light of the risk factors shared above, determine where your group is in their life cycle. If just beginning, center your questions on "history giving," the safe past. When you assess that trust has been growing, you may move into the future and present tense. Even further trust is required for a question of "affirmation" or one that requires personal accountability. "How have you seen yourself or another grow in the time we've been together?" In the course of a group's life, persons appear ready and desirous of moving into these areas of greater openness and commitment.

Questions asking for factual information are low threat as long as they do not involve expertise. "What was your placement in the family? Firstborn? Baby? Only?" Good sharing questions usually evoke some kind of emotional response. Combine the informational question with a request for personal self-disclosure and a feeling response. "What was your placement in the family, and what did you like about it?" Add feelings or inner emotions to the following fact questions that focus on various needs of the group.

History giving: "When is a time you remember being in the limelight for something and . . ."

Present: "What is a good thing happening in your life right now and . . ."

Future: "What is one change you would like to make in your life in the next year and . . ."

Affirmation: "What is something you appreciate about someone in this group and . . ."

Accountability: What is one responsibility you have to carry out this week and . . ."

Keep questions simple so they don't require explanations and they can be answered in a brief amount of time. (No more than three to four minutes if your group is over five in number.) There is a major difference between asking "What kinds of things would you like to change about your job?" and "What one aspect of your work last week made it enjoyable?"

Beware of asking questions that could be very psychologically revealing or painful. This could include asking persons to confess sins or to admit negative things about themselves. Groups that have been together for a long time may be open to this kind of trust, but not beginning groups. It can be helpful to identify the primary feeling that your question will likely arouse. Feelings of regret over the past where nothing can be done, or anger and depression over unfair treatment can color what goes on in the group for the rest of its life together.

Good questions reveal something about the individual that is helpful in understanding and caring for him or her. Don't take up time sharing trivialities that give little insight into the person; i.e., "What is your favorite fruit?"

Avoid superlatives like the *best*, the *most*, and the *worst* because they force persons into evaluation and hair-splitting. "What was the best birthday present you ever received?" *Best* can be interpreted many ways—best for that age? Best in terms of desire? Best in terms of size or expense? Also persons fear inadequacy in remembering the top selection and will change the question to provide credibility—"Well, I don't know if this is the *most* important, but. . . ." Change superlatives to *a very memorable,* or *a difficult* or *highly appreciated*.

Check your questions' inclusiveness—can they be answered by all, not just a few? Experience and expertise can exclude persons from responding to a sharing question. "What are your childhood memories of Sunday School?" can eliminate those who did not attend Sunday School while growing up.

Sharing questions are not intended as occasions for discussion, comment, or critique. Members should have permission to reshape a question into one they feel comfortable answering, or to pass and be given another chance to share after others.

The leader can begin the sharing and set the pace, or can call on an individual known to be comfortable with disclosure. The group depends upon the leader to keep the sharing from bogging down, and from becoming controversial, judgmental, or painful for anyone in the group.

Examine the following sharing questions. Which need to be revised because they don't meet the criteria listed above?

1. What's an area where you feel like a failure?
2. What is a prayer you are glad God didn't answer and why?
3. Share your most significant learning experience.
4. What is your opinion of rock music?
5. How do you feel about foggy days?
6. What's one thing you like about our church and one thing you'd like to improve?
7. What did God do to get you into this group?
8. What one thing have you worried about the most this week?

Answers: 1. Negative, arousing guilt. 2. Confusing, interpreted differently. 3. Superlative, hard to select. 4. Controversial and divisive. 5. Not significantly helpful in getting to know person. 6. Good—balanced and realistic—not everybody likes everything. 7. Good as long as it involves how you felt about it in the answer. 8. Psychological striptease, superlative.

Relational activities also provide opportunity for self-disclosure, utilizing materials or activities as expressions of inner feelings. An example of such is the drawing of your dining room or kitchen table as you remember it at age 10. Colors identify relational feelings as each person draws where family members sat around the table. This picture becomes the gist for discussion questions about the family of origin. Other relational activities utilize sculpting an individual's perspective in clay or paper, sharing from card or board questions in *Ungame* fashion, or creating want ads that describe one's person. Using media frees some persons to express inner thoughts and feelings. It can frustrate others who are not used to such creative expression. Because of their nature, relational games tend to take longer to process, and may be remembered for a greater period of time because of the involvement required.

The best self-disclosure grows out of the purpose or content of the group so there is a relationship between what is shared and what goes on in the group.

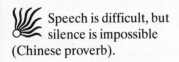 Speech is difficult, but silence is impossible (Chinese proverb).

Hearing is one of the body's five senses. But listening is an art (Frank Tyger).

Hear twice before you speak once (Scottish saying).

Ross, 206

LISTENING
Charlie Brown comments to Lucy as they prop themselves against a brick fence, "In a good conversation, one person talks while the other listens, then *that* person talks while the first person listens." Looking thoughtful Lucy admits, "I like talking. I hate listening," and Charlie Brown affirms, "I realize that." Lucy looks at him blankly and asks, "What?" Once again Charles Schultz has captured the reality of our hu-

manity. For most of us it seems easier to talk than to listen. We ignore, interrupt, misinterpret, get defensive, argue internally, and find it very difficult to "hear out" another's point of view.

Jesus frequently finalized His teaching of truth with "Let the one who has ears to hear, hear." In this manner, He suggested that the listener must become involved if hearing is to truly take place. In the Old Testament, when given opportunity to request anything of God, Solomon asked for a listening heart. He wanted to hear with the inner ear. Though usually translated "understanding or discerning," the Hebrew literally means "hearing." God granted Solomon a wise and listening heart—made competent to hear with the inner ear and discern wisdom in ruling his people (Wakefield, 12–13).

The Chinese characters that depict the verb meaning "to listen" incorporate these elements.

EAR

EYES

UNDIVIDED
ATTENTION

HEART

Calligraphy by Angie Au (p. 107, *Understanding Human Communication*, 4th ed. by Ronald Adler & George Rodman, 1991.

Sperry Corporation's senior news specialist Cynthia Swain documented that 80% of a person's waking hours are spent in some type of communication. Writing occupies 9% of that time, reading 16%, speaking 30%, and listening a whopping 45% (Bittner, 71). We spend at least six elementary school years learning to read and write, and both high school and college offer specialized courses in speaking. Yet little, if any, formalized training in listening skills is given. The student graduates into a society in which he or she will spend three times as much time *listening* as reading and five times as much time as writing. Though we pick up our speech habits from our environment, we spend time correcting and perfecting these habits so as to be successful. Yet we do not deliberately work at improving listening skills. In job interviews we rarely test for listening competence. In his autobiography, Lee Iacocca stresses the importance of listening.

> I only wish I could find an institute that teaches people how to listen. After all, a good manager needs to listen at least as much as he (she) needs to talk. . . . You have to be able to listen well if you're going to motivate the people who work for you. Right there, that's the difference between a mediocre company and a great company.

(Iacocca, 54–55)

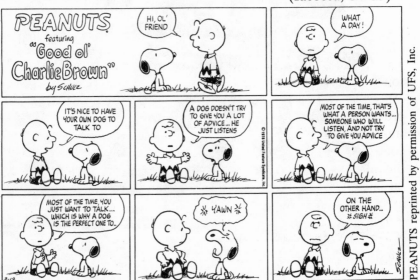

Therapist Franklin Ernst suggests that we are typically trained in anti-listening by such edicts as:

"We don't listen to those things in our family."
"Don't pay any attention to him (her)."
"Pretend you don't notice."
"Don't take it so seriously."
"He (she) didn't mean what he said."
"Don't give them the satisfaction of knowing that you heard them (and that it bothers you)" (Bolton, 160).

One of the reasons that listening is difficult is rooted in the fact that an average person speaks at approximately 125 to 150 words per minute while listeners can easily process some 500 words per minute (Wolvin, 3rd edition, 88).

This leaves listeners with "time on their hands" to use in ways other than concentrating on the words of the speaker. Such "spacetime" creates various listening hazards as persons listen to self-disclosure in small group sharing.

One of these pitfalls is pseudolistening. Pseudolisteners appear to listen but are actually thinking of something else. They may nod, murmur some response like "Great," and look the speaker straight in the eye while their minds are focused on issues of concern to them.

Other ways persons fill up the lag time created in processing faster than the speaker can talk may be silent arguing, evaluating the validity of what is said, and preparing advice or correction for what has been deemed faulty information or assumptions. Persons who know each other well often think they know what the other will say before they say it, so they tend not to listen. Others prematurely prepare to make remarks before they fully understand another's statements or questions. Sometimes persons become emotionally involved, and project their own experiences on the speaker. They cease to hear specific information from then on and may become sidetracked as they mentally recall a past experience triggered by the one sharing.

The most common hazard for persons newly formed into a group is to focus more on what they are going to say when it is their turn than on what the speaker is currently saying. This is especially true if one is nervous about making a good impression. Often listeners cannot even remember another's name because of this preoccupation. To foster concentration sometimes leaders will ask persons to share in twos, with each partner then asked to share the other's information with the whole group. Others will stimulate focused listening by suggesting listeners listen for something specific such as "things you have in common with this speaker." Sometimes a summary statement enables persons to be heard and understood. "So you are struggling with a job that tends to undermine how you feel about your value as a person?" Helping another get into a conversation and share what is inside their person is a ministry. In groups it is called "gatekeeping" or "door opening." Typical door openers include:

1. Describing what you see. "You look like you identify with that experience." "A frown just creased your forehead."

2. Tentatively describing what you hear. "It sounds like you may have some regret over that."

3. Inviting another to share. "Would you care to elaborate on that?" "Do go on." "Umm."

4. Providing relaxed silence so the person can make a decision to share. Silence tends to seem longer and unnerving to the leader or questioner more so than to those thinking about the question or preparing to share.

5. A posture of attending with eye contact and demonstrated interest.

Of particular benefit in self-disclosure is listening for the feelings being expressed. Reflecting back those feelings can enable the speaker to know understanding has taken place. Reflecting feelings is of greater importance than reflecting facts. New facts that affect a situation may only be heard after the listener has accurately reflected the feelings shared. More will be discussed on this in the chapter on Communication. For now try to identify the feelings expressed in the following self-disclosures.

Statement	Feeling Expressed
"I guess I've never had a feeling of being real close to God. I hear people talk about God being a Friend but it seems hard for me to know how to go about making Him my best Friend. He's always been God at a distance."	
"I'd like to trust you in this group, but don't be surprised if I don't. I trusted my spouse and he left me. I trusted my boss and she took advantage of me. I don't even know if I can trust God at this point."	

Advice giving or cheering come across as judgment with feelings of not having been heard. To reflect back feelings to the speaker in each of the above scenarios, identify the feelings above and complete this phrase, "It sounds like you. . . ."

Self-disclosure is absolutely vital to the building of Christian community. Being known, accepted, and cared about is the seedbed for growth and transformation. Remaining hidden may seem safe, but it also conveys the doubt of acceptance and the possibility that no one may care. Small groups can be climates for healthy self-disclosure, relational support, and major growth in understanding and commitment.

> O Lord, You have searched me and You know me.
> You know when I sit and when I rise;
> You perceive my thoughts from afar.
> You discern my going out and my lying down;
> You are familiar with all my ways. . . .
> Such knowledge is too wonderful for me. . . .
> When I awake, I am still with You (Ps. 139:1-3, 6, 18).

"HOW DO YOU EXPECT ME TO HEAR YOU WHEN I WASN'T EVEN *LISTENING*?"

DENNIS THE MENACE®
used by permission of Hank Ketcham and © by North America Syndicate.

9

ONE OF A KIND: THE INDIVIDUAL IN A GROUP

Am I the same as we? And us the same as me?
Do groups exist for members or members exist for groups?
If I join a group, will I lose my individuality?
Is a group more than a collection of individuals?

How would you respond to each of the above? Every group member lives with this tension. We long to be individuals—unique and distinct from any other. But at the same time we fear being alone, being excluded because we are different, or isolated because we don't fit in. So we crave affiliation, connectedness, and inclusion but vacillate in our commitments because we don't want to be consumed, absorbed, or obliterated by the ones we join. We are driven to the one side as we contemplate the painful extremity of the other. We then retreat as we fear the hazards of the chosen state. We vacillate between a desire for autonomy and a compulsion for inclusion.

While we are made for community, ambivalence characterizes our attitude toward inclusion in a group. Being creatures of imperfection whose adaptation to community bears the marks of that imperfectedness, we find ourselves constantly dissatisfied and in conflict when in a group (Gibbard, et al., 177). Even the most group-minded person feels a gnawing anxiety over whether she is giving up too much, and if this group is worth it. And the most confirmed isolationist feels the tug of loneliness and faces facts that he is free but perhaps missing out on the "good life."

161

While the nature of the fusion-abandonment tension may not be self-evident to the individual in the group setting, the anxiety that emanates from it usually is. The experience for the individual joining a group is primarily one of a low-grade anxiety that surfaces as an amalgam of forces such as excitement over the possibilities represented in group membership, uncertainty about how he or she will fit in, fear that he or she will be less competent than when acting alone, and frustration over earlier group experiences. When such anxiety is stirred, the individual usually becomes preoccupied by a secondary fear, that this anxiety may escalate and get out of hand. An initial goal for the individual in the group is to keep a lid on this anxiety by pretending that it does not exist or by replacing it with behaviors that seem acceptable to others in the group. While the individual may be aware of the anxious feelings, the underlying roots of that anxiety are rarely recognized. As a result, the methods used to manage it can very often be self-defeating.

(Smith and Berg, 66–67)

This anxiety often shows up in excessive talking, followed by a pulling back and aloofness to regain a sense of feeling individuated and in control. Others may withhold any kind of involvement until the lay of the land is clear, but then fear being "left out" of the developing community and quickly try to connect.

William C. Schutz, in his landmark book *FIRO: A Three-Dimensional Theory of Interpersonal Behavior,* targets three major interpersonal needs that every individual sustains: inclusion, control, and affection. These three needs drive a person to communicate and to develop cohesiveness with others in a group (Schutz, 1958). Conflict arises when commitment to one's own needs, goals, and convictions is in opposition to group acceptance, security, and care. This clash is inevitable and most persons approach a group wondering what they will have to give up if they are to belong. Groups themselves struggle with whether their goals can be accomplished by the individuals comprising the group. Thus it is that some persons look for "good" groups where they feel that little of their individuality will have to be given up. And groups look for "good group members," meaning those who will place the group development above their own.

Our identity is seen in an either/or perspective rather than individual and group identity being integral parts of each other. This either/or mind-set is illustrated clearly in the case of the deviant. Norms express the rules of the group. They are the usually unwritten but powerful guidelines about ways the group operates. When someone deviates from these norms and asserts an individual identity, the group moves quickly to bring that individual back into conformity or to restrain the influence of that individual from spreading to the remainder of the group. "That's the way we've always done it in our group," is a powerful rebuke to individualism. Should the deviant one persist in this anti-communal way, the group uses its greater power to withdraw privileges and to "freeze out" the offending one. The group identity *as currently formed* is the only *acceptable* one.

Consider, however, the person who expresses an individual perspective which is received as revelatory of the group and gives the group insight into an area where it needs to grow or change. If the group realizes that the individual gained this insight from experiencing a deficiency in the group, they will see that the group created the individual who is now re-creating the group. This simultaneous tension that occurs between the individual and the group is in reality a tension occurring within the individual and within the group as the individual struggles to live in the group and the group struggles to live with individuals. Each feeds the other rather than competing for an either/or supremacy (Smith and Berg, 91–93).

Our individuality drives us to groups and groups foster our individuality. To be developing fully as individuals, we must be in community. To be a true community we must nurture and protect the individual's uniqueness. The Apostle Paul recognized this in God's design of the body of Christ. "Though all its [the body's] parts are many, they form one body. . . . The parts of the body that seem to be weaker are indispensable, and the parts that we think are less honorable we treat with special honor. . . . If they [the parts] were all one part, where would the body be?" (1 Cor. 12:12, 22-23, 19) The parts are enhanced and valued by being in the body, and the body is enhanced and energized by the parts.

This reciprocity principle is frequently found in God's kingdom. In dying, we live; in giving, we receive; in serving, we lead; in losing, we gain. The way up is down. It is as if the Creator has built within us a symbiotic relationship of focus on the opposite of what is natural. In this way we can receive that on which we *do not* focus. Groups reflect the reciprocal nature of God and group dynamicists are discovering this truth to be present as they research behavior in groups. Consider these insights.

> The group gains its solidarity as individuality is legitimated, and individuality is established when the primacy of the group is affirmed.
> Most of us have the tendency to be cautious, to hold back our energies, our individual wishes, our secrets, until we know what the group is like. . . . The dilemma is that our very withholding is what contributes to making the group unsafe. The refusal of members to engage makes the group a hollow cocoon that no one wants to be part of. A group can become a group only when individuals put themselves into it. . . .
> Members usually join a group because they feel some sense of inadequacy — to cope with aloneness . . . to develop competencies that cannot be acquired in isolation . . . to meet intimacy and social needs. . . . Hence, individuals come to a group looking for what they can get. Yet the overwhelming message is often, "You can't get anything from here until you give!"
>
> (Smith and Berg, 100–101)

Thus, whenever an individual risks expressions of his or her uniqueness which seem "different," there is the hazard of disconnecting with the group. But there is also the possibility of connecting based on expression of something which another thinks or feels but has not yet expressed. Any expression of similarity or conformity, while creating bonding with another, also runs the risk of creating a stagnant community which may prompt the withdrawal of individuals who refuse to live in that stagnation. Community is energized by the very aspects that threaten its existence, and individuality is strengthened and valued by the very facets that could jeopardize its continuance. To express difference could result either in disconnection from the community or in the creation of new paradigms of community. To express similarities could result in connectedness that enriches or in conformity that stifles. Both individuality and community are needed; they are integral to each other. "So in Christ we who are many form one body, and each member belongs to all the others" (Rom. 12:5).

How have you experienced this ambivalence of group and individuality? What fears in this dichotomy have surfaced in your group life? How do persons express these fears of being left out or absorbed by the group?

IMPLICATIONS FOR INDIVIDUAL/GROUP SYMBIOSIS

This individual/group symbiosis has many different implications. An individual's self-worth affects how he or she perceives the group. Groups are affected by individual perceptions. Luft records that persons with low self-esteem tend to see a group's performance as the same as their own performance, regardless of how effective the group has been. Persons with high esteem tend to assume credit for the successes but not the failures of the group. Others are blamed for the failures (Luft, 29).

Likewise, when groups fail and do not meet the needs of the members, there is a tendency to look for blame in an individual person. Though the source of difficulty may be within the system of the group itself, the possibility of considering this versus individual blame is usually not considered. The leader may be targeted as victim or a person who displayed deviant behavior in the group. Witness this characteristic in the firing of a coach when the team does not function as expected, or the focus on the "acting out" teenager in the family when the family's dysfunctional system is at fault.

On the other hand, groups often foster individual roles which aid the whole group in development. Persons find fulfillment in exercising these roles unique to their personalities and gifts. Those roles usually fall into one of two categories: persons whose primary interest lies in getting a task accomplished and persons whose primary interest lies in promoting good relationships between members. The first are labeled task oriented and the second, maintenance or relationally oriented. Which is better? A group composed of task oriented persons who focus on getting the job done? Or a group of persons who want persons to feel good about themselves and their relationships in the group? Or is the best group a mix of types? Most groups are made up of persons from each category. Some feel that dual leadership, with one leader being task oriented and the other maintenance oriented offers a healthy, balanced group. Generally, productivity research suggests that groups composed of like types—either all task focused or all relationship focused—are more productive than a mixed group where personality clashes interfere with output. However, the nature of the goal or task also affects which groups are more effective, some achieving the given task better with relational focus and some with task focus (Napier and Gershenfeld, *Groups: Theory and Experience,* 199–200).

INDIVIDUAL PERSONALITY STYLES

How does individual personality style affect group productivity and process? Carl Jung is credited with identifying and labeling dual responses for four different functions in processing life. The first is the function of gathering information from one's world: *Sensing* or *Intuiting.* The second function relates to how persons make decisions: *Thinking* or *Feeling.* The source of energy which decides where and how a person gathers information and makes decisions is the third function: *Extrovert* vs. *Introvert* perspective. Finally, how a person prefers to relate to the world, their lifestyle orientation, is categorized by *Judging* or *Perceiving.* An understanding of these different styles will enable us to see why persons perceive a group differently and prize a group for different reasons. It will help us understand why individuals respond the way they do and ask the questions they ask. It can help to explain why what is important to one person seems pedantic and nitpicking to another. Realizing that persons process the *same information in different ways* can reframe an act by another from seeming belligerent to making sense. Such information can help us understand ourselves and our responses in the context of a group setting.

Jung's theory suggests that personality is made up of various composites of the above-mentioned four functions. For example,

someone may be a Sensing-Thinking-Introverted Judger by preference whereas another may be an Intuitive-Thinking-Introvert-
ed Judger. While persons have preferred functions in varied proportions, seldom is one person totally one category or the other.
It is also important to realize that these are not concrete, un-
changing boundaries, and are not prescriptive but descriptive of
the usual response made by an individual. Circumstances and
value changes may cause a person to develop an "at homeness"
in the opposite type. A graduate school student who by nature
prefers to make decisions as a Feeler (subjective evaluation of
data) may by virtue of prescribed academic exercise become
more of a Thinking (objective evaluation of data) decision-mak-
er. Or a natural Introvert may learn to enjoy being an Extrovert
and find that energizing as she responds to job demands for
success. It is also vital to understand what Jung includes in the
different explanations that accompany the labels and not to assess your own meaning to the particular labels he selected. Neither is one bad while the other is good.

THE INFORMATION-GATHERING PROCESS: SENSING VS. INTUITING

We are continually taking in information from the world around
us. Keirsey and Bates claim this difference in how persons gather
information is the most basic of the differences (Kroeger and
Thuesen, 50).

Sensors are literalists—they see things realistically and are practical in the way they perceive things. Called *Sensor,* they rely primarily on the five senses for gathering information. They major on facts
and details without making interpretation and prefer to learn
through organized, sequential, and carefully constructed information. Exactness and accuracy are factors important to the Sensor.
"There were 65 people present who ate lunch in the first 40 minutes and then broke into fifteen groups of 4 and one group of 5."

The Intuitors see meaning in the facts and in contrast to the
literalism of the Sensor, Intuitors are figurative in their information gathering. They look for meaning and relationships between
and within the facts. A yawn is not just a yawn—it has significance. Exactness in information is not nearly as important for
them, but they like to see the whole picture and gather informa-

tion in terms of a holistic framework. The Intuitor puts together the yawn with a previous statement made by the yawner and the way the yawner is sitting.

While samples vary somewhat, a number of researchers estimate that Sensors outnumber Intuitors about seven to three (Kroeger and Thuesen, 25). These two types often see things in entirely opposite ways. Recall the report of the 12 spies Moses sent to check out the land of promise. Some saw and reported in detail the size of the people, the barricades and fortifications built around the cities, and what peoples lived in which terrain. Others saw the size of the grapes and claimed it was a "land flowing with milk and honey." All saw the same land but picked up different information. On the whole, Intuitors tend to be more optimistic than do Sensors who collect hard facts and are inclined to see things more objectively. This literal-figurative conflict in perception has provided laughs for great comedy routines. Gracie Allen was a deadpan literalist who took off on George Burns' comments. Jean Stapleton as Edith Bunker, Woody and Coach from "Cheers," and Rose Nyland (Betty White) from "The Golden Girls" are laughed at for their literal interpretations of life. But Intuitors, also, can become sources of humor when they absent-mindedly drive miles in an opposite direction, can't remember where they put the keys, or walk the parking lot looking for their car because they failed to note with exactness the important details.

Such communication is not always funny in real life when these two information seekers interact in a group.

Sensor: "What time is it now?"
Intuitor: "Oh, it's getting late!"
Sensor: "Well, what time is it?"
Intuitor: "It's time we should be starting!"
Sensor (impatiently): "But I asked you what time it was."
Intuitor (also impatient): "It's after 6."
Sensor (exasperatedly): "Can you tell me the exact time, please!"
Intuitor (frustrated): "I told you already. It's time we were beginning. It's already past 6 o'clock and we have to be through by 7:30."

And so the conversations go. She says, "Did you notice the new couch the Andersons have in their living room?" He says, "No, I didn't even see it." Or one member says, "Did you see the resistance the new members had when you brought up the idea of time?" And another says, "Naw, they asked those two questions and after that they didn't say a word."

- Consider how these personality types will approach contracting for a group differently. Who will probably want it in writing?
- How would they learn in a different fashion?
- What kinds of questions will Sensors ask? Intuitors?
- How would each respond to a proposed new format before accepting it?
- What aspects of the one might "bug" the other as they work together in a group?
- What could each do to let the other know he/she is heard and valued as a person who is "different from me" but valuable?

Of course, most of us exhibit some Sensor and some Intuitor aspects while selecting one as our primary type and the other as secondary. It's easy to believe your information gathering is right and to distrust the others' way of processing data.

DECISION-MAKING PROCESS: THINKING VS. FEELING
But gathering information is only the first step. Then comes our preferred process of making decisions. Thinkers are analytical, logical, and can remain objective and detached. Feelers are much more subjective, being able to identify with others, and become personally involved with the information collected. Thinkers tend to be result driven and can remain uninvolved and firm. Actually the terms "objective" and "subjective" would be better descriptors for Jung's classification than Thinking and Feeling. Thinkers also feel and Feelers also think. A Thinking decision maker contributes clarity and objectivity to a dilemma. A Feeling decision maker cultivates awareness of what happens to persons in the process of making that decision. Both may agree on the decision but contribute different perspectives in deciding. Thinkers base

decisions on principles and objective criteria. Feelers ask, "How would I feel (or have I felt) if I were the recipient of this decision?" This function of decision-making is the only one that falls along gender lines with two-thirds of American females selecting the more subjective Feeling for making decisions while two-thirds of American males select Thinking. The remaining one-third who go counter to their gender often are ridiculed or rejected (Kroeger and Thuesen, 28–31).

This decision-making function affects personal relationships in many ways. In terms of intimacy, Feelers want to experience it while Thinkers want to understand it (Kroeger and Thuesen, 129). Each senses the other is out of sync and doesn't understand the other's perspective. In making group decisions Thinkers, after examining the facts, may be irritated by the Feeler's comment, "I just don't feel good about the way we've handled this." In response, most Thinkers will go over the facts and principles "one more time," not realizing that Feelers are asking to explore more than just facts. Feelers often identify with the subject so much that they personalize decisions. And they may feel that the Thinkers with their brutal analysis of facts and detached mode of operating are insensitive and uncaring. This can lead them to feel that the group devalues them and their way of operation. A more subjective group can frustrate Thinkers as they endlessly explore subjective areas and seek to have everyone "on board" and harmonious in the decision-making. Neither is actually seeking to thwart the other. But the paradoxical focus, unless valued for being "right and left" not "right or wrong," can become a major battleground with the stronger members winning over the weaker. Personality choice in decision-making affects the climate and goals of the group. Feelers want to be in harmony with self and with everyone else in the group. Thinkers may challenge another and jeopardize relations in order to get the facts. This decision-making process also impacts self-disclosure by establishing what each thinks/feels is important to contribute in order to know and be known.

SOURCE OF ENERGY: INTROVERT VS. EXTROVERT

This decision making and information gathering is energized by a preferred setting. Extroverts are stimulated by persons and action, talking out their ideas in order to find out what they think. Introverts are drained by these same elements. They would prefer to think through issues on their own, listening and working out decisions internally. The Extrovert becomes impatient with solitude, introspection, and reflection which seems to recharge the Introvert. Introverts want time to concentrate. Extroverts crave intense interaction to help them work through facts and feelings. Introverts guard their "space" carefully, resenting intrusions from the phone or persons who break into their protected thoughts and time. Extroverts will talk to anyone at any time and never cease to amaze their counterparts with the amount of time they spend in "useless chatter." Introverts may think they have communicated their thoughts when in actuality they have rehearsed them only in their minds. Introverts feel uncomfortable with praise while the Extroverts thoroughly enjoy it and need such responses from others to keep them going.

LIFESTYLE ORIENTATION: JUDGING VS. PERCEIVING
While Introverts will join groups, they prefer to process internally and will often contribute only when asked. The challenge for group members who find energy in intense discussions is to be aware of the member who is not as vocal. After giving him or her time to work through ideas privately, it is important to ask for input from the introverted member. The person who doesn't show visible stimulation caused by active verbal interchange may be intensely involved on the inside and be able to contribute insight more open co-members have overlooked. This preference for outer world or inner world as the setting for collecting and processing information into decisions is probably the one of which most group members will become aware.

The final function in Jung's personality preferences deals with which function a person most naturally selects as he/she interacts with the world outside of self. Judgers lean toward decision-making while Perceivers prefer to collect information and withhold making a decision on it. Because they bring facts to conclusion, Judgers come across as structured, scheduled, controlled, and doing everything in an ordered and planned way. They make decisions fairly easily and set up choices as right and wrong. Perceivers, on the other hand, appear to be in a holding pattern as they continue to collect new information. This creates the impression of being flexible, spontaneous, and open-minded.

Judgers want a sense of closure—an opinion formed, a plan made, a definite time schedule, yes and no answers. Such definiteness disturbs those who prefer to keep open on a subject—new input could change their plan—and they don't want to be locked into a time frame or way of thinking. Creativity is at home in the Perceiver but follow-through to conclusion is hard. Judgers are often bugged by the Perceivers getting side-tracked or expressing fluidity in thinking. They may be late because of encountering some new phenomena, or because they get wrapped up in a conversation and forget commitments. Judgers need the freedom to explore alternatives which Perceivers provide. Perceivers need the focused attention that leads to the conclusions which Judgers naturally offer when they take charge. Perceivers may appear to be unable to make up their minds, while Judgers often come across as being closed-minded.

This conflict between structure and spontaneity, between resolution and remaining open can lead to small group conflicts and tension among members. Some want straight, decisive answers while others don't want to be bound by predetermined structures. The stronger the preference for one of these alternatives, the greater the irritation at the opposite preference (Kroeger and Thuesen, 37–43).

IMPLICATIONS

How would a group session led by one who strongly prefers decision-making (Judger) differ from one led by a person who prefers openness to the ongoing gathering of information? How would their schedule and plans differ? Judgers will have structure and time frames with fixed goals while Perceivers will probably work off of several general statements that point out topics and suggest the method will be to follow the flow of conversation.

How would the processing of ideas differ? Judgers will give a sense of control in the questions they ask (such as wording for specific answers) and will move from one organized point to the next. Perceivers will pose open-ended questions of a broad general nature. "How do you feel about the church?

The wrap-up? Judgers will want to come to at least one definite conclusion, with an issue resolved or a plan of action decided upon with a deadline established before the group ends. Perceivers will prefer a tentative conclusion or leave with no decision made but with lots of information and pending possibilities available. There will be an openness for persons to take what is important to them or to remain unchanged and undecided.

What differences in response would you get from a group of Extroverts and a group of Introverts if you asked the question, "How do you know that you are loved and cared for by this group?" Extroverts will probably point out their freedom to share openly and to talk through their most radical ideas with a group that listens carefully. Introverts will value the freedom to be different and to be included whether they say something or not, the freedom to "pass" when their ideas aren't worked through sufficiently to be expressed.

How would Thinkers and Feelers respond differently to the above question? Thinkers will probably list facts about what the group does for all its members. Feelers will identify specific circumstances that took place in the group where they personally experienced love and care.

Suppose a leader wanted to sell a group on participating in a specific project. How would a Sensor present this project differently from an Intuitor? Sensors would list actual facts about number of persons needed, practical goals accomplished by participating or competencies gained, and realistic amount of time or money required. Intuitors would give purposes in theory and possibilities inherent in being involved. They would aim at inspiring members to commit to the cause per se without necessarily being aware of what was involved.

- How have you realized that a preference of yours affects your response in a group?
- Do you lean toward Sensing or Intuiting? Thinking or Feeling?
- Are you energized by persons and activity, or do you prefer to internally work out conclusions?
- Do you make decisions and state opinions, or keep open and spontaneous?

Of course most persons are a mix of the preferences and exhibit characteristics of both preferences while leaning to one as primary. The preferences of the other functions in Jung's theory will color how a specific function displays its preference. A Sensing Perceiver will respond differently than a Sensing Judger. A wise leader who wishes to involve persons of both preferences cultivates awareness and characteristics of each so as to communicate and challenge group members. A good leader also accepts the perspectives of both styles and enables each to express his/her primary style while cultivating understanding of the other style as different—not wrong—and the person as adding to group understanding and balance, not thwarting or stalemating the members of the differing preference.

Personality types of individuals color responses and affect the climate and productivity of a group. Such preferences have developed over a long period of time and many experiences. It is important to remember that in no way is an indicated preference an absolute and neither preference is to be valued over the other. One of the merits of community is the exposure to those who are "different," forcing one to grow and recognize the need for others with different perceptions. Building Christian community gives group members opportunity to practice the realities of what it means to claim allegiance to Jesus as Lord, not to self as the only right perspective. It calls for a broadening of insight and acceptance, and reveals our need of one another since no one has a monopoly on truth. It provides a setting for being together with others whom we might not naturally select as friends.

And individual differences, while constantly changing, are esteemed in constructing the "whole" of community. Both "sameness" and "variety" are of worth. The individual and the community offer valuable uniquenesses not available to the other. But the recognizing of those uniquenesses enhances their worth rather than rejecting them as being unnecessary or wrong. To fully be an individual, one must be in community. To be in community, one must retain individuality—otherwise there is a sameness that destroys the very possibility of genuine unity. Community is the harmonizing of variety. God reflects both individuality and community, and created us to exist as both in His image. *Let's celebrate our differences!*

PERSONALITY NEEDS

Personality needs vary from one person to another. However, the motivating factors that prompt us to join others in groups can be categorized into three basic interpersonal needs.

Inclusion speaks of our desire to belong to and feel a part of others.

Affection includes our need for intimacy, giving and receiving love.

Control refers to needs of influence, power, and authority.

Group theorists believe that these three factors drive us toward togetherness with others. We need to receive these dimensions from others and express them toward others. The greatest degree of compatibility seems to take place when persons' needs are similar in the affection and inclusion dimensions and are complementary when it comes to control. There is greater satisfaction and less conflict occurring between persons who enjoy similar needs for expressing a sense of care and intimacy. Likewise a higher degree of harmony is found when one needs to coordinate and initiate, while another feels most comfortable supporting and cooperating. The variables of personality seem to affect behaviors and both verbal and nonverbal responses regardless of the type of group (Tubbs, 49).

For example, the need for achievement focuses on the drive to accomplish, to perform well, and to do things more quickly than others. A high need in this area usually leads to extreme focus on the task in groups, major stress on efficiency, and a resentment toward those who slow down or interfere with this goal of getting the task done. Persons with this personality need will give the group momentum in task accomplishment. Others will do the same thing out of a fear of failure. Because they cannot fail, they propel the group toward achieving what it set out to do.

Persons who have a high need to control will usually seek some form of leadership where they can influence the group more than the average member would. They are high participators and usually appear as Extroverts. Other persons exhibit a high need for approval, which comes out as a willingness to be controlled by others. These personality types watch for clues as to how they are

175

to behave and are quick to adapt and defer to authority.

In the area of control, some persons display a tendency to exhibit demanding, unbending, almost abusive behaviors in seeking to compel others to subscribe to their closed-mindedness. These dogmatic persons show great confidence in their perceptions, ideas, and ability, while demeaning others who have differing views or less power. Their opinionated and ridiculing statements breed resentment and reduction of trust.

Persons with high needs for affection, care, and a sense of togetherness will look for a group that openly expresses those qualities or allows one to be a caregiver. They build a sense of cohesion and bondedness between members in a group, often by fostering social interaction between persons. These members are the nurturers and "warm" personalities who are sensitive to what is happening to themselves and to others in the group. They score high in group maintenance and support, which may become the task focus of groups they lead. Their need for belonging and being liked may get in the way of achievement that requires focus on more objective issues. Needs of *inclusion, affection,* and *control* have effects on each other and on the way an individual responds to and has impact on the group. Groups themselves develop personalities that express the dominance of one or more of these dimensions. For some, the emphasis is on group identity, "I'm with you and you're with me and so we are all together." Others join Streisand's appraisal of relational intimacy, "People who need people are the luckiest people in the world." Still others become centers for having and being influenced, for expressing and experiencing power (Tubbs, 51–57).

Johnson has conceptualized a four quadrant model of personality variables called D-A-S-H (Dominance-Affiliation-Submission-Hostility). The characteristics of each are noted in terms of descriptive behaviors.

The personalities of individuals who join together to become community shape and adjust what the group will become. They affect its goals, process, and final outcome. They in turn are affected and shaped by the community in which they participate. This is a symbiotic relationship that can result in the enhancement of both individual and group without the domination of one over the other.

	High Dominance	Low Dominance
High Affiliation	advises coordinates directs initiates leads	acquiesces agrees assists cooperates obliges
Low Affiliation	analyzes criticizes disapproves judges resists	concedes evades relinquishes retreats withdraw

(David Johnson, 35)

10

TERMS OF ENDEARMENT: COMMUNICATION

I know you believe you understand what you think I said,
but I'm not sure you realize that what you heard
is not what I meant.

S uch is the dilemma of communication. More books have probably been written on the topic of interpersonal communication than on any other subject dealt with in small groups. We are able to define it, can recite rules that govern it, continue to perfect phones and faxes that enable it, and yet it remains the number one issue among persons. The Son of God encountered this curiosity in His listeners and commented on those who rejected His message, "Though seeing, they do not see; though hearing, they do not hear or understand. In them [the listeners] is fulfilled the prophecy of Isaiah: 'You will be ever hearing but never understanding; you will be ever seeing but never perceiving' " (Matt. 13:13-14).

We live in an age when the communication of information has been perfected to a technological degree previously unreached. Yet misunderstandings and inadequate or inaccurate information remain as the number one cause of marital difficulties, a major factor in employer-employee conflicts, and a great promoter of international disruptions.

For most beginning small group leaders, the quality of communication plays a predominant role in their fears about small group leadership. "What if my group won't talk? What if they talk too much? What if they misunderstand my motives? What if I can't get anything across? What if they don't get anything out of the group? What do I do if they don't get along?"

Communication is a glorious indication of life. As often said, "We cannot *not* communicate." Even silence communicates. What then causes it to be so difficult to correctly ascertain meaning? Much is due to the complexity of the process. Communication has meaning both in its content and in how it is said or how that content is intended. (The latter is often conditioned by the relationship of the communicators.) Communication has verbal and nonverbal components. Interpretation of meaning is filtered by our needs or emotions, our context, previous history, and patterns of interaction developed over time. For example, consider all the meanings the following sentence could convey depending on which word is emphasized:

"I didn't say you were stupid."

Now consider the same sentence communicated with each of the accompanying nonverbals:

- Said with a teasing smile.
- Said with a frown.
- Said in wide-eyed, eyebrow lifted surprise.
- Said without looking you in the eye.
- Said with a wave of the hand.

Consider the added meaning if you hear this statement after spending hours trying to solve a frustrating problem. Or after years of competing with a brilliant older sister. Or having lived under a teacher's influential pronouncement that you would never understand arithmetic because you were "slow." Multiply these scenarios by the number of persons in a group and the number of interactions possible between those persons and the magnitude of the hazards of communication becomes evident.

Another complication that thwarts our gaining an accurate understanding comes from the effort and time required to request and give adequate feedback necessary for true comprehension to have taken place. Consider the following exercise adapted from one developed by Virginia Satir. Ask one person in a dyad to make a statement about themselves such as "I like this group." The listener is to give feedback beginning with "Do you mean. . . ?" until he or she receives three "yes" answers. The speaker may respond with only "yes" or "no." E.g., "Do you mean you feel comfortable here?" "Yes." "Do you mean that I should like this group too?" "No." "Do you mean you are glad you got into this group as opposed to another one?" "No." "Do you mean you feel happy to be present tonight?" "Yes." etc.

Be aware of the effort it takes to zero in on the exact meaning another attaches to specific words. Most of us don't have the time or the energy to fine-tune each communication—life would bog down in the process. However, we often jump to conclusions that the communicator never intended unless we "check it out" with the sender. Many a "But I thought you said. . . ." is the result of this incorrect leap of understanding.

Expectations too lead us astray in that they promote selective listening. We tend to "hear" what will confirm our already formed perceptions. Thus we filter out important variables that convey what a person really said.

EXPECTATIONS

Christian small groups have expectations placed upon them— sometimes unrealistic expectations—that hinder communication in the group.

1. We expect to be understood by other Christians and it comes as a shock to realize that they do not understand.
2. We believe that perfected understanding will eliminate conflict. We often gloss over misunderstandings to maintain the illusion of harmony.
3. We often live with the assumption that "complete" understanding means we will all think alike or agree on everything.
4. We live under a strong right/wrong orientation and find it difficult not to label ideas and behaviors rather than seeing differences as "left and right."
5. Because of a strong "do right" perspective, many find it

difficult to be honest in communicating in Christian groups. We find it easier to share what we *should do* or our success stories than our real feelings and struggles.

6. The one verse that most Christians remember is "Judge not, that you be not judged." While Christians do not hesitate to "judge another" internally, they fear being judged harshly by others if they voice any kind of negative communication or critical assessment.

7. Certain types of personality styles and communications are accepted within the Christian culture while others are rejected. Such restrictions may limit our understanding. A person who appears as a deviant to the acceptable norms will be "frozen out."

Of course, there are many positives of our faith that enhance small group communication. Among them are a climate of genuine love, acceptance, a spirit of grace, allegiance to Jesus as Lord, a willingness to forgive, the presence of the Spirit of God, the insight of the Word of God to enable good communication, a sense of being accepted by God, and a God-given desire to know and be known by the family of God.

TWO LEVELS OF COMMUNICATING
Communication involves two levels of message sending:

1. The informational level
2. The metamessage level

The informational level conveys the meaning of the words used. The metamessage level deals with the meaning conveyed to the recipient of the communication. Metamessages "frame a conversation, much as a picture frame provides a context for the images in the picture. Metamessages let you know how to interpret what someone is saying" (Tannen, 33). We usually react more to the metamessage than we do to the information message given in the words. For example, the question, "Why do you bring that up?" could be a simple request for connecting information. The metamessage could be, "You're way off the track. Get with it." Or "You must have some hidden agenda you're

181

trying to work in." The metamessage frames interpretation of the informational message and conditions our response. It is helpful to check out metamessages to avoid misinterpretation. It is incorrect to assume that others mean what we would mean if we said the same thing in the same way.

Reframing is extremely helpful in avoiding jumping to conclusions and misinterpreting communication. Ask yourself, is there any other way this statement could be interpreted? Many persons have "read into" communications things that weren't intended. Reframing communication by rephrasing/clarifying the message or acting in a different way is a powerful way to change interaction in a group. Conflicts arise when the metamessage is read as, "You are not valuable, loved, or esteemed." The informational level is not the issue, the metamessage is.

NONVERBAL INFLUENCE
A major component of the metamessage is the nonverbal communication accompanying the information. Facial clues, body animation, vocal pitch, volume, and rate convey information about feelings, attitude, mood, and intended interpretation. Reflect on how the following statement by a leader could be impacted by varied facial expressions. "We need to get this settled before we move on." Now think through various gestures that would color interpretation. What is an interpretation conveyed by a deliberate, slow punching declaration of each word? "WE-NEED-TO-GET-THIS-SETTLED-BEFORE-WE-MOVE-ON." Say the statement in a depressed mood. How did you express your feelings? Now say it in a mood of serious concern. What conveyed your seriousness? Even without visual contact persons on the telephone convey impressions.

IMPACT OF DISTANCE
Distance impacts communication and sends a metamessage. Picture a person moving closer as she talks. What does this convey about the content, the attitude, or intention of the speaker? While much of this is cultural, distance affects the tone and effectiveness of interpersonal relationships. Imagine conveying "I care for you" or "I want to share this secret" across a large room. Group seating that affects the distance between members has an

effect upon the kind of communication experienced. Members need to be seated within four to twelve feet of one another (social distance). Group members will probably stake out their territory and sit in the same general area. To move out of that area affects communication and creates discomfort.

Immediacy—the sensation of closeness—is enhanced or diminished by nonverbals. Sitting side by side tends to diminish arguing with one another. Touching deliberately seems to increase our effort in listening. Sitting outside a circle, persons tend to contribute less and seem less interested in the comments of others. We momentarily look away when experiencing intense anger, laughter, or an overly personal remark (Grove, 144).

OTHER FACTORS
Environment also influences the comfort level of persons and determines the communication of meanings. Picture the difference that sitting around a table makes compared to sitting in a living room. Sitting on the floor sets up a different communication tone than sitting in classroom chairs.

The credibility of a speaker decreases as the number of nonfluencies (content-less words such as *uh, well, you know,* pauses and repetitions) increases (Miller and Hewgill, 1964). Whatever the nonverbal, the effect is more powerful than we usually credit. Researchers suggest that the contribution of the nonverbal to a message ranges from 55% to 65% while the vocal way a person speaks the words contributes 38% and the words spoken contribute about 7% (Mallison, 61). Nonverbal aspects must be considered if communication is to improve.

INFLUENCE OF METAMESSAGE
Conversation serves two purposes: it gives information and it maintains relationship. What makes metamessages tricky is that they strongly influence relationships. When a person says, "I forgot to send you a birthday card," there are many communications going on. The metamessage more important than a mention of the lapse in memory is the why and what that says about the relationship. "Does this mean our relationship is deteriorating? Does it mean I am no longer valuable to you? Does it mean you no longer care?"

METAMESSAGE AND GENDER

Gender differences, while not stereotyped, appear to play a part in communication interpretation. In general women are more attuned to metamessages. She will say, "Did you notice the tension between Bill and Susan tonight?" He will answer, "No, I didn't see anything unusual." She mentions that Bill ignored Susan's request for attention. Susan argued for accuracy in his descriptive comments. Also, each of them used *I* a lot more than *we* in their conversation. Metamessages are more apparent to women because they tend to be more aware of how persons relate to one another (Tannen, 136).

Another major difference between women's small groups and men's small groups is the need most women have for talking to maintain relationship. If someone doesn't talk, the metamessage is, "Something must be wrong with our relationship." The interchange assures a woman that the relationship is intact and that the other is still involved. The content of the conversation is not that important. American men, on the other hand, at times find it difficult to know what to say unless some important information is to be conveyed. Culture has taught them to "not waste time talking, but to get down to the business at hand." This adaptation dominates the American business culture, but it is a definite disadvantage in cross-cultural exchange with counterparts in countries where establishing relationship is primary for conducting business.

In a mixed gender group, the women will usually want to chat just to "keep in touch," while the men will prefer to "do what we came to do," and then go home. This difference in styles explains why men are characteristically seen as inept when it comes to building close personal relationships with other men and why women have those personal contacts that give support and enable them to survive. This does not mean that women do not want information or that men do not want relationships. But the primary focus and basis for evaluating good communication for women will be on "Did we relate?" and for men, "Did we solve the problem or get the information?" Each gender tends to devalue and make jokes about the style of the other without recognizing the need for both informational messages and relational maintenance. When she wants to talk, she probably wants relational connecting in "talking things out," and when he says, "Let's talk," he means, "Give me facts and let's respond to them." The tension goes back to the balancing act between being an individual and being involved in community. To show involvement threatens the pull toward individuality, and to keep our distance and our thoughts to ourselves threatens involvement (Tannen, 32–34).

DIRECT AND INDIRECT SPEECH

Another conversational variable that impacts small group communication is the difference between "Hinters" and those who use directness. Hinters express their wants and opinions indirectly whereas their counterparts say exactly what they want and mean. Each runs the risk of being misunderstood.

In her excellent book, *That's Not What I Meant,* Deborah Tannen explores this conversational style difference that affects communication in groups. Tannen found this diverse way of talking caused persons to draw conclusions never intended and often led to baffling behavior. At times others seem to be totally oblivious to the motives so obvious to us as we talk to them because their style is different from ours. Realization of one's own style and the effect it has on others is a big plus in interpersonal communication (Tannen, 26–27).

Some of us grew up with rules for social situations that sounded like this:

- "If you want it, be polite. Don't ask."
- "Don't tell people what you really want, then you won't be hurt when you don't get it."
- "It's not good to 'speak your mind.' "
- "Always find out what the other person wants first. Don't be pushy."
- "If you say what you think, people will write you off."

These kinds of rules conditioned us to be very aware of others' responses and helped us adapt to or figure out a more acceptable way of getting what we wanted. Tannen writes,

People prefer not to say exactly what they mean in so many

185

words because they're not concerned only with the ideas they're expressing; they're also—even more—concerned with the effect their words will have on those they're talking to. They want to make sure to maintain camaraderie, to avoid imposing, and to give (or at least appear to give) the other person some choice in the matter being discussed.

(Tannen, 21–22)

Hinters have found that asking questions works for them so they interpret questions as hints of agendas behind the words.

"Do you want to study the Book of Revelation?"
"Sure, if that's what you want. It's a hard book to understand."
"Well, would you rather not tackle it at this time?"
"As leader you're probably going to have to do the most work."
"So are you saying you want to study Revelation or you don't want to study Revelation?"
"We don't have to study Revelation if you don't want to."
Exasperatedly, "But I didn't say I didn't want to."
Heatedly, "Why are we even having this conversation? Let's just vote!"

And so it goes. Sometimes both parties end up doing what they don't want to do because neither wants to offend the other. Both are trying to get comfortable and to do the right thing. At other times, one party can feel manipulated by the other who forces him to make the decision *they* should have made. "Testing the waters" before making a statement of conviction is a protection device. We then can reshape our thoughts and statements as we move through the conversation. But hinting is risky because signals can be overlooked and sometimes meaning can be garbled. Hoping the office crowd picks up on your subtle hints that Friday is your birthday can lower your esteem if you read a meta-message in their obvious absence of remembrance. In groups, hinters face the same pain and isolation when no one picks up on their indirect suggestions. Interpersonal pain is often caused because no one knew the importance of something to a member.

Blurting-out directness is not the answer either.

The Author of community suggests wise guidelines for healthy communication. "Speak the truth" to one another, not hiding or distorting it but speak that truth "in love," with motives and conditions that reveal genuine care for the one receiving the communication. "Let your conversation be always full of grace, seasoned with salt, so that you may know how to answer everyone" (Col. 4:6). Maintain conversation that is gracious, but always flavored with the truth of the Gospel. "Let the word of Christ dwell in you richly as you teach and admonish one another with all wisdom. . . . And whatever you do . . . in word . . . do it all in the name of the Lord Jesus" with the authority and Spirit of Jesus behind it (Col. 3:16-17). This is the message and the metamessage; it is the information and the maintaining of relationship—truth spoken in the attitude and condition of love.

COMMUNICATION THROUGHOUT GROUP LIFE

Ironically communication is an ongoing concern in small group encounters. We never reach the point when it is automatic and perfect. New challenges are constantly arising. At the beginning of a group, as already discussed, communication is threatened by awareness of self and what others will think, by a preoccupation to impress with the right thing, and to present our best face only. We tend not to listen to others because of overwhelming sensitivity to how we are being perceived.

Being together longer or becoming closer in relationship can cause the communication to be more fragile than ever.

1. When we feel we are loved, we expect to be understood.
2. The longer you have been with people, the more you expect to be understood. "If you don't understand me, who will?" As the relationship grows, so do unrealistic expectations and thus the misunderstanding becomes more painful.
3. The closer you are to someone, and the longer you have been close, the more you have to lose when you open your mouth (Tannen, 123). When a relationship has been formed, you don't want to lose it by saying things the other won't like.

187

4. Misunderstandings are often seen as signs of a failing relationship. "We don't understand each other in this. Maybe this group is falling apart." In getting acquainted whatever prompted understanding or togetherness was seen as building the group. Now, however, any sign of misunderstanding or difference is registered as moving persons away from each other.
5. Because relationships have been built, much is at stake so information is now framed in the metamessage question, "Do you still love me *enough?*"
6. The more time persons spend together, the more their differences will surface and be misunderstood. These differences may threaten the group that wants to hang on to the unrealistic relationship that was.

(adapted from Tannen, 121–126)

Being aware of these factors and not labeling them with more weight than they deserve is a first step in improving communication. *We will never have perfect understanding.* One of the acts that binds us together as a community is having to work out understandings and absorb differences. Being in community is a call to commit oneself to the work and time required to develop healthy interpersonal communication—not to enter a community where there is no miscommunication. Talking about communication hazards, checking in, and reframing with redirected actions are all gracious, caring responses to sharing the truth framed in love. Helping persons grow in communication skills within a group is helping them grow in life.

11

TOO CLOSE
FOR COMFORT:
CONFLICT IN GROUPS

I plead with Euodia and I plead with Syntyche
to agree with each other in the Lord.
Yes, and I ask you, loyal yokefellow,
help these women who have contended at my side
in the cause of the Gospel.
Philippians 4:2-3

T here is probably no topic more controversial in the study of Christian small group dynamics than the subject of conflict or controversy within a group.

Think for a moment about your own personal experiences in this realm.

How was conflict handled in your home? Did you or your family members withdraw into silence? Yell and slam doors? Hold a family council?

What has experience taught you?

- "Let sleeping dogs lie."
- "It pays to speak your mind."
- "Don't get mad. Get even."
- "Keep the peace at all cost."

Our culture gives mixed messages in this area. We are taught

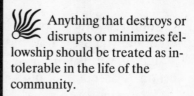 Anything that destroys or disrupts or minimizes fellowship should be treated as intolerable in the life of the community.

Richard C. Halverson
How I Changed My Thinking About the Church, 55

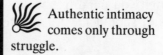 Authentic intimacy comes only through struggle.

Richard C. Halverson
Somehow Inside of Eternity, 63

to view anger as unladylike, not gentlemanly, and immature. Conflict is viewed as uncomfortable and embarrassing. Many persons believe that conflict causes marriages to break up, divides organizations, causes church splits, is responsible for employees being fired, and breeds disintegration and demoralization. At the same time we are taught "to speak up for what we believe," "we are responsible for our own happiness," "people won't respect you if you don't stand up for what you are thinking," "our idea is as good as another's," and "do not gunnysack grievances." Generally, it is not the conflict itself which causes a severing of relationships but an inadequate way of dealing with that conflict.

Conflict is usually seen as negative, and we learn few strategies for dealing with it in a positive way. Most persons see conflict as a "win-lose" situation. Personal aggressiveness is disliked and devalued. We want friends who are unassuming, don't put restrictions on us, don't cross us, do anything for anyone, never raise their voices, aren't pushy, and don't contradict us.

In some situations, however, conflict and being personally aggressive are acceptable. On the athletic field, in contests, as an entrepreneur, in debates, and in games, these qualities are valued in a teammate and opponent. "Although anger and aggressiveness are officially taboo, as a society we apparently admire and are fascinated by aggressive people" (R. Weaver, 324).

> Conflicts with peers are all right if you have been stepped on and you are a boy, but talking back to parents when they step on you is not all right. Having a conflict over a promotion is acceptable, but openly vying for recognition is not. Competing over a girl (if you're a boy) is admirable, but having a conflict over a boy (if you're a girl) is catty. ... Thus, persons emerge with a mixed feeling about conflict, and many simply learn to avoid the whole subject. Clearly, one of the dysfunctional teachings about conflict is that you need to check with those in power to determine if you should have a conflict and, if so, how to carry it out.
> (Hocker and Wilmot, 6–7)

We are taught many dysfunctional generalizations that shape and reinforce our feelings about conflict. For example:

Harmony is normal; conflict is abnormal. Such a statement suggests that to be in conflict is unusual, temporary. "Observation of people in relationships shows that conflict is not a temporary aberration. It alternates with harmony in an ebb and flow pattern. But common expressions such as 'I'm glad things are back to normal around here' or 'Let's get back on track' express the assumption that conflict is not the norm" (Hocker and Wilmot, 7).

Conflict is always a win-lose situation: someone will be a winner and someone a loser. Such belief results in dysfunctional behavior where one competes to apply enough power to come out on top, lives with the mixed feelings of giving in so the other can feel good, or feels devalued by personalizing the loss.

Conflict is the natural result of personality clashes. This belief is founded on the premise that some people just can't get along. It was popularized several years ago in terms of having an "Irregular Person" in your life. Many Christians found this an affirmation of something they wanted to believe—some people are impossible to get along with. Now they had confirmation of this suspicion and it justified their being "bugged" by certain persons. Grove points out the lack of substantiation in this dysfunctional excuse. In the phrase "personality clash," " 'personality' is one of those illusive abstractions that connotes more specificity than it can support. Sometimes we are said to 'clash' because our personalities are 'so different.' Other times, it is because we are 'so much alike.' Not a lot of information there. Yet many people seem to cling to the idea that we carry little valences around in our bodies which outside of our control, set us up for conflict conversations with certain others who house valences of the opposite sign" (Grove, 291). "Personality clashes" result from learned human behavior which is under our control and can be changed. "Personalities don't conflict—behaviors that people do conflict" (Fisher, 104).

Christianity has added to these misconceptions generalizations of a moral nature.

All conflict is wrong. It is true there are dysfunctional responses to conflict. James writes, "What causes fights and quarrels among you? Don't they come from your desires that battle within you? You want something but don't get it. You kill and covet, but you cannot have what you want. You quarrel and fight" (James 4:1-2). Note the four dysfunctional ways of handling conflict: fight, quarrel, kill, and covet. However, in Acts 6 the conflict that arose because the Grecian widows were being overlooked, prompted improved organization and resulted in the involvement of others in ministering to alleviate this conflict situation (Acts 6:1-7). Conflict between two major missionaries who saw Mark differently resulted in two teams being sent out and may have "saved" Mark for the ministry. Though they conflicted in their point of view, neither Paul nor Barnabas is depicted as being in the wrong. They simply had different values and perspectives (Acts 15:36-41). Jesus Himself aroused conflict. "Do not suppose that I have come to bring peace to the earth. I did not come to bring peace, but a sword. For I have come to turn 'a man against his father, a daughter against her mother, a daughter-in-law against her mother-in-law—a man's enemies will be the members of his own household' " (Matt. 10:34).

Christians must never conflict but are commanded to live in conformity. As Christians we are commanded, "Live in harmony with one another. . . . If it is possible, as far as it depends on you, live at peace with everyone" (Rom. 12:16, 18). But harmony and peace speak of living positively with differences, not being uniform in thinking. When harmony is interpreted as everyone being alike, groups cultivate a pseudoharmony which gives the impression of peace and togetherness but which in actuality declares that Christians cannot be honest and real in their differences. The Gospel is thus removed from real life, and hypocrisy and guardedness sets in. True harmony comes from different notes played at the same time in an enriching, not discordant, manner.

The Christian way to handle conflict is to give in, esteeming the other out of Christian love. Again we have one side of the coin. In the Sermon on the Mount, Jesus advocates not only giving in, but giving more than asked for. "If someone wants to sue you and take your tunic, let him have your cloak as well" (Matt. 5:40). But He also teaches, "If your brother sins against you, go and show him his fault. . . . If he listens to you, you have won your brother over" (Matt. 18:15). Paul illustrates this way of handling conflicting values in reporting his opposition to Peter. "When Peter came to Antioch, I opposed him to his face, because he was clearly in the wrong. Before certain men came from James, he used to eat with the Gentiles. But when they arrived, he began to draw back and separate himself from the Gentiles because he was afraid of those who belonged to the circumcision group. . . . When I saw that they were not acting in line with the truth of the Gospel, I said to Peter in front of them all, 'You are a Jew, yet you live like a Gentile and not like a Jew. How is it, then, that you force Gentiles to follow Jewish customs?' " (Gal. 2:11-12, 14)

There are different kinds of conflicts that occur and different ways of handling conflict. At times, conflict can result in negative reactions or it can produce positive responses that lead to improved conditions and relationships.

Generally speaking, conflict is inevitable in every group because no two persons are exactly alike. Getting in touch with one's own attitude about conflict is important because the more negative a person's assumptions about conflict, the more difficult it will be to face conflict in a productive fashion. When experiencing conflict, a commitment to positive results is key to working through that conflict to a positive end. Self-disclosure and making others aware of your assumptions leads to improved conditions for working together.

FUNCTIONS OF CONFLICT

Conflict can lead to improved conditions and growth. It can bring to our attention hidden values and assumptions that need to be examined, verified, modified, or discarded. A group that allows itself to experience conflict can be a healthier group. People feel that they can express both negative and positive feelings without fear of being rejected. New levels of understanding grow out of the revelation of differences. Where those differences are not allowed out, tension builds that will eventually affect group relationships and group goals. For example, a group that must always be conciliatory in spirit may never develop a level of trust that leads to high commitment and investment because they realize they are only dealing with half truths. Witness the polite but strained conditions in beginning groups where each person is trying to put his or her "best foot forward." Though conflict is absent in these early stages, so also is depth of commitment. This is natural during this beginning period, but groups who are still experiencing this situation four weeks later are probably stuck in pseudocommunity.

Paradoxically, conflict increases involvement and involvement increases conflict. When members care, they get involved risking greater investment of themselves in the group. Likewise, the greater the investment a person has in what is happening, the more likely that person is to come into conflict with another. High commitment means greater risk which translates into increased self-disclosure and involvement because "I have a vested interest in the issue." A group that cares deeply about its members is torn between being agreeable and being honest with one another (which could disrupt harmony temporarily). Persons in this tension will often "test the waters" with statements such as, "Can I tell you how I really feel?" or "Please don't misunderstand me. I really like this group but. . . ." How have you seen conflict propel a person into active participation in a group where otherwise he or she would have remained a spectator?

Conflict also has the potential for promoting a sense of cohesion. Cohesion is defined as "the degree of intensity with which group members are bonded together and motivated to work as a unit toward the achievement of group goals" (Palozzo, 256). Sometimes called morale, cohesion keeps persons a part of the group and is a result of members' satisfaction with what the group is becoming and what *they* are becoming *in the group* (worthwhile and cared for individuals). On the surface, most would see conflict as destructive to group morale. In actuality, a lack of conflict can be more destructive because of what its absence represents. Working through difficulties together binds members to one another. Just knowing that they like each other and the group enough to reveal and work through issues of deep emotional ownership, develops a feeling of commitment to others who shared in that revelation and process. "Not running away" says "while I am committed to this issue, opinion, perspective, I am also committed to you and our relationship." As Fisher and Ellis paraphrase, "The group that fights together stays together" (Fisher and Ellis, 264). Can you think of a group experience where you saw this happen?

Group conflict also can cause a group to become creative and more productive. Challenging the status quo or working through a dilemma means that members must look for new or improved conditions and the result will probably be a better group. Groups with differing members push the boundaries that often limit and restrict solutions. New paradigms emerge out of conflict. Effort is increased as members clash over alternatives. Increased effort can mean higher productivity. Of course, mismanaged conflict can result in unhealthy deteriorating relationships which will definitely undermine work on the task (Wilson and Hanna, 248–249). Both of the conflicts cited earlier in this chapter (conflict over ministry to Grecian widows, and Paul and Barnabas' conflict over John Mark) led to increased productivity in quality and quantity.

> If you're going to fight . . .
>
> Fight for the relationship—not against it!
>
> Fight for reconciliation—not for alienation.
>
> Fight to preserve the friendship—not to destroy it.
>
> Fight to win your spouse—not to lose him/her.
>
> Fight to save your marriage—not to cash it in.
>
> Fight to solve the problem—not to salve your ego!
>
> If you're going to fight, fight to win . . . not to lose!
>
> Richard C. Halverson
> *Somehow Inside of Eternity,* 63

SOURCES OF CONFLICT

Where does conflict come from? James tells us that fights and quarrels grow out of conflicting desires within us, probably determined by self-centered motives (James 4:1, 3). Often the cause is a power struggle. There is only so much of a resource to go around and we come in conflict as we compete for control, attention, reward, and so on. The Grecian widow conflict grew out of differing values when it came to who got helped and who didn't. Paul and Barnabas separated because of a difference in perspectives or aims. Conflict is more than an argument—it is tension between persons who are in sharp disagreement.

Sometimes conflict is ideational. We express strong commitments to differing principles, priorities, and values. Our goals may compete or simply differ from those of the group. Hidden agendas house personal, unspoken objectives that are often of a personal nature. Our behavior causes conflict. The behavior of the group as a whole or as individuals irritates us because it cuts across agendas counter to ours.

One faction of a group believes the way to handle a group is to take control and accomplish the task. Another faction puts higher priority on building relationships and taking time to know one another in a mutual way before focusing on the project to be done. Competing goals and processes cause conflict to be expressed overtly or to be a running undercurrent as one faction holds sway.

How have you seen differing principles, priorities, or values create conflict in a group?

Other conflicts may be labeled interpersonal. Members jockey for power or status, maintain a running disagreement—whatever A suggests, B is bound to debate—express irritation and disagreement with another's personal or group habits.

Some group conflicts are the result of "carry-over" of dysfunctionalism in an individual's personal life which affects others who are in community with that individual. For example, a person who finds it difficult to take responsibility for himself can cause conflict by exercising that dysfunctional pattern in a group. We all bring to a group our own learned patterns of operation. Sometimes these patterns are curbed or changed by the fact that a desire to be accepted and loved takes priority over that pattern. In what ways have you experienced this personal "carry-over" into a group?

At other times the individual's learned behavior pattern disrupts the group and creates a conflict. The situation is often exacerbated because neither party is aware of or can identify the real source of conflict. The real issue is hidden and what triggers the conflict is only a minute symptom of the deeper conflict. Miller, McNully, Wackman, and Miller's Awareness Wheel is helpful for getting in touch with root issues in situations that cause emotional tension and anger or anxiety within us. How do we deal with conflict when it has arisen?

CONFLICT STRATEGIES

Persons develop patterns of response to conflict. Experience is an effective teacher. Our chosen style of response has been learned by trial and error in the situations of conflict. Styles of operation may be conscious or unconscious.

We usually have a preferred way of dealing with the tension of conflict and a secondary system that we use as backup. "I usually see conflict as a situation to be avoided at all costs, and if somehow I get pushed into it, I try to accommodate the other person as quickly as possible to alleviate the tension I'm feeling inside." Or "I've found that changing the subject helps me avoid conflict."

Persons develop patterns of response that make sense to them. Years of having to cope with conflict have created a rationale for the way we operate. What works for us fits in with our understanding of what we have experienced and who we are. Though the style a person uses may appear inappropriate, self-defeating, or surprising to us, to that person it has a logic that has been created out of the will to survive in stressful conflict.

One style of behavior is not necessarily better than another. There is no one style that works every time. Joseph, in conflict with his boss' wife, used withdrawal. Paul and Barnabas, in the sharp conflict over circumcision in Acts 15, utilized confrontation and collaboration. But in addressing Philemon over the issue of Onesimus, Paul calls primarily for accommodation.

Persons can learn to use new styles of managing conflict. When a chosen style no longer works or when the reward for utilizing another style is attractive, we can make a decision to change. In this process we develop new logic to compensate for now operating in these new ways.

Groups are often powerful means for changing a person's way of operating in a conflict situation. The pressure of group acceptance and the support of group relationships are strong factors in helping a person move to another style (Hocker and Wilmot, 37–39).

There are many conflict-managing strategies identified in research on this topic. The interesting study on page 198 records five styles observed in interpersonal conflicts and the way they are expressed in relational contexts.

197

1. Strategy of Manipulation
   Act so nice that he/she later cannot refuse when I ask him/her for my own way.
   Be especially sweet, charming, helpful, and pleasant before bringing up the subject of disagreement.
   Make this person believe that he/she is doing me a favor by giving in.
2. Strategy of Non-negotiation
   Refuse to discuss or even listen to the subject unless he/she gives in.
   Keep repeating my point of view until he/she gives in.
   Argue until this person changes his/her mind.
3. Strategy of Emotional Appeal
   Appeal to this person's love and affection for me.
   Promise to be more loving in the future.
   Get angry and demand that he/she give in.
4. Strategy of Personal Rejection
   Withhold affection and act cold until he/she gives in.
   Ignore him/her.
   Make the other person jealous by pretending to lose interest in him/her.
5. Strategy of Empathic Understanding
   Discuss what would happen if we each accepted the other's point of view.
   Talk about why we do not agree.
   Hold mutual talks without argument.

(Fitzpatrick, Winke, 7)

Because it is helpful to be aware of the strategies we use and to see how these compare with strategies used by others:

1. Mark the following proverbs according to how typically each expresses your behavior in a conflict situation.
2. Provide copies of the proverbs for several others who are in your group and ask them to mark their responses to the proverbs.
3. Next read the description of styles that follows the questionnaire and on separate pieces of paper write the names of the others who also completed the question-

naire and select the conflict strategy description that best describes their actions as observed in your group. Ask them to do the same for you and the others.

4. Hand each the slip of paper describing the style most often observed in them and receive from each their observation of your style.

5. Score and rank your questionnaire according to the strategy frequency of use that follows the proverbs. Share how others see your style of conflict management as noted on the slips of paper and how you scored yourself. Ask the others to give examples of how they have observed your use of the style they chose to describe you in conflict. Move to the next person to follow the same process.

Use the following scale to indicate the degree to which each proverb expresses your response in a conflict.

Proverbs

5 = very typical of the way I act in a conflict
4 = frequently typical of the way I act in a conflict
3 = sometimes typical of the way I act in a conflict
2 = seldom typical of the way I act in a conflict
1 = never typical of the way I act in a conflict

____ 1. It is easier to refrain than to retreat from a quarrel.
____ 2. If you cannot make a person think as you do, make him or her do as you think.
____ 3. Soft words win hard hearts.
____ 4. You scratch my back, I'll scratch yours.
____ 5. Come now and let us reason together.
____ 6. When two quarrel, the person who keeps silent first is the most praiseworthy.
____ 7. Might overcomes right.
____ 8. Smooth words make smooth ways.
____ 9. Better half a loaf than no bread at all.
____ 10. Truth lies in knowledge, not in majority opinion.
____ 11. He who fights and runs away lives to fight another day.
____ 12. He hath conquered well that hath made his enemies flee.
____ 13. Kill your enemies with kindness.

____ 14. A fair exchange brings no quarrel.

____ 15. No person has the final answer but every person has a piece to contribute.

____ 16. Stay away from people who disagree with you.

____ 17. Fields are won by those who believe in winning.

____ 18. Kind words are worth much and cost little.

____ 19. Tit for tat is fair play.

____ 20. Only the person who is willing to give up his or her monopoly on truth can ever profit from the truths that others hold.

____ 21. Avoid quarrelsome people as they will only make your life miserable.

____ 22. A person who will not flee will make others flee.

____ 23. Soft words ensure harmony.

____ 24. One gift for another makes good friends.

____ 25. Bring your conflicts into the open and face them directly; only then will the best solution be discovered.

____ 26. The best way of handling conflicts is to avoid them.

____ 27. Put your foot down where you mean to stand.

____ 28. Gentleness will triumph over anger.

____ 29. Getting part of what you want is better than not getting anything at all.

____ 30. Frankness, honesty, and trust will move mountains.

____ 31. There is nothing so important you have to fight for it.

____ 32. There are two kinds of people in the world, the winners and the losers.

____ 33. When one hits you with a stone, hit him or her with a piece of cotton.

____ 34. When both give in halfway, a fair settlement is achieved.

____ 35. By digging and digging, the truth is discovered.

Scoring

Withdrawing	Forcing	Smoothing	Compromising	Confronting
____ 1	____ 2	____ 3	____ 4	____ 5
____ 6	____ 7	____ 8	____ 9	____ 10
____ 11	____ 12	____ 13	____ 14	____ 15
____ 16	____ 17	____ 18	____ 19	____ 20
____ 21	____ 22	____ 23	____ 24	____ 25
____ 26	____ 27	____ 28	____ 29	____ 30
____ 31	____ 32	____ 33	____ 34	____ 35
____ Total	____ Total	____ Total	____ Total	____ Total

Too Close for Comfort

"The higher the total score for each conflict strategy, the more frequently you tend to use that strategy. The lower the total score for each conflict strategy, the less frequently you tend to use that strategy" (Johnson and Johnson, 304–306).

FIVE BASIC STRATEGIES
Johnson and Johnson describe the following strategies for dealing with conflict:

The Turtle (Withdrawing). Turtles withdraw into their shells to avoid conflicts. They give up their personal goals and relationships. They stay away from the issues over which the conflict is taking place and from the persons they are in conflict with. Turtles believe it is hopeless to try to resolve conflicts. They feel helpless. They believe it is easier to withdraw (physically and psychologically) from a conflict than to face it.

The Shark (Forcing). Sharks try to overpower opponents by forcing them to accept their solution to the conflict. Their goals are highly important to them, and relationships are of minor importance. They seek to achieve their goals at all costs. They are not concerned with the needs of others. They do not care if others like or accept them. Sharks assume that conflicts are settled by one person winning and one person losing. They want to be the winner. Winning gives sharks a sense of pride and achievement. Losing gives them a sense of weakness, inadequacy, and failure. They try to win by attacking, overpowering, overwhelming, and intimidating others.

The Teddy Bear (Smoothing). To teddy bears the relationship is of great importance while their own goals are of little importance. Teddy bears want to be accepted and liked by others. They think that conflict should be avoided in favor of harmony and that people cannot discuss conflicts without damaging relationships. They are afraid that if the conflict continues, someone will get hurt, and that would ruin the relationship. They give up their goals to preserve the rela-

201

tionship. Teddy bears say, "I'll give up my goals and let you have what you want, in order for you to like me." Teddy bears try to smooth over the conflict out of fear of harming the relationship.

The Fox (Compromising). Foxes are moderately concerned with their own goals and their relationships with others. Foxes seek a compromise; they give up part of their goals and persuade the other person in a conflict to give up part of his goals. They seek a conflict solution in which both sides gain something — the middle ground between two extreme positions. They are willing to sacrifice part of their goals and relationships in order to find agreement for the common good.

The Owl (Confronting). Owls highly value their own goals and relationships. They view conflicts as problems to be solved and seek a solution that achieves both their own goals and the goals of the other person. Owls see conflicts as a means of improving relationships by reducing tension between two persons. They try to begin a discussion that identifies the conflict as a problem. By seeking solutions that satisfy both themselves and the other person, owls maintain the relationship. Owls are not satisfied until a solution is found that achieves their own goals and the other person's goals. And they are not satisfied until the tensions and negative feelings have been fully resolved.

(Johnson and Johnson, 307–309)

Conflict in small groups can be buried in group process and task achievement — it may be squelched by a leader or dominant member. It may go underground, but it will not disappear without being dealt with. Members may drop out based on other excuses. Tasks will never be fulfilled with the blame often placed on circumstances. Groups will never quite gel and the reason given will be "the members just didn't hit it off." In all probability, conflict has arisen but never surfaced, or been faced and worked through.

WHEN AND HOW CONFLICT SHOULD BE CONFRONTED

When differences of opinion arise or two conflicting perspectives are evident in a group, be aware that for most persons the esteem postures that are involved in these differences are as important as the issues themselves. What creates emotion in conflict are the personal interpretations and esteem connections to the conflicting facts that differ. Identify and reflect tentatively the emotion being expressed by the person in conflict before dealing with the factual issue. "This seems to have triggered anger in you: is that true?" "You're feeling some anxiety at this point?" By stating the emotion expressed, the other person feels heard and can move on to facts. Unless an individual senses that feelings are "heard" those feelings will continue to be expressed no matter what facts are presented. This same principle is operant when a child cries over a nonexistent scratch. The parent who argues that there is "nothing there" will continue to receive wailing. A wise parent responds, "You hurt your finger. Let me kiss it." And the "heard" child returns to play. Hear feelings when expressed, before dealing with facts.

When opposing views arise, give opportunity to present facts about both sides of the issue without interruption. Keep focused on the issue and be alert to others' resistance to crucial information presented.

Cultivate dialogue that checks perceptions for accuracy. Use phrases such as, "What do you hear _____ saying?" "Is this an accurate statement of what you are saying?" Conflict often occurs because persons are operating out of distorted perceptions of what another wants. By temporarily leaving one's own comfort zone (position) and accurately restating another's position, a person feels heard and usually becomes more cooperative.

Look for and identify areas where both conflicting parties agree. In a conflict we tend to magnify our differences. Wherever possible, express items of agreement or blending.

Focus on what each wants and options available rather than on positions. Positions polarize. Needs and wants have many creative ways of being satisfied, some of which are probably mutually acceptable (S. Miller, et al., 291–294).

Where the issues, values, and perspectives are incompatible and resolvable only by choosing one over the other, focus on the

203

reasons for the choice while esteeming the persons who differ. "It's been helpful to look at different aspects of this issue. Carol's comments have deepened our awareness of the implications of our choice and given us as a group opportunity to choose, while realizing the cost." Never identify a position with a person (Jack's idea versus Carol's proposal). A good leader always ends with a sense of "ourness" with the deviant view having been fairly treated.

INTERPERSONAL CONFLICTS IN THE GROUP

What about interpersonal problems that cause conflict and hinder goal achievement in the group? Decisions must be made as to where these are best handled—in the group or with individuals. If the problem is a personal habit pattern (such as negativism), it may best be handled individually. However, if an interpersonal conflict erupts in an incident between persons within the group, it is best worked out within the group. This assures that those who were exposed to and impacted by the interpersonal conflict can also be part of its solution. Such resolution as an agenda item not only deals with the disrupting emotional stress, but also models how to deal with conflict in a positive way. When an incident of conflict disrupts a group session, it is best dealt with before the group disbands. "Let's talk about what just happened and how we are feeling." When an individual's behavior is chronic and appears to be wearing away at group morale or creating an ongoing underground conflict among persons in the group, it can be brought up as an issue needing to be resolved before the group can go on. This can be delicate and such confrontation requires prayer and careful guidelines.

CONFRONTING DISRUPTIVE BEHAVIOR WITHIN THE GROUP

Here are eight hints for confronting disruptive behavior within your group.

1. Make certain that you want to confront. Check your perceptions and concerns with several others to see if they are valid. Discretion here is vital—both in whom you select and in how you approach the situation so your inquiry does not become judgmental. "What is your perspective on. . . ?"

2. Determine goals you would like to see accomplished by this action. What do you desire for the person? For the group? For the experience of dealing with conflict? For you? What resolution would be satisfying to all? It is important to voice shared goals at the beginning of group confrontation so all can identify the focus and can express ownership in their positive direction. "We as a group have agreed that we want to create a community where we are accepted and loved for who we are and where we are challenged to become all that God intends us to be. Those challenges are risky and mean changes for each of us who participates in community. If we are to grow toward that goal, we at times will have to pass through risk and perhaps pain to reach safety and health. That challenging step lies before us right now."

3. Think through specific behaviors observed as having a disruptive effect. Specifics are much better than general statements here. Descriptive stuff is important. Judgmental statements must be avoided. "When you said this to Joan, she . . ." rather than "You were critical of Joan." The person cannot do anything about past actions, so stick to the present tense for solution. What is the condition of the group now? What needs to happen now?

4. Personalize the confrontation by limiting statements to what you observe or feel. Take ownership of your judgments, weaknesses, and wants. Do not use the bandwagon technique that marshals and speaks for others. "I feel irritated when I hear you, and I see _____ happening in our group," rather than "the group feels you create anger and dissension by your statements and then we ignore you."

5. Invite others to express their views so you get a balanced and honest perspective. This is not to turn the group against an individual but to allow persons to take ownership of their feelings and actions. It also permits expression from those who see the one confronted differently

than you do. The "offender" who has caused conflict needs to hear true responses. Caring for the person means being truthful in a loving way. For this to happen the group must be convinced that it is OK to talk about conflicts, problems, and feelings. The leader usually establishes this as a norm by modeling and verbally accrediting such actions. In a group where this kind of honesty and acceptance have become a norm, the group feels comfortable in discussing how it sees itself. A nonthreatening discussion can be opened with, "Let's see how we are doing. What are you thinking and feeling about what is going on in our group at this point? What seems good and what needs to be examined and dealt with so we can maintain our close relationship?"

> ⚡ Look over the following statements. Which are personalized (P) and which are directed toward others (O)?
> a. ___ I feel that you don't care when you continually show up late.
> b. ___ You make me so angry when you interrupt.
> c. ___ Your behavior seems inconsiderate to me. I don't like it.
> d. ___ Your reasoning is ridiculous — nobody said you were stupid.
> e. ___ It's uncomfortable to me when you cut me off.
> f. ___ You must learn to listen more carefully.
> (a, c, e = P; b, d, f = O)

6. Carefully listen to others' points of view. Most persons' behavior is not unreasonable to them. Listen for logic, for feelings, for implications, and perceptions. Ask questions. Check out statements for accuracy by rephrasing them. Reflect feelings back to the person, regardless of whether or not you agree with those feelings. Protect the boundaries of all involved.

7. Prepare for and utilize supportive measures. Esteem persons and relationships through statements of goals and ways of responding. Express an attitude of hope and confidence in positive outcomes. See the conflict as mutually owned. Hear and accept a person's views as real to them. Share what you want for the other person and the group

as well as your desires for yourself. Take responsibility for your feelings and behaviors and allow others to do the same (adapted from Wilson and Hanna, 256–257).

8. Bring closure to the confrontation with specific steps of action taken or to be taken. Affirm participants in steps taken. Check to be certain each person has said all that he/she wants to say and affirm that nothing more will be said about this incident outside of group time. List positives occurring in the group and ask members to participate in expressing gratitude for specifics in prayer or praise to God.

AWARENESS WHEEL

Miller, McNully, Wackman, and Miller have developed a tool called the Awareness Wheel that is useful in helping persons and groups get in touch with roots of conflict. Their Awareness Wheel is made up of the following segments: Sensations, Thoughts, Feelings, Wants, and Actions. When a person senses anger, uneasiness, or general anxiety over another's behavior or comments, checking out the awareness wheel can reveal the place where the conflict arises and thus open possibilities for working it through. Let's examine each of the segments and the questions they pose.

SENSORY DATA

Each of us is constantly monitoring what goes on around us. We observe facts through seeing, hearing, smelling, tasting, touching, and intuiting. In a brief and wonderful way, the mind integrates all of these together to provide us with sensory data. Amazingly, we are often not consciously aware of many of these messages. Thus in an instant we hear loud words, see flashing eyes and furrowed brow, and sense pressure from another. Our memories flash sensations from the past and our hunches feed us information. Contexts and the actions of others provide us with raw material for answering, "Who/what did I hear/see? Where? When?"

Intuitors, sensitive to group atmosphere, often "sense" stress within a group of persons. No one may have mentioned conflict, but the nonverbals suggest tension and disagreement. Nonverbals are probably more accurate in their projection of what is really taking place than are verbal statements about attitudes and conditions. Look for the following nonverbals that betray stress or tension.

1. The lower lip is extremely hard to control with conscious effort. It can tell you when a person is reacting with tension, is relaxed, and reveal other emotional states.
2. Skin color changes also express what is going on internally. Watch especially the face for flushing or paleness.
3. The corners of the eyes and the muscles around the mouth betray the amount of stress a person feels.
4. Listen and watch for rapid or deep breathing which reveals the emotional state of an individual.
5. Rapid and loud speech also indicate emotional involvement and pressure.

(S. Miller, et al., 81–86)

Thoughts

Thinking interprets the above collected facts to make meaning out of them. These thoughts come in many forms: expectations, assumptions, judgments, beliefs, reasons, conclusions, impressions, and principles. Thoughts incorporate memories from the past, interpretations in the present, and possibilities of the future. Such thoughts become filters by which we perceive and interpret what is happening. For example, if a person believes that conflict is wrong, she will judge strong difference between persons as undermining their relationship and will shape her actions to eliminate that conflict. If her expectation is that good relationships don't experience conflict, she may feel that its presence is a sign of deteriorating intimacy when in actuality it may be the opposite. That is one reason why it is important to view interpretations and the perspectives we hold as working hypotheses.

Since most conflicts stem from interpretation, it is extremely helpful to ask, "Is there any other interpretation possible from this data?" Reinterpretation or alternate possibilities may eliminate the cause of conflict. Also we tend to select an interpretation that reinforces what we already believe. Another question to ask in sensing a conflictual possibility is, "How do my preconceived beliefs and expectations affect my interpretation of this event?" If I believe that the group doesn't accept me, an objective question such as, "Why do you think that?" becomes an expression of judgmental disdain, questioning my credibility. This interpretation may cause me to become defensive and stressed. Under stress, thoughts solidify to become even more set, which then results in my imagining, ignoring or denying the actual sensory data being given. In a conflict situation check your thinking dimension with "What do I think is going on?" (S. Miller, et al., 87, 90)

Feelings

Our emotions are often the first indicators that conflict is going on. When what we experience does not measure up to our beliefs and expectations, our feelings spontaneously erupt. You have a great idea and share it with the group whom you expect will treat it and you as brilliant. The group, however, is slow to accept your insight and even subjects it and you to numerous penetrating interrogations. Hurt and anger accompany a feeling of rejection and disappointment and these quickly move into insecurity and sensitivity. To cover those vulnerabilities you manifest forcefulness and stubbornness. The issue has moved from your idea to your standing in the group and your value as a person. An important question to ask when you experience such stressful signs is "What am I feeling?" This will then probably lead to "What am I thinking?" which grows out of "What am I picking up that leads me to that interpretation?" Becoming aware of what you are feeling is a primary step in changing behavior and managing conflict. Until feelings are dealt with, a person is likely to continue irrational and detrimental actions to self and others. All of us have preprogrammed physical reactions that serve as gauges to what we are feeling. Clenched teeth, tiredness, knotted stomachs, tight shoulders, and shallow breathing are only a few flags that should get our attention. Because our emotions tend to "lock in" our thinking, a dramatic shift in our actions from the expected to the unexpected opposite can break the emotional "lock" and allow you to think in new dimensions. This can change how you feel. For example, when angry—help—don't resist (S. Miller, et al., 91–96).

Wants

Each of us has desires and intentions that drive us to do what we do. Conflicts can grow out of competition with or a thwarting of reaching these priorities. Your objective was to lead the group to accomplish a certain level of trust-building in the group session. By the end of the session, you felt angry at them and ready to turn in your leader's badge because they seemed so uncooperative and self-centered. Their actions and joking around left you uptight and in conflict over minor issues.

Becoming aware of your wants—not just for yourself but for them as a group—may be the source of strong feelings of conflict that seem the opposite of what you felt going into the group session. Clarifying what you want can be a first step in managing conflict that exists between you and them.

Close to this is finding out what *they* want. Are *your* wants unrealistic when laid alongside *theirs?* Do they contradict each other? What intentions lie buried beneath those expressed? Are those the driving force behind the intensity of the conflict? For example, you want to come across as a leader who has a good group. And the group doesn't seem to care about your reputation. Or you want your group to prove that meeting once a month is not hurting your community building. However, the group has no interest in disproving this trend and wants a group that fits their schedule more than anything else.

Stating intentions and examining motives can clarify conflicting feelings and unify competing actions. Motives that are very clear to us may not be clear to another. "What do you want?" is extremely valuable to know if conflict is to be managed effectively.

Think of an area of frustration to you right now, a "hot spot." What is your *want* in this area? For others? For yourself? Is this motive clear to others involved? Is it desirable to them? Is it translated or interpreted differently by them? Is your true motive masked by a pseudo-intention? Is their priority intention different from yours?

Wants may be in competition for limited resources or they may be collaborative, realizing that one helps promote the other. Realizing that some motives are "unworthy" or unrealistic ones can cause us to take the pressure off ourselves and others and reduce conflict (S. Miller, et al., 97, 102).

Actions

Behavior incorporates what we have done, what we are presently doing, and what we will do in the future—plans and promises that we intend.

Patterns of behavior are interesting insights into how we think and feel. Is there any action that you use in a conflict situation that causes reaction, either negatively or positively in others? What are your reactions—verbal and nonverbal in a conflict situation? Some people are not aware that they tense up whenever the possibility of conflict arises. They do not realize how relaxation would put others into a more accepting frame of mind. Their rigidity brings out irritation in others. Or they are oblivious to the fact that under stress they lower their gaze and voice so that persons see them as victims and react against them. "What have I done? What am I doing? What will I do?" are questions that help put us in touch with our actions and the part they play in managing conflict (S. Miller, et al., 103–105).

How would your best friend describe your patterns of action in a conflict situation? What things do you do that help manage conflict and work it out? What would be listed as increasing the tension?

Not only do individuals have awareness wheels, but groups also need to become aware of the norms they convey in these areas. For instance, being late may convey a different interpretation in one group from the meaning expressed in another. Group cultures seek to cause everyone to subscribe to their norms and conflict arises where a deviant questions or resists "the way we always do it in our group." Changes in groups often occur when members get in touch with their own awarenesses and reevaluate validity and desirability of that aspect.

CONFLICT: PROBLEM? PHASE? OR WHAT?

Most approaches to conflict treat it as either a problem or a phase. Those who view it as a problem seek to do everything possible to promote cooperation, to bring resolution to the conflict that arises, and if possible, to design the group so as to minimize and preempt conflict of any kind.

Those who see it as a phase that groups must go through (similar to the terrible twos or adolescence which offer a helpful differentiation) treat it as a necessary and helpful—in its resolution—passage. It is labeled as Power and Control stage, Storming, or just plain CONFLICT. This is a time of rebellion against the leader and reaction against others who differ.

Another perspective sees conflict as always present in groups, never avoided, resolved, and passed. Because groups are composed of persons who are fluid, constantly changing in emotional reactions and conditions, conflict inevitably recurs. Responses are paradoxical, causing opposite feelings in the same individual. The group itself will often divide into subgroups that read the same situation differently. The presence of conflict itself brings excitement to some and dread to others as they realize the movement that is taking place. Contradictions throw the group into subgroups and polarizations.

Our paradoxical emotions and actions betray the ever-present contradictions found in groups. Community can create double binds. In joining and staying in a group to work through loneliness, the group experience itself may actually cause greater loneliness when we retreat into ourselves to resist being absorbed. Just being with others evokes a fear of their power as a group. We may be attracted to a group to gain a sense of personal competence or adequacy. Yet the collective pressure of peers in a group may limit options and cause the individual to feel less competent. A person may find his/her need for power fulfilled by a role in the group while at the same time being dependent upon the group (and thus powerless) to not fulfill that role because of being "locked into it" by the group. Such contradictory reactions are typical of being in community with others.

Each of us comes to a situation with preconditioned emotional and behavioral expectations, and the dynamics of being with others who are different from us in their group identification reaffirms those expectations or cuts across them in conflict. At times, we will divide as to whether individuals exist for the group or the group for the individuals in it. As we make judgments we set up a paradox: the very judgments we make judge us and cause us to want to "take away their power" by playing the role of the deviant and changing the rules that now rule us. Group life accentuates these tensions by providing more alternatives, greater differences, and more opportunities to divide (Smith and Berg, 38–42).

Such inner and group ambivalences become a constant frustration to the person who wants group life to be all harmony and peace. Holding the perspective that conflict is a normal part of being alive frees one to accept the coexistence of opposing emotions and reactions.

> When groups stop "holding" the opposites and move instead toward extruding or subjugating one "side" of a conflictful issue, they often get "stuck," because the balance in the group so necessary for member involvement and participation is threatened. It is indeed a paradox that while the existence of conflict and opposition threatens a group's life, the *absence* of these same forces is also a serious threat. Emotionally, a group that does not provide room for the conflicting and ambivalent reactions evoked by group life is not a place where either the individuals or the group as a whole can thrive.
>
> (Smith and Berg, 82–83)

By looking at the conflict through a paradoxical lens we learn to live with it productively.

Think of a conflict situation you've experienced in a small group setting. What were the opposing sides? What was your emotional reaction to the conflict? How did this help/hinder your response? How was the group affected? If you could replay the experience, what would you change?

CONFLICT AND GENDER

Conflict managing has some interesting observable phenomena along gender lines. Although more of this will be dealt with in Chapter 13 on gender variables in small groups, in general, conflict is viewed stereotypically as more in line with masculine than feminine traits in our society. When asked to note adjectives or words to describe the meaning of conflict, students chose terms such as *hostile, aggression, turmoil, opposition, tension,* and *problem.* To deal with the above, students noted these characteristics as being required: *aggression, assertiveness, strength, power, understanding, intellect*—most of which they perceived as masculine characteristics (Borisoff, 96–97).

While conflict itself is often locked into stereotyped images,

213

assumptions about men's and women's behavior that is viewed as limiting their ability to engage in productive conflict management likewise reflects stereotypical images. But as suggested under the Awareness Wheel, these assumptions condition our expectations and evaluations.

Gender Assumptions	
Women	Men
Women are compliant and tentative in their assertions.	Men make generalizations and sweeping claims.
Women's speech lacks power and is hyperpolite.	Men's speech is forceful, often offensive.
Women's voices belie weakness and emotion.	Men are inexpressive.
Women are unable to assert their concerns – they are often silenced.	Men dominate conversations and interrupt others.
Women listen too much.	Men do not listen enough.
Women's smiling behavior often masks their true feelings.	Men are unable to express their true feelings and emotions.
Women can better read the nonverbal behavior of others because they are less powerful than men.	
	(Borisoff, 98)

While some studies dispute the validity of many of the above statements, these assumptions and others like them often determine the way we think about the way men and women communicate in a group setting.

Deborah Tannen sees conflict as a complicated blending of self-display and a means of becoming involved with others. In general, "To most women, conflict is a threat to connection, to be avoided at all costs. Disputes are preferably settled without direct confrontation. But to many men, conflict is the necessary means by which status is negotiated, so it is to be accepted and may even be sought, embraced, and enjoyed" (Tannen, 150).

An interesting self-study is to ask yourself how you feel about direct confrontation. What belief or feeling prompts that evaluation? In what ways do you fit in with your gender response as described above? In what ways do you differ? Picture a men's group and a women's group handling the same conflict issue — perhaps one of opening the group to new members. How would each typically handle the problem issue?

APATHY

The opposite of conflict may not be harmony but apathy. Conflict speaks of vested interest, the will to be involved, and stand up for concerns. Apathy represents indifference, lack of enthusiasm, refusal to invest self, and satisfaction with less than adequate results. In many respects it is easier to deal with a group in conflict than an apathetic group. A common assumption is that a leader can overcome apathy by being inspirational. "An outgrowth of this belief is the prescription of pep talks which, unfortunately, have only momentary effects, if any, and become less and less effective the more often they are used" (Bradford, 67). Dealing with apathy requires identifying and treating the cause rather than the symptoms.

Apathy—withholding interest and involvement—may be due to one or more of the following causes.

1. Persons feel powerless to influence. Authoritarian leaders who make all the decisions and hold all the control can create apathetic groups who simply "follow the leader" in meaningless motion. Group sessions become ritualistic without involvement or investment.

2. The purpose of the group—why they are together does not seem to be important to persons in the group. Being assigned to a group where they have little choice in the goals, direction, and outcome undermines commitment. The existence of the group seems meaningless because the goals and activities are not related to the existing needs of the members. Overcommitment to a printed

curriculum that exists to promote denominational goals but is unrelated to present member needs can result in a spirit of apathy "when it's time to do our study."

3. Fear of results also leads to apathetic response. When a person is asked to do something that he/she knows could be detrimental, that person will avoid becoming involved. A group that has experienced a crisis such as divisional conflict or betrayal after complying with instructions where these crises have never been dealt with and worked through becomes a group that fears to be real. It is easier to go through the motions with no intention of reaching conclusion or congruency. No one wants to be open to ridicule, attack, or judgment.

4. Likewise a group where hostility exists between members but is treated as though it doesn't, is a candidate for apathy. Where a power struggle exists between one part of a group and another, or between a portion of the group and the leader, persons may withdraw their participation and support to undermine the opposition.

(Bradford, 67–68)

Such causes produce unhealthy, diseased groups with no loyalty, usually little accomplished, and rigor mortis setting in. Some may be salvageable if the cause is faced and structures changed. Often "new blood" is needed to give a sense of hope and energy to change behavior. Changed attitudes and probably confession of sinful responses that have set in will be necessary.

Apathy-prone groups need a new vision of their calling to community and of the Creator of community. The church in Laodicea, charged with being neither "cold nor hot" in their response was threatened with being "spit out of My mouth" because of their apathy. They were called to take it seriously, repent, and renew relationship with the one who stood at the door knocking (Rev. 3:14-20).

Conflict in itself is not evil. Our response to it can be functional or dysfunctional and for the Christian, an opportunity to grow in understanding and practicing the will of God. While some

216

observable strategies are out of the question for one who has made a commitment to Jesus as Lord, no *one* strategy is good and all the others bad.

Scripture suggests and describes various means of living with conflict that leads to the growth of persons and the building of relationships. Going through conflict, while being committed to one another and to living out the principles of our faith can be a tremendous enabler of community. In conflict we also can refine and expand our understanding of life together as God intended.

Growth will inevitably be linked with conflict, producing it, and growing out of it. Because now we only see through a glass darkly, conflict is an inevitable part of intimate relationships. Because of the complex nature of us as persons and of the multifaceted aspects of conflict, principles for exploring and processing conflictual issues are extremely difficult to put into practice, especially in an emotion-charged situation. Thus we must continually express our need of assistance from one another and from the One Called Alongside to Help us in our inadequacies as we live life in community.

> Lasting relationships are not negotiated. . . . They are forged. That means heat and pressure. It is commitment to a relationship which sustains it . . . not pleasant feelings. Treat a relationship as negotiable — it is easily lost. Consider it nonnegotiable — a way is found to make it work.
>
> Richard C. Halverson
> *Somehow Inside of Eternity,* 63

Our conflicts call us to experience forgiveness and to live dependent upon Jesus who calls us to Himself and together.

Leonardo Boff writes:

In a certain sense it is unrealistic to struggle for a "classless society" — a society that would be simply and totally a community of brothers and sisters, without any conflict at all. Realistically one can only struggle for a type of sociability in which love will be less difficult, and where power and participation will have better distribution. Community must be understood as a spirit to be created, as an inspiration to bend one's constant efforts to overcome barriers between persons and to generate a relationship of solidarity and reciprocity.

(Boff, 5)

To live above with saints we love,
O, that will be glory.
But to live below with the saints we know,
Now that's a different story!

12

TURNING POINTS: PASSAGES AND CYCLES OF GROWTH

A life cycle must be lived to be genuine, and to
understand the behavior of any phase of life
we must look at the special story of the
flesh-and-blood people traveling through it.
William Strauss and Neil Howe, Generations, 47

Organizing is part of being human. Seeing similarities, labeling, and cataloging gives us a feeling of mastery and being in control. Time is one of the most difficult resources over which to gain control. We divide it into years, months, days, hours, minutes, and seconds, and that's the best we can do. In history, we divide time into the Medieval Period, the Industrial Revolution, the Age of Technology, and so forth. In like manner, we seek to section off life into infancy, toddler, early, middle, and late childhood, adolescence, and adulthood.

Researchers and writers have further defined these life span years by mental age: sensory motor, pre-operational, concrete operational, conceptual, and so on. Gail Sheehy wrote a book called *Passages* describing adult years, suggesting that all adults pass through predetermined stages of development, facing similar life issues. While somewhat controversial, the manuscript brought reassurance to many people who wondered if they were alone in the things they were experiencing. It also provided security in knowing what was ahead and helped to reduce anxiety over the unknown.

Change within a group is also the subject of observation and patterning. Do groups move through predictable developmental stages? Do they face similar challenges during corresponding stages? Is development random and spontaneous? Does behavior differ in each developmental era? Do groups have common characteristics when in the same phase of group life?

Despite highly varied approaches, findings, and explanations, current research suggests three models that illustrate group development: the linear-progressive model, the life-cycle model, and the pendular or recurring-cycle model.

LINEAR-PROGRESSIVE MODEL
This descriptive approach looks for patterns to develop in a given order. The group progresses through one stage to another in the direction of completion of the task and functioning group relationships. The linear movement suggests steps in a given order with resolution of one phase of problems prerequisite to the solving of the next stage of dilemmas. This straight line approach in growth describes behavioral and attitudinal symptoms that will occur in each group who passes into each stage. Such responses are unavoidable.

Tuckman (1965) notes the following stages of group development: (1) *Forming,* the period of dependence and beginning; (2) *Storming,* the stage of conflict and testing, of vying and struggle; (3) *Norming,* a stage where the group establishes boundaries and comes together; (4) *Performing,* a stage of functioning and relating as the group task is accomplished. Others noting the same characteristics label them: Orientation, Conflict, Emergence, and Reinforcement (Fisher). Peck utilizes the provocative progression of Pseudocommunity through Chaos and Emptiness to Community.

The linear-progressive element is revealed in the movement from hesitant exploration through struggle to cohesion and on to accomplishment of the goal. Of course there are not well defined boundaries where one session the group is in one stage and in the next session moves to another stage. The movement is subtle and may not be decisive, but it is there as the community evolves in its understanding and development. A preliminary predisposition that will especially impact the first stage of group life is that of precontracting. Without the group even present, leaders get together and consciously or unconsciously begin to formulate what the group should be about. Decisions made here will affect much of what the group will go through in its subsequent formation. Climate, procedures, structures, direction, and leadership style may all be impacted by the results of this interaction.

A closer look at these subphases reveals important information that conditions response and explains behavior.

Orientation-Exploration Stage

The first meeting is conditioned by guardedness. Most participants come with ambivalent feelings—high expectations and nagging fears. There is a tension between the desire for empathy and closeness and the necessity of distance for protection and survival. Persons come with expectations, individual histories, previous group experience, and questions. Napier and Gershenfeld liken participants to children on the first day of school who tend to:

> keep our feelings to ourselves until we know the situation: look more secure in our surroundings than we might feel . . . lack a feeling of potency or sense of control over our environment; act superficially and reveal only what is appropriate; scan the environment for clues of what is proper: clothes, tone of voice, vocabulary, who speaks to whom; be nice, certainly not hostile; try to place other participants in pigeonholes so that we can feel comfortable with them.
> (Napier and Gershenfeld,
> *Groups: Theory and Experience,* 471)

Because fear is the dominant emotion—whether recognized or not—the group will seek to build security in the following ways.

Create structures and rules which give a fragile sense of stability. Groups often appoint timekeepers or enablers who gingerly exercise their rights of "control" and "decision" so there is some sense of order.

Engage in safe chatter as though it was of extreme interest and importance in your life. Or utilize delaying tactics such

as quibbling over details, semantics, being legalistic, or overly elaborate in the making of plans. All this helps delay
entrance into unknown and feared territory.

Become overly polite and formal to keep people at a distance and to avoid all disagreement. Peck sees this as an
attempt to ignore or minimize individual differences. He
describes this well manneredness as being automatic, even
unconscious.

In pseudocommunity it is as if every individual member is
operating according to the same book of etiquette. The
rules of this book are: Don't do or say anything that might
offend someone else; if someone does or says something
that offends, annoys, or irritates you, act as if nothing has
happened and pretend you are not bothered in the least;
and if some form of disagreement should show signs of
appearing, change the subject as quickly and smoothly as
possible — rules that any good hostess knows. . . . The members pretend — act as if — they all have the same belief in
Jesus Christ, the same understanding of the Russians, even
the same life history. One of the characteristics of
pseudocommunity is that people tend to speak in general-
ities. "Divorce is a miserable experience," they will say. Or
"One has to trust one's instincts." Or "We need to accept
that our parents did the best they could." Or "Once you've
found God, then you don't need to be afraid anymore. . . ."

Another characteristic of pseudocommunity is that the
members will let one another get away with such blanket
statements. Individuals will think to themselves, I found
God twenty years ago and I'm still scared, but why let the
group know that?

(Peck, 88–89)

At times fear in these early stages drives groups to focus on
being fanatical about the task. They avoid confrontation and
depth by making lists, and ritualistically going through routine
tasks (reading minutes, checking addresses). At the same time

they clearly avoid defining the problem on which they are working (Bradford, 108–110).

Persons want to avoid conflict and will use any available means to keep from allowing it to erupt. At the same time, they paradoxically want to be able to trust others and to know that others find them likable and trustworthy. To do this they need to give a little of themselves away. Too much intimacy too soon frightens persons at this stage. Thus the leader who forces intimacy on participants (physical hugs or psychologically revealing sharing) may find they won't be back. But if they don't eventually move in the direction of closeness, neither will they feel satisfied.

Dependency upon the leader is central in this stage. The leader builds security, is in control, knows what is going on, and has the power to value or destroy. Giving members opportunity to make choices and to participate in other ways increases their sense of inclusion and at-homeness. Lots of safe sharing—information particularly about past experience—creates awareness and opportunity for bonding. At this stage group members look for anything that suggests, "We are alike. You think like I do, so I must be OK."

Power and Control Subphase
When members move in the direction of "being real," differences come out. Some resent the authority they have given to the leader and begin to vie for recognition and power with the leader by rebelling and presenting countersuggestions. Others reveal antagonisms and evaluations of group members and a pecking order develops.

From trying to blend into a pseudocommunity there is often a reciprocal attempt to preserve one's own distinctiveness and to react by being an individual. This is displayed by arguing, jockeying, and withdrawing from others. During this time some may seek to overwhelm others with their Bible knowledge or their experience and reputation. Persons are working through "Who am I in this group?" and "How are we going to work together?" If these issues do not get worked through, it is unlikely the group will ever come to cohesion. Questioning, critiquing, and open expression of feeling is legitimized. There may be more anger revealed as well as more laughter. In the linear-progressive mod-

223

el this is the one time that conflict is seen as helpful to the group process. The tentativeness of the early stage is gone. Members state positions with more definiteness and rigidity. Polarization is evident. It is a lively time with lots of energy displayed, but it is also a draining experience as members struggle over whose norm will prevail.

The leader—so needed in the earlier stage—is no less needed now, but often becomes the object of attack. The leader is blamed for what is going on and is often ignored as persons in the group seek to "rescue" it by proposing leadership remedies such as organization. "Let's divide into groups of four and accomplish something." or "We're going nowhere—let's set up task forces to study the problems and report. We want to get this done." Each spokesperson feels he/she is the savior of the group and has the solution to the struggle in some form of organization. The leader must be very secure during this phase, realizing that in moving toward, not running from, the issues, there will come balance. Encouraging self-disclosure, valuing differences, identifying similarities, and demonstrating "bendability," are behaviors that provide strong, stable leadership during this experience of extremes and realism.

Trust Phase—Emergence
This stage is ushered in with a developing feeling of "we-ness," a reopening of communication, a growing acceptance of deviations, and a recognition that personal aims are not being met as a result of competitive actions to gain power and to force others to conform. The group moves into accepting one another as having strengths and weaknesses and into seeing itself as an integrated unit that can be open and harmonious. The leader is recognized as a facilitator and becomes more a member of the group during this period. Persons in the group, as they contribute strengths, are recognized as contributing to the building up of the group. It is a relief to enjoy the group relationships and any disruption of the harmony is feared. Therefore, group members discuss and work through problems with new flexibility and understanding (Napier and Gershenfeld, *Groups: Theory and Experience*, 473–474). Peck describes the action that propels a group into this phase of growth as an Emptying—of one's expectations, preju-

dices, need to control or to provide solution — barriers to communication (Peck, 94–99).

The Productive Stage
In the linear-progressive plan this is the be-all and end-all of the group. It represents being able to get along with others, enjoying them, and functioning well as a unit housing differences. It includes carrying out the task and goals that are a part of the group and feeling good about the group and about self and self's contribution. In a Bible study we no longer have to prove how spiritual we are or who knows the most. We are comfortable with these people and we help each other achieve.

More About the Linear-Progressive Model
A three-phase development is noted by Kaplan and Roman (1963) who describe groups progressing from dependency to power issues and resolution, and finally to intimacy issues and resolution. Bennis and Shepard capsulize development into two stages, each of which is divided into subphases. Reflecting on the dependency described above, the first stage is the authority phase with the second being the interpersonal phase, dealing with the problem of interdependence. They see groups passing through submission, rebellion, and compromise; wrestling with intermember identification ("enchantment") and on to individual identity — climaxed by the resolution of these two.

LIFE-CYCLE MODEL
The Life-Cycle model arose to reflect a more complete view by adding a terminal stage that compares to the "decline and death" aspect of life. This is the phase when the group must cope with its own death — reflecting on the success or failure of time together and preparing for the act of separation from one another. Still progressive in nature, the Life-Cycle model moves the group from the inadequate dependency of childhood, through the imbalances of adolescence, into the productivity of adulthood and then deals with the reflective assessment and decline of old age (Gibbard, et al., 83–86).

Hestenes adds another stage before termination that is comparable to the role change and reassessment of mid-life. Called

"Differentiation," this period reflects the realignment that takes place in groups that stay together with the same people for a long time but want to change and grow within the relationship. The person who has been the "responsible one" may wish to assume less responsibility; the "clown" may want to be taken seriously. Differentiation may also occur in the group's goal and process. They may move from being a Bible study to becoming more involved in social action or from always having potluck sessions to eliminating them. Such radical movement can allow the same persons to remain together but add an element of risk and growth for persons who like each other but whose needs are changing. If the group is open to this change taking place, Differentiation becomes a period of readjustment and newness (Hestenes and Gorman).

Subphase Termination
The major emphasis added to the Life-Cycle to cause the group pattern to parallel life is this concluding summation stage. It incorporates relational reaffirmation with a bringing of closure to group relations as they have been, reflection, and review of the group to evaluate accomplishment and growth. Sometimes groups move into this stage without being aware of what is happening. The group becomes static and boring. It has lost its purpose. Persons in the group like each other so much that they cannot be honest anymore. Such honesty would threaten the relationship so they don't push or challenge each other. They settle down to maintenance. Somewhere in this process the group dies, but nobody acknowledges what has happened. Other groups realize that ending a group is part of group life. They focus on celebrating what has been accomplished and the relationships they have enjoyed. They rejoice over needs that have been met and no longer drive them to be a part of this group. They ask such questions as, "Was all this worth it?" "What have we gained by being together?" "How am I different?" "How are you different?" "What is God calling us to at this point?"

Groups usually encounter ambivalent feelings at this parting—sadness in leaving what was known and excitement over moving on with a sense of accomplishment. *Never force this stage on a group.* They must come here on their own. Questions can stimulate action. "Do you want to renegotiate? To develop a new purpose? To end the group?" Assurance of the naturalness of this closing is important here since some persons feel guilty and unfaithful in leaving a group. It may be translated as "failure" or disloyalty to the leader. In actuality, concluding is as vital as beginning and fulfills commitments made in contracting to end by a certain time or when the goals have been reached. Concluding allows for new beginnings. Talking about a group's future is necessary to allow persons to voice what God is calling them to — whether it be renewed commitment to this group, renegotiated purpose for continued growth or closure in group existence. Better to give participants a choice in determining the group's life cycle than to slowly watch them drop out one by one while the remaining ones live with resentment or envy.

Stages of relational disintegration as they appear in personal friendships suggest similar counterparts in a group where commitments are changing. A decision must be made to renew or to conclude with positive review.

Stages of Relational Disintegration

1. *Differentiating.* A focus on self, rather than on the other person and the relationship causes persons to put emphasis on differences. Instead of finding joy in shared experiences, greater importance is placed on enhancement of the individual and the differences seen in each other.
2. *Circumscribing.* Communication becomes limited to certain "safe subjects." Players begin playing with a new set of rules, often refusing to even talk about something. Personal rights determine what is acceptable and unacceptable. This limits conversation and interactions with frequent topic changes to avoid the personal issues.
3. *Stagnating.* Such limited conversations evolve into silence. Farthest from reality is talk about the relationship. Avoidance of confrontation, pain, and facing what is happening is a central motivation.
4. *Avoiding.* Persons in this stage remove themselves from being with the other in relationship. If present, they may

act as if the other were not there. They withhold any positive affirmation — an act which tends to lower the other's self-esteem.

5. *Terminating.* Distance and disassociation break off talking and the relationship. Persons are usually left with lowered esteem, hurt feelings and an abrupt sense of closure with much unfinished business but no opportunity to work it through.

(R. Weaver, 404–407)

Awareness of these progressively deteriorating steps can help persons in groups honestly face what is happening and deal with it in a more constructive way than simply letting it happen.

Johnson and Johnson have developed the following exercise to help members finalize unfinished business, reflect on group experiences and on what members have received from the group, and express in a positive way their feelings about this termination. "The theme of the exercise is that although every group ends, the things you as a member have given and received, the ways in which you have grown, the skills you have learned, all continue with you. . . ."

1. Discuss the topic, "Is there anything that needs to be resolved, discussed, dealt with, or expressed before the group ends?"

2. Discuss these questions: "What have been the most significant experiences of the group? What have I gotten out of being a member of the group? How has being a part of this group facilitated my growth as a person? What skills have I learned from being in this group?"

3. Discuss how you feel about the group winding up its activities and what feelings you want to express about the termination. The following alternatives may generate a productive discussion:

   a. Each of you in turn says good-bye to the group and leaves. Each of you then spends five minutes thinking about your feelings and returns to express anything you wanted to but did not express before.

  b. Each of you nonverbally shows how you felt when you first joined the group and then shows nonverbally how you feel now.

4. As a closing exercise, stand up in a close circle. You are all to imagine that you have the magical power to give anything you wish to another group member. You are then to give the person on your right a parting gift, each taking your turn so that everyone in the group can hear what the gifts are.

(Johnson and Johnson, 486–487)

Other groups may want to write psalms of praise listing benefits gained from God having been in the midst of and working through members. Another helpful and affirming action is to share changes seen in members and self as a result of having been together in community and then close by thanking God for having done this within a person.

In whichever manner you choose, *celebrate* the final chapter in your group experience.

An excellent overall summary of the various passages a group experiences follows.

Stages:	Exploration	Transition	Action	Termination
Group Members' Thoughts	Do I belong? What is expected of me? What can I expect of others?	Can I trust this group? Whose group is this? Is this group going to work?	Let's do something. I'm willing to risk and give to others.	Was it worth it? What did I learn about myself? God? Others?
Group Members' Feelings	Anticipation Anxiety Excitement	Low enthusiasm Beginning tensions Anxiety Impatience	Acceptance Determination Warmth Freedom	Warmth Respect Appreciation Sadness
Group	Giving infor-	Attending	Sharing posi-	Expressing

Members' Actions	mation; accepting others initially.	sporadically; expressing irritation; giving biographical information.	tive feelings; distributing leadership; taking risks; giving feedback.	love and respect; showing appreciation to individuals.
Leader's Actions & Attitudes	Empathy Warmth Concreteness Caring Effective communication	Empathy Encouragement Confrontation Self-disclosure Flexibility	Challenging Supporting Giving feedback Risking Keeping goals clear	Reflecting Reinforcing Reviewing Being thankful
Leader's Planned Activities	Self-descriptive sharing Socials One-to-one times	Trust-building exercises Self-disclosure Covenanting Prayer partners	Risk taking Outreach Gift identification Feedback	Review Celebration Gift giving

Reprinted from *Small Group Leaders' Handbook* by Ron Nicholas, et al. © 1982 by InterVarsity Christian Fellowship of the USA. Used by permission of InterVarsity Press, P.O. Box 1400, Downers Grove, Illinois 60515.

PENDULAR OR RECURRING-CYCLE MODEL

A third model bears the label Pendular or Recurring-Cycle Model. In a sense, Hestenes' Differentiation stage starts the process of group formation all over again. This is the accent of this third model: it describes recurring cycles or issues that must be dealt with or suggests oscillation between issues. One of these cycles that continues to recur is that of dependency, fight/flight, and pairing as alternatives to work. These situations are always present, never resolved completely, presenting themselves in new guises and dilemmas (Bion, as described in Gibbard, et al., 86). Schultz (1958) in his FIRO schema presented earlier, offers three interpersonal areas that continually require attention: inclusion, control, and affection. Both of the above illustrations contain sequence but differ from the previous two models in that they view the concerns as constantly reappearing, challenging the group to accommodate to them. It becomes difficult to see progression in this state of recurring patterns (Gibbard, et al., 86–

88). Thus it is difficult, if not impossible, to combine these models into one.

THE DYNAMICS OF MOVEMENT

While many have attempted to describe and pin labels on the behavior of groups that occurs during different time periods of their existence, few have wrestled with what causes movement *within* a group. Which factors seem to release a group to lurch toward an unexplored state? What causes them to become "unstuck"?

Smith and Berg suggest the answer may lie in the way groups respond when confronted with coexisting opposites. The paradoxes of group life present contradictory extremes in many arenas. There are opposing factors in preserving one's identity as an individual and developing one's identity with the group; in remaining independent, free, and isolated; or in developing interdependence, being obligated, and knowing intimacy. We vacillate between self-disclosing vulnerability and self-protecting withholding. Between wanting authority and not wanting it. Between being distant and uninvolved and being intensely involved.

As groups confront innumerable paradoxes, they embrace or risk extremes and in so doing create movement. However, as persons we normally fear intensity, and value living somewhere in the middle. Groups become "stuck" by refusing to immerse themselves in extremes. They invent coping mechanisms that enable them to live in the tension, or they seek to change the paradoxical conditions so they are nonexistent and the tension is released. Seeing threat to the group's progress or even existence in the opposing reactions aroused by the group, members call upon all their skills to keep the boat from rocking and thus capsizing. How do they seek to rid the group of these painful paradoxical feelings?

1. Groups look for compromise—a middle ground—where the frustration of contradictions disappears. Such action sets up a "stuckness" as group energy is used up trying to maintain a balance of emotions by incorporating elements from both perspectives. The resultant mix may keep peace for a time but it also prevents the group from

moving ahead because no one dares venture into territory that is "off limits" for fear of upsetting the balance created by reconciling the offsetting forces. The group is imprisoned in a cage of its own making. And keeping fragile existence in the middle ground uses up group resources. The group enjoys a harmonious state on one front, but new frustrations arise.

2. Groups can call for a show of force between contrary positions and seek to eliminate one of the troubling forces. The proverbial "calling for the vote" is an attempt to get rid of the tension created by opposite reactions. Working with a "quorum" even though some members cannot be present is a way of getting on with life — eliminating the troublesome problem of conflicting schedules. Citing authorities who favor one over the other eliminates the opposition. But such domination often has the opposite effect of causing the "defeated ideas and emotional expressions" to become appealing so as to keep from "going off balance." In subjugating one side, the winner grants power to the loser and groups remain in stand-off stuckness.

3. Some groups attempt to "overlook" or "put aside" opposing views in order to get on with the decision. However, the polarization defining each group is not that easily set aside. The group who wants intimacy continues "doing their thing," while the group that stresses autonomy makes decisions proudly affirming their right to individuality.

(Smith and Berg, 207–214)

Speaking of attempts to eliminate paradoxes, Smith and Berg summarize:

Such efforts produce stuckness because they seek to change the inherent character of collective life, a character that reasserts itself because the group's survival depends on its ability to serve as a forum for the expression of the opposing reactions evoked by group membership. . . . If groups experience their realities as paradoxical and groups evoke contradictory reactions expressed through individuals and subgroups, then attempts to eliminate the paradox, to separate or split the elements and to divorce the two opposing forces from their common source, will create a reaction to assert the link and to pull the paradox back into the group so that both sides can be expressed. For groups trying to separate the elements of the paradoxical tension or eliminate them altogether, stuckness is an indication of the survival instincts of the group.

(Smith and Berg, 214–215)

Stuckness results from trying to eliminate tensions within groups. Movement, on the other hand, grows out of living within the paradox. In moving toward the paradox, not away from it, by immersing oneself in both of the contradictory forces, it is possible to gain insight into what links them together and thus be released to explore new territory. Movement means exploration of new paradigms — new framing for ideas and concepts being discussed.

Even as beginning groups reflect hyper-politeness to "play it safe," there is a pull toward risk and "telling it like it is." By immersing itself in both of these, by daring to explore the highly feared territory of each, there is a regathering of emotions denied and thoughts that had to be subjected to making a good impression only. As groups reclaim this holistic view of contradictory emotions and reactions, formerly discarded as tension producing, they set themselves up for movement. In the case of the beginning group, members may be propelled into the more honest but realistic stage of individualism. Whereas formerly all pretended as if differences didn't exist, now each reveals blatantly his/her difference. "Viva la difference" feels good until members seek to obliterate all difference in favor of theirs. In seeking to "cure" others of their differences we find a dissatisfaction and frustration that results in stuckness until both diversity and uniformity are embraced. By accepting the contradictory nature of our emotions and reactions rather than trying to eliminate the paradox we open ourselves to movement. In facing the fear and opposite reaction we open ourselves to the possibility of moving into unexplored territory previously forbidden. When emotions of fear or anxiety arise, these are signals that the concern that provoked them is to be explored, not avoided. Only in engaging will the group move through them (Smith and Berg, 216–224).

Thus, movement in groups occurs when we face and live in the opposites that arise in group experience. This willingness to explore what we react to or fear in our interpersonal relationships is key to that movement. Such is experienced in a conflict situation which everyone fears facing because they fear that the group will be torn apart. For a period of time they act as if the conflict is not there or they try subtle ways to remedy the situation, giving careful attention to both sides to prevent eruption. Finally, worn down by the energy it takes to keep the contradictions in line, the group faces the conflict openly, recognizing the realities in both sides. It is only then that they can move beyond the conflict. Up to that point it has remained a tyrant that controls the group through the anxiety it generates. By retrieving emotions and thoughts that have been denied or split off, new energy is gained. This is reminiscent of nuclear fusion. "If enough energy can be marshaled to hold opposing forces together, in spite of the forces acting to drive them apart, a tremendous amount of energy can be released and a new 'element' created" (Smith and Berg, 225).

Maturing in life comes from embracing paradoxical reactions instead of retreating to one polarity or living within the boundaries of compromise. As Christians, we live in the paradox of humanity and our new spiritual natures. We have new life in Christ Jesus with our hearts set on what is above, yet are never free from our bodies with the humanity they bring. Dallas Willard has dared to look at both of these as a paradox to live in and as a result has moved beyond the dichotomy paradigm. He embraces the concept that God never devalues the body. Though the body has limitations, it is also the temple of God (Willard).

Movement between the extremes in this paradoxical world is cyclical. For example, the group oscillates between the extremes of disclosure and concealment until another has disclosed. "If they knew me, would they really like me?" is a question that limits our disclosure. At the same time we struggle with, "How can they really like me unless they know me?" When members face the emotions and important responses involved in both conflicting issues the group is propelled toward trust. While realizing the fearfulness of being known, they also recognize the anxiety that goes with not being known. The result is the building of trust. One needs to trust others but can one trust unless trust exists? The dark side of trust is being taken advantage of, and we wait for some demonstration of trust before we trust.

Someone must expose the weak, anxious, ugly side of trust so it can be implemented. When faced, this contradictory circumstance moves us to intimacy with its paradoxical nature. In the course of constructing this deeper relationship, further self-disclosure is required. Since this new disclosure is on a deeper level which requires more trust, the previous contradictions return in new guises. And they will return again as new conflicts arise. This flowing back and forth between extremes continually provokes other paradoxical states which prompt movement within the group. It is like a flowing amoeba constantly changing as resistance is encountered, necessitating new boundaries which may move it in an opposite direction until it readjusts to move ahead. This process will occur many times before the termination of the group as paradoxes resurface resulting in stuckness or movement. Issues such as authority and intimacy will reappear many times with each resolution introducing new contradictions to be dealt with. Preoccupation with authority relationships leads to preoccupation with personal relationships which introduces new complications in authority relationships (Smith and Berg, 225).

ROLE OF THE LEADER
What is the role of the leader in this development? It appears that no leader can force a group to go from one phase to the next. The leader can only be instrumental in helping members to focus on—becoming immersed in—the exploration of paradoxical tensions that arise, looking for how they are related. The leader provides stable caring for members as a climate for their exploration and growth as an ongoing process.

Finally, Peck suggests a stance for both leader and group member if community is ever to be born. He describes it as leading from the chaos phase with its individualism and flight to the community stage that carefully handles vulnerability and values differences. He calls this act *emptying* and labels it as the "key to the transition from 'rugged' to 'soft' individualism" (Peck, 95). The barriers to communication that we must "give up" include:

1. Our expectations and preconceptions. Being terrified of the unknown we enter groups with false expectations and seek to shape the group experience to conform to those expectations. This prevents our really listening and seeing persons and our relationships for what they are and is destructive to community.

2. Our prejudices. These are the judgments we make about persons locking them into preconceived molds—quick conclusions we draw or pigeonholing persons without knowing them.

3. Feeling we have the only right ideology, theology, and solutions while discounting any perspective that is different.

4. Our need to heal, convert, fix, or solve. Our actions in this direction are usually motivated out of a need to make ourselves feel better. "I feel uncomfortable when you are in pain or when you call my convictions into question so I must change you," is our mind-set. Our solutions often stand in the way of coming to know and appreciate the uniqueness of one another.

5. Our need to control. To be out of control is scary. It could lead to failure. It leads to manipulation and hidden agendas and forcing upon persons my way so I can feel at ease. Control says I am taking more responsibility for this group than I should. If it fails, I fail.

(Peck, 94–99)

The sooner we achieve this "emptying" the more exciting will be our development in the group and the group's development. As we see persons released to be who God wants them to be at this stage of relationship, as we recognize freedom to explore unknowns in the company of our brothers and sisters who also are desirous of experiencing more in this field of interpersonal relationships, the group develops. As we embrace the challenges that "life together" brings, we find movement, not just motion, in our lives. The group becomes a womb of maturing—a laboratory for experience and insight. We never leave the challenge to grow more in this community climate, to increase our understanding and commitment to one another, to develop in our ability to work together for a common goal.

PART IV
SPECIAL CONCERNS
OF COMMUNITY

13

WHAT'S THE DIFFERENCE? WOMEN AND MEN IN GROUPS

Our sexuality penetrates to the deepest metaphysical ground
of our personality. As a result, the physical differences
between the man and the woman are a parable of the psychical
and spiritual differences of a more ultimate nature.
Emil Brunner

R esearcher and author Carol Gilligan asserts that women and men do speak *In a Different Voice.* Gilligan suggests that while completeness for men is focused primarily on achieving and separating themselves as individuals, a woman finds her identity primarily in interpersonal attachments and in creating interdependence in a relational network. Thus, while a man tends to define himself in terms of his professional achievements, a woman usually defines who she is in the context of her relationships (Gilligan, 159–60). This, of course, does not infer that women do not rejoice over achievements nor that men do not enter into relationships. But the central focus for femininity is connecting and relating, and for masculinity, individual achievement.

Both of these factors—task achievement and relationship building—are at the core of small groups. Many questions arise. Is there a difference in how men and women approach and behave in groups? What differences are found in men's groups and women's groups? How are mixed groups affected by the presence of both genders?

There is major debate today over whether gender roles primar-

241

ily result from nature (biologically inherited differences between males and females) or are conditioned by nurture (environmentally learned behaviors fostered by culture as to what it means to be male or female). Both of these sources probably contribute to the formation of these roles. The roles themselves are well known in their stereotypes, some of which are probably true while others are inaccurate assessments.

When a person enters a group and sees all men or that it is made up of entirely women or that both genders are represented, automatic assumptions and expectations begin to operate with the individual probably being largely unconscious of these. Previous experience, values that the individual has learned, popular categorizations come into play just as mothers-in-law provoke stereotypical mother-in-law jokes which may be totally inappropriate for the present mothers-in-law. Jokes about men and women that focus on accentuating negative factors are a part of folklore. Everyone knows what is meant by a "woman driver" even though statistics show that women drive more carefully than men and have fewer accidents.

What is your awareness of some of these stereotypical assumptions about men and women in groups? Complete the following sentences.

In a small group:

men _____ women _____
men act _____ women act _____
men speak _____ women speak _____
men tend to _____ women tend to _____
men avoid _____ women avoid _____
men enjoy _____ women enjoy _____
men are expected to _____ women are expected to ____
men _____ more than women _____
women _____ more than men _____

One thing I would like the opposite gender to know about what it's like to be a man (woman) in a group is _____ .

Groups consisting of the same gender usually _____ .
Mixed gender groups usually _____ .

Look over your answers to the above. Which do you think are actually true? Place an asterisk (*) by them. What is your overall reaction to the picture of gender in groups that you have described? Can you recall specific incidents that have conditioned your response to any of the above?

While there are wide variations within a gender, researchers have found enough similarities in various factors to assert that in this important area of interacting, in general men align in certain characteristics with others in their gender in a way that is different from women. One author writing on power argues that "sex role turns out to be one of the most important determinants of human behavior" (McClelland).

Our preconceived notions about gender actions condition our behavior and succeeding evaluations. These perceptions lend predictability and enable us to function successfully in our culture. However, they also lead us to incorrectly prioritize one gender's behavior over the other's as being more right, effective, and acceptable. In general, those different from us or from the accepted norm are seen as deviations and less valuable. Such assessments, which are unjustified, limit growth and lock persons into labeled behavior. The theory of cognitive consistency holds that once boundaries are assigned we look for happenings and interactions that will give confirmation to these beliefs. If we believe that women should be noncompetitive, supportive, and politely agreeable we will be frustrated with a woman who is contrary to the above and will probably write her off. Our attitudes that grow out of beliefs condition our responses and can effectively block the alteration of beliefs. We avoid the disequilibration of inconsistency.

> "Do you not think that the reason why women talk so much is that men hardly ever listen to them? It is a vicious circle: The more silent the man is, the more the woman talks, and the more she talks, the more silent he remains."
>
> Paul Tournier
> *The Gift of Feeling*, 99

Our identity also becomes tied in with gender roles—we must behave as dictated by appropriateness for our gender. Thus a man's identity may prevent him from being responsive and tender in a painful situation. "Be a man" exhorts him to toughness and moving on as though untouched by the dynamics of a relationship. A double-bind situation for women is set up when showing emotion is seen as "acting just like a woman," but also viewed negatively in being unstable and weak as a leader. As much as we may hate stereotypes, they often become the influencing factors in our identity building—either to not become "one of those women" or to capitulate with "that's what they expect" (Borisoff and Victor, 99–101). Differences between men and women in group interaction may often fall along the lines of psychological gender roles rather than biological gender roles. Women who learn the usually male-attributed skills of instrumental problem solving and males who cultivate the female-attributed socioemotional skills create an androgynous focus within the small group.

MIXED GROUPS VERSUS GENDER-LIKENESS GROUPS
Targeting specific audiences is becoming more and more evident in advertising. In a metropolitan community ethnically targeted billboards display ads that appeal to certain groups. Why do advertising companies develop different ads for the same product when aiming for an audience largely male or female? How have you observed this is done?

Look above at your expectations for how men's and women's groups differ. In general, women prefer an all female group if the group is small but prefer a mixed group if the number is large. This is probably due to their perception that conversation in a small group is personal and thus should be shared only with those of their sex. Men, however, showed preference for including women in small and large groups. Men in an all-male group take longer to become a cohesive group (Marshall and Heslin, 952–961). Competition tends to be greater in an all male group while women appear to be more willing to share resources and to be cooperative even with opponents. The presence of women in a group seems to increase relational awareness among men and thus creates a favorable group climate. Research documents that men in a mixed group become more personally oriented, speak about themselves more frequently and address individuals (as opposed to the group) more often than they do in a same-sex group. However, women gave evidence of being less dominant, initiating less, and sharing in leadership less than in all female groups. In general persons in same-sex groups seem to focus more on task while those in mixed groups appear to show more concern for interpersonal relations than the task, with less conformity found in same-sex groups (Blumberg, Hare, Kent, and Davies, 93).

COMMUNICATION AND GENDER
Contrary to popular thinking, women do not talk more. Studies show that men talk equally as much if not more in mixed-sex situations and interrupt women far more than women interrupt them (Doyle and Paludi, 226). Women, on the other hand, ask more questions than do men in mixed-sex conversations.

Focus of Conversation: The Motivators
Women appear to talk for different reasons than do men. Primarily they communicate for understanding or empathy whereas men communicate for information and problem-solving (Adler and Towne, 185–186). Women's so-called "chatter" is not so much a bid for information as a sense of connectedness and an assessment of the relationship. Men often see these conversations as wastes of time because the information communicated seems so trivial and unimportant. But the metamessage of well-being in the relationship is all-important to the women communicating. Such differences in communicating often lead to frustration between the sexes as each assesses the other's style in his/her own terms. For example, Tannen cites male complaints about women's refusal to take action in solving the problems they complain about. When women bring up problems,

> "For most women, the language of conversation is primarily a language of rapport: a way of establishing connections and negotiating relationships. Emphasis is placed on displaying similarities and matching experiences. . . .
> For most men, talk is primarily a means to preserve independence and negotiate and maintain status in a hierarchical social order. This is done by exhibiting knowledge and skill, and by holding center stage through verbal performance . . ."
> Deborah Tannen
> *You Just Don't Understand,* 77

males usually focus on solving the problems—the message level of talk.

For women, the metamessage is far more important—a bid for reinforcement of rapport and understanding—not solutions. This sense of mutuality is found in words like, "I understand how you feel" or "I feel the same way," not in "Here's what you need to do." Hence, a woman who doesn't receive satisfaction in seeking this rapport talk, will probably bring up the issue over and over while the man incredulously shakes his head over why the problem hasn't been solved. Men want to solve problems and get them over with. Women want a sense of someone sharing an understanding of how they feel in the situation even more than they want resolution (Tannen, *You Just Don't Understand*, 52–53).

This does not infer that women do not want solutions or that men do not seek understanding but primarily the feminine side focuses on connectedness in conversation whereas the male side focuses on accomplishment and resolution, using verbal skills to give a report on what he knows. Of course, it is possible for some women to seek solutions.

Consider the marriage of a man who has had most of his conversations with other men, to a woman who has had most of hers with other women. . . . He is used to fast-paced conversations that typically stay on the surface with respect to emotions, that often enable him to get practical tips or offer them to others and that are usually pragmatic or fun. She is used to conversations that, while practical and fun too, are also a major source of emotional support, self-understanding and the understanding of others. Becoming intimate with a man, the woman may finally start expressing her concerns to him as she might to a close friend. But she may find, to her dismay, that his responses are all wrong. Instead of making her feel better, he makes her feel worse. The problem is that he tends to be direct and practical, whereas what she wants more than anything else is an empathetic listener. Used to years of such responses from close friends, a woman is likely to be surprised and angered by her husband's immediate "Here's what ya do. . . ."

(Adler & Towne, 184)

In the world of relationships intimacy is key whereas in the world of achievement and ambition, autonomy is key. Tournier, the Swiss psychotherapist, states it thusly, "Women . . . do not aspire so much to autonomy as to a successful, stable, profound relationship; not to dependence, as is sometimes said, but to a relationship in which they will find true freedom" (Tournier, 130). They therefore tune in to "the negotiation of connections: Is the other person trying to get closer or pull away?" Meanwhile men are checking out conversations through a different filter: Is the other person winning by gaining a dominant position and trying to get me to do his bidding? (Tannen, *You Just Don't Understand,* 38) With both the elements of power and relationship always present in small groups, the same conversation may be interpreted differently according to which element is focused upon. Perhaps this difference in viewpoint is foundational to the masculine desire to resist asking for help or directions and to "find it on his own," whereas women evaluate such independence as foolishness and see nothing wrong in requesting assistance and collaboration. The information—the message—is not the issue. The metamessage of what such action signifies (control or connection) is the significant motivator (Tannen, *You Just Don't Understand,* 62–63).

In mixed groups, task fulfillment and decision-making may be affected by such motivations and cause frustration and resentment in the group whose motivations differ.

What rewards one sex in communication may not be satisfactory to the other. In the arena of decision-making men take pride in their ability to focus on a task and bring it to completion while women show more concern for being open-minded (Pearson, Turner, and Todd-Mancillas, 70).

GROUP ROLES

Men tend to introduce more topics in a mixed-sex group. Stated another way, the topics men bring up are more likely to be explored. Topics brought up by women are viewed as tentative. Women, however, work harder to maintain conversation once it is directed (Borisoff, 107; Adler, 186). This masculine initiating style is labeled proactive behavior as opposed to the responding or reactive behavior of women in groups (Pearson, et al., 220).

How do these differences fit in with motivations, metamessages, and focused issues as mentioned earlier? What effects could these differences have in a group discussion on personal needs? On task accomplishment? In the arena of conflict? In what areas do you observe women initiating? Men being more reactive? As mentioned earlier persons who have adopted the psychological gender role of the opposite sex (a woman who works in a competitive male-oriented position) may display characteristics more common to that gender.

COMMUNICATION SKILLS

Self-Disclosure

As already stated, the presence of women in mixed-sex groups appears to foster more personal and expressive disclosure in men, and women appear to prefer other women as constituents of a small group because of the personalness assigned to their conversations when the group is small. In fact, both men and women have been found to self-disclose more to women than to men (Pearson, et al., 169). One author observes, "the presence of a female has a powerful effect on the social behavior of another; it makes him or her more self-disclosing, more open, and less lonely" (Winstead, 93). Generally speaking, men seem to reveal cognitive information—facts, while women appear to be more inclined to share affective information—feelings (Pearson, et al., 165). Also as expected, the disclosure of the masculine gender generally concerns the task before them in their focus on achievement. Of concern is the fact that women tend to share more negative information about themselves, confiding weaknesses and concealing their strengths (Critelli and Neumann, 173–177; Hacker, 401).

Pearson (1981) found that men will disclose more about themselves in a dyad than in a small group made up of three or more. Females were the opposite, sharing more in a small group than in the dyad (Pearson, et al., 168). Another observable nonverbal difference that occurs as men and women self-disclose is that in disclosing, women tend to move closer through eye contact and physical proximity while men as they self-disclose tend to avoid eye contact, move away from each other, or move from facing one another to a side-by-side position (Pearson, et al., 172–173). Witness males talking, staring off into space while fishing side by side or looking straight ahead while walking and talking. Women turn toward the recipient of their self-disclosure and move closer, probably to pick up on the nonverbal signs of how the message is being received. The reasons for women being more oriented toward disclosing and receiving self-disclosure are probably numerous. Four possibilities are: Women are expected to be more open and expressive in our culture whereas men, being competitive, do not disclose for fear of losing advantage and opening themselves to exploitation. Relationships and accompanying openness to others are more important to women than to men. Women, who are seen as lesser-status people fulfill their position of disclosing more to superior status persons than vice versa. Disclosure patterns are perpetuated through generations as females — having greater identification with the usual primary caretaker, the mother — are nurtured into disclosing as males in their differentiation from the mother are not (Pearson, et al., 177–178). A summary chart from Pearson on gender differences in self-disclosing follows.

GENDER DIFFERENCES IN SELF-DISCLOSURE ARE DEPENDENT UPON A VARIETY OF FACTORS

Positive or negative nature	• Both sexes are equally likely to offer negative information. • Men are less likely to disclose positive information than women. • Women offer more negative than positive information.
Cognitive or affective information	• Women offer more affective information than men.
Intimate or nonintimate information	• Women report that they disclose more intimate information than men. • In interactions, men set the pace of intimacies and women match the pace set by men.
Topics under discussion	• Men and women do not differ on the amount they self-disclose on nonintimate topics, such as politics. • Women self-disclose more on intimate topics such as sex and religion.
Gender of the target person	• Females prefer other females to whom to self-disclose. • In mixed-sex dyads, females and males do not self-disclose to a different extent.

GENDER DIFFERENCES—continued

Attractiveness of the target person	• In general, both women and men self-disclose more to an attractive person than to an unattractive person. • Attractiveness may be a more relevant variable for women than for men.
Interaction of attractiveness and the gender of the target person	• Both women and men self-disclose more to attractive individuals of the same sex. • Both women and men provide less negative self-disclosure to attractive persons of the opposite sex.
Attractiveness of the discloser	• Men who perceive themselves as attractive self-disclose more than men who perceive themselves as unattractive • Women who perceive themselves as attractive self-disclose less than women who perceive themselves as unattractive.
Age of the discloser	• In general, women self-disclose more than men of all ages. • For both women and men, self-disclosure increases as they mature and become older.
Nonverbal behaviors	• Increased eye contact encourages self-disclosure in women, but inhibits self-disclosure in men. • As the amount of personal space decreases among interactants, women self-disclose more while men self-disclose less. • For both women and men, increased touch is associated with increased self-disclosure. • Increased movement on the part of a male target of disclosure and decreased movement on the part of a female target of disclosure resulted in increased self-disclosure on the part of clients in a counseling setting.
Influence of sex-related variables	• For men, increasing levels of femininity and decreasing levels of masculinity are associated with an increasing level of self-disclosure. • For women, increasing levels of masculinity coupled with decreasing levels of femininity are associated with increasing levels of self-disclosure; however, the addition of masculinity to stationary levels of femininity is not associated with increased self-disclosure. • Homosexual men and heterosexual women are similar in self-disclosive behavior, while homosexual women and heterosexual men are not.

What's the Difference?

Select several of the above factors and reflect on how group discussions will be affected by this element.

Language
Language is seen by some as a communication strategy. How do men and women utilize language in different ways to accomplish different metamessages in communicating? In general men, being confident and encultured in having authority, are more likely to utilize direct forms of language to gain compliance from others. Studies have shown that as far back as childhood, little boys appear to use direct commands with higher frequency while little girls use the more suggestive "Let's. . . ." A woman expects behavior to be influenced by others and sees herself as requesting cooperation from others, not demanding it. Is this learned behavior conditioned by culture or does it reveal different goals pursued by the different genders? Tannen observes this pattern of command parallels the differences in the social structures the genders grow up with.

> In the hierarchical order that boys and men find or feel themselves in, status is indeed gained by telling others what to do and resisting being told what to do. . . . But girls and women find or feel themselves in a community that is threatened by conflict, so they formulate requests as proposals rather than orders to make it easy for others to express other preferences without provoking a confrontation. It is not that women do not want to get their way, but that they do not want to purchase it at the cost of conflict.
> (Tannen, *You Just Don't Understand,* 154–155)

However, the very condition women seek may be endangered because of their intentions being translated negatively by the opposite style that fears a different threat. Men do not fear conflict as much as control. "Insofar as men perceive that someone is trying to get them to do something without coming right out and saying so, they feel manipulated and threatened by an enemy who is all the more sinister for refusing to come out in the open" (Tannen, *You Just Don't Understand,* 155).

Another difference in language is that women tend to use

more "fillers" in their speech. This includes phrases such as "You know, well, let me see, ah, uhm, oh." Such fillers indicate nervousness or discomfort on behalf of the speaker and perhaps indecision and lack of firm conclusions.

A third characteristic is the addition of "tag questions" after a statement is made. Examples are: don't you think? wasn't she? isn't it? This is a polite form that allows another to express his/her opinion on the subject. While showing consideration, such language usage also conveys indecisiveness and tentativeness that weakens the statement.

Qualifiers further undermine women's statements. A qualifier discounts or weakens a statement. "I may be wrong but I think. . . ." brings an escape from criticism but reveals a lack of conviction and presents an ambivalence that undermines her opinion. Even worse is, "You've had more experience in this than I, but . . ." or "I'm only a homemaker, but. . . ." In a self-effacing way, the statement that follows "but" is discounted by the speaker's first words (Doyle and Paludi, 223–224).

To some, the above language strategies express consideration and a willingness to negotiate. To others they express a recognition that the speaker's contribution is lesser in value or the speaker is less credible and less able to make such a statement. Such discounting causes frustration to women who have been socialized into speaking this way but find the resulting disaffiliation of the receiver causes dissatisfaction and awareness that all is not well in the relationship. Thus attempts to be considerate and compliant in order to keep others feeling good and in relationship ricochet and the female ends up feeling devalued and rejected. On the other hand, the masculine direct, commanding style can also be misinterpreted and cause rebellion or a feeling of subservience and devaluing in the receiver.

Of course the above language usage characteristics are descriptive, not prescriptive, and while utilized with high frequency by women in general, are not limited to the feminine gender and do not reflect inherent diminished value. Some women include more direct styles such as command giving in their behavior while some men incorporate some indirect characteristics of speaking. Although our culture places more value on the direct, assertive power style reflective of masculine language style, this is a learned response and the opposite unobtrusive, collaboration style which Americans view as more feminine is esteemed in other cultures.

Nonverbals

Of much greater variation is the difference in genders when it comes to nonverbal communication, both in sending and receiving. Women are particularly good at reading and communicating through body movements and facial expression. Men, on the other hand, seem better in evaluating and expressing cues in the voice. Women lean toward the visual while men express emotion, strength, and control in the vocal. Hall observes that each gender may "specialize in the modalities that are most relevant to them"—women in the visual that reveals degrees of positivity and negativity of emotions and interpersonal harmony and men in vocal that reveals degrees of dominance and submission (Hall, 140). A woman will often pick up unspoken conflict or pain as she monitors eyes and facial expression while words spoken convey the opposite. Body movements tend to be more congruent with our true emotions than words which can be consciously controlled. One of the most revealing parts of the face is the lower lip which seems to be difficult to control.

Women tend to maintain more sustained eye contact which increases as the conversation increases in personalness. While men may be more assertive verbally, women express assertiveness in approaching others more closely than men do. Male conversationalists are characterized by asymmetrical gaze in conversation and appear to react more negatively to face-to-face intrusions (Grove, 197). They maintain greater space between conversationalists and converse less as the space between them diminishes. Crowded conditions therefore cause men to respond less (Pearson, et al., 172). Women express more affiliative behaviors, smiling and nodding at a latecomer or showing empathy and concern for a participant sharing some significant personal material (Grove, 198). These gender variables are most pronounced when one is participating in a group of one's own sex. In other words, the greatest variation is seen in comparing men's groups with women's groups whereas in mixed-sex groups each gender tends to adapt to the other.

If women feel that they are underestimated, the feminist problem will not be solved simply by giving them rights, political rights, the right to education and a career to be paid as men are paid to be heard and to be read. If a woman is not listened to, she will not fully regain confidence in herself, in her own value as a person.

(Tournier, 98)

Listening

Listening is probably the form of communication that we engage in the most. Research is inconclusive as to whether men and women listen differently. One author argues that "men listen to find out how to solve a specific recognizable problem, while women listen to understand something they did not understand before" (Pearson, et al., 39). Another study emphasizes the goal-orientation of males which enables them to give focused attention to certain elements without being distracted by details (Halley, 79–82).

Males tend to restructure observations in terms of their own goals, whereas, females tend to accept the pattern as it is to determine relationships. The female hears more of a message because she rejects less of it, while the male derives more coherent meaning from the message because he is building a structure of the general message as he listens.

(Pearson, et al., 39)

Listening appears to be a skill that affects the self-esteem of the participant. Women and children seem to need the gaze and nonverbal affirmations of the listener to feel "really heard." Tournier offers some insightful observations in this area. "It seems to me that generally speaking men do not listen to women as seriously as women listen to men. . . . The demand to be taken seriously is a fundamental one for women. . . . Women do not feel that men take them seriously" (Tournier, 96–97). "If a woman is not listened to, she will not fully regain confidence in herself, in her own value as a person." "Do you not think that the reason why women talk so much is that men hardly ever listen to them? It is a vicious circle: the more silent the man is, the more the woman talks, and the more she talks, the more silent he remains" (Tournier, 98–99).

The Swiss psychiatrist suggests that Jesus was a man who took women seriously and listened to them truly and intensely. Drawing upon Francoise Dolto's *L'évangile au risque de la psychanalyse,* he alludes to the dialogue of Jesus and His mother in Cana at the wedding (John 2:1-11) and the comment made regarding Mary who anointed Him with perfume (Luke 7:36-50). In both cases Jesus in listening to the word of these women sees in it a revelation of the will of the Father. Intuitively, they reveal to Him the decisive "hour of public revelation" and the "hour of sacrifice." In summary, Tournier sees Jesus listening to feminine sensitivity and responding to it seriously, "At certain decisive moments Jesus allows Himself to be led along the path that they reveal in front of Him" (Tournier, 96). Listening skills may or may not be gender related. They are, however, esteem building in all group participants. Listening with the whole person, listening for information, for affective feelings as well as accuracy, and attending to the whole person strengthens group communication regardless of gender mix.

Conflict
Attitude toward and behavior in conflict situations reveals variation that falls along gender lines. As you think about the nature of conflict and the nature of women and men as depicted above, how would the typical masculine approach to conflict differ from the feminine? How would you expect behaviors to differ in the midst of conflict?

The feminine focus on maintaining community and strengthening interpersonal relationships usually causes women to view conflict as a threat to such connectedness. It is therefore to be avoided or if unavoidable, resolved before it causes separation. Direct confrontation is to be avoided because it offers the possibility of loss. Attachment is the priority. She looks for similarities—for ways of promoting togetherness and closeness. From the masculine perspective conflict is not fatal, but exhilarating. Discussion and arguments are but contests in which to prove self. They become chances to spar with another which enhances the sense of being different and independent. ". . . To many men, conflict is the necessary means by which status is negotiated, so it is to be accepted and may even be sought, embraced, and enjoyed. . . . Because their imaginations are not captured by ritualized combat, women are inclined to misinterpret and be puzzled by the adversativeness of many men's ways of speaking and miss the ritual nature of friendly aggression" (Tannen, *You Just Don't Understand,* 150).

Women may act as if nothing is different or conflictual in order to maintain a form of togetherness on the surface when in actuality there exists profound difference and competition. Power strategies appear to fall along gender lines. Women tend to report more indirect strategies of a collaborative nature whereas men seem to utilize more directness and unilateral ways of getting what they want. That is, women may undermine the opposition through subtle maneuvering outside the group or through appearing to join the opposition in certain aspects. In many ways they seek to persuade in nonconfrontive ways. Men, in general, seem to feel greater confidence in revealing their desired outcomes and what needs to take place for that to happen. Both genders need to accept the other's perspective if community is to be developed. Forthrightness and sensitivity are both needed. As mentioned in the chapter on conflict, we live with continual ambivalence, a situation that often causes constant vigilance and an uneasiness in one who fears eruption of conflict. The ability to see likeness and to move closer is an asset in healing and bringing balance and harmony.

Leadership
In mixed-sex groups leaders are men more often than women. This appears to be the case even though women appear to be equally as capable as men when it comes to serving as leaders. The major issue seems to be perception: men are perceived to be more successful in leadership. This perception may be due in part to the preponderance of men in authority positions in our society. Masculine attributes that are readily associated with leadership are verbal initiation, dominance, confidence in their ideas, aggressiveness, and independence (Pearson, et al., 222–223).

Instrumental skills that lead to the accomplishing of a task are often valued over socioemotional skills that create relational harmony in a group. Women are more frequently associated with the expressive acts that build relationships than with accomplishing direction and developing plans. For women small group leaders the major hurdle may be the negative attitude that perceives them to be less desirable as leaders. As our culture changes, small group studies may reveal reversals in this perspective. Already some studies are showing males utilizing the more socially oriented styles (Winter and Green, 41–56). *Harvard Business Review's* "Ways Women Lead" identifies women's general style of leadership as "interactive leadership" and explains, "women encourage participation, share power and information, enhance other people's self-worth, and get others excited about their work" (Rosener, 120). Women seem to naturally share resources and demonstrate more cooperative behaviors than men (Pearson, et al., 219).

In many cases, the leadership of women may be more subtle because women tend to talk less in the presence of men while men show an increase in their expressive remarks when in a mixed sex group with women (Blumberg, Hare, Kent, and Davies, 425). It may be that a woman's effectiveness in leadership is affected more by personal attributes such as initiation and confidence than by her gender. However, the influence of sex-role stereotypes on leadership perception is still strong in some circles and this may limit women in serving in leadership capacities. Women are often seen as having less competency in problem solving or decision-making. However, some evidence indicates that women appear to be better in learning instrumental skills to bring about such problem solving and the making of decisions than men are at developing socioemotional skills (Pearson, et al., 222).

A balanced approach to small-group work appears advantageous. Whether the traits are gender linked or not, both instrumental and socioemotional skills are needed in a group. Task achievement and good group relations are interdependent. Consulting others and seeking agreement has advantages in building community, but not being afraid of conflict is also a strength in groups. Tannen notes, "Many women could learn from men to accept some conflict and difference without seeing it as a threat to intimacy, and many men could learn from women to accept interdependence without seeing it as a threat to their freedom" (Tannen, *You Just Don't Understand,* 294). Community is made up of persons. Tournier observes that the "foundation of the person — the 'image of God' who is Himself the person par excellence, and the harmony and fullness implicit in the notion of the person — is the indissoluble complementarity of man and woman." Both are given the command to "Be fruitful, and increase in number; fill the earth. . . ." But also the command, "and subdue it" (Gen. 1:28). He concludes, "Man and woman are to build the world together — not a masculine history filled only with the vicissitudes of an endless race for power, not a masculine civilization which asserts the priority of things over persons" (Tournier, 131). So with the world of community — men and women are to build it together, contributing as his or her part what each has to offer.

14

SERVANT POWER

Give us a king to lead us (1 Samuel 8:5).

*Nowhere is the radical nature of the Christian perspective
more evident than in the conceptualization of leadership.
It is a subject often spoken of in Scripture.
Leadership is also a topic of major interest in
today's world. In the early nineteenth century essayist
Thomas Carlyle projected that leaders possessed certain
innate qualities that others did not have.
H. Lloyd Goodall, Jr., 124*

Theories of leadership have tantalized researchers from
the 1920s on. Early studies picked up on Carlyle's observation and taught us that "Leaders are born, not
made," and we were accordingly told that leaders were taller
(Caldwell and Wellman, 1926), larger and healthier (Bellingrath,
1930), neater (Partridge, 1934), more intelligent and self-confi-
dent (Gibb, 1947), better adjusted (Holtzman, 1952), more out-
going and dominant (Goodenough, 1930), and more empathetic
(Chowdry and Newcomb, 1952). But this trait theory produced
such diversity and fragmentation that it lost its credibility. "All
we know about leadership traits . . . is that some leaders differ
from some followers on some traits, sometimes" (Baird and
Weinberg, 208).

Kurt Lewin's studies in the late 1930s revealed the qualitative
differences between autocratic, democratic, and laissez-faire
(leaderless) styles of leadership. Ten years later Stogdill postulat-
ed the "situational" approach to leadership. This theory suggests
that characteristics of the nature of the task and the situation
define which style of leadership will be most profitable. Function
theory focused on the things a leader does which can be learned,

Tubbs cites a study done by Wilson that verified our cultural view that higher status is sometimes accorded those who are taller. Mr. England was introduced by the following different titles in five different college classes.

Class 1 — a student from Cambridge

Class 2 — a demonstrator in psychology from Cambridge

Class 3 — a lecturer in psychology from Cambridge

Class 4 — Dr. England, senior lecturer from Cambridge

Class 5 — Professor England from Cambridge

When required to estimate the speaker's height, students' average estimates rose from class 1 to class 5. As speaker England's title became more prestigious, so did students' estimate of his height.

"In a study conducted by a Madison Avenue employment agency with branches in 43 American cities, it was found that overweight persons may be losing as much as $1,000 a year for every pound of fat."

Stewart L. Tubbs
A Systems Approach to Small Group Interaction, 161–162

and identified the categories of task functions and the maintenance of socio-emotional conditions functions.

Fred Fiedler at the University of Illinois led a team of researchers in developing the "contingency theory" of leadership. Dividing leaders into task-motivated leaders and relationship-motivated leaders, this theory suggests that the contingencies of the situation determine which kind of leader will be most effective in maximizing performance. Others felt that leaders combined varying degrees of task and relationship-motivated styles in themselves and the goal was to sustain high performance in both in order to be a successful leader (Goodall, 126–127). One of the most popular theories involving situational determinants was developed by Hersey and Blanchard. This theory is depicted in quadrants representing four combinations of task and relationship factors in the situation. The level of maturity of followers is represented by a bell-shaped curve which passes through each quadrant illustrating growth in the followers matched by a change in style of leadership. The leader thus must adjust both task and relationship behaviors to compensate for the maturity level of the followers. For each of the following theories, there are dozens more representing the complexity and the perplexity of what it means to be a leader.

LEADERSHIP STYLES

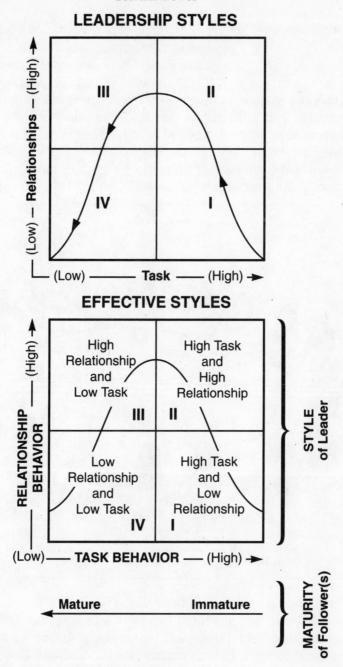

Regardless of how it is defined or explained, whenever the term "leadership" is used in contemporary culture it is closely associated with other words: power, influence, control, authority, initiative, direction. "If . . . a people's language not only describes but shapes the world they live in, then our culture's synonyms for leadership tell us something important about our commonly held understandings and assumptions regarding leadership among us. What they tell us, in essence, is that we take it for granted that leadership is primarily a matter of having effects of a certain kind on others" (Lee and Cowan, 187).

"Now, the round table symbolizes our equality while my fancy chair and golden crown signify that I, perhaps, am just a smack more equal."

But leading necessitates following. There are no leaders without followers. Nor are there followers without someone leading. Both leading and following are "interrelated aspects of the same relational dance." To lead means to affect and also to be affected by those who follow. It involves influencing and being influenced, initiating and responding, being giver and receiver. As wrestlers locked together there is a mutuality about any movement. There is a delicate balance of leading by giving and receiving. A leader is one who has the capacity for receptivity as well as initiation. Leading well means facilitating the capacity of group members to fulfill their function. Leaders lead for the satisfaction of others. Fulfilled followers affirm the effectiveness of leaders. Leadership is never a one dimensional, unilateral process (Lee and Cowan, 187).

Influence is a reciprocal process. In an essay entitled "Two Conceptions of Power" Bernard Loomer identifies "relational power" as "the ability both to produce and to undergo an effect," "to influence others and to be influenced by others" (Loomer, 17). He states, "the conception of relational power, in contrast to power conceived as unilateral, has as one of its premises the notion that the capacity to absorb an influence is as truly a mark of power as is the strength involved in exerting an influence" (Ibid.). Relationships by their very nature are interactive and reciprocal — not necessarily balanced or symmetrical — but both parties receive as well as give.

Relational power portrays the strength of being open to the influence of another. Allowing another to have an effect upon me is as great a sign of personal strength as having an influence upon another. Loomer writes:

> "The empowering leader will attempt to establish power in another person. Empowering leadership will not, however, merely yield to the wishes of another person, nor give up one's own power to someone else. Rather empowering leadership engages in an active, intentional process of enabling the acquisition of power in others. The person who is empowered has gained power — the ability or resources from which to lead — because of the empowering behavior of the leader. . . . Empowering leadership is the process of helping the other to recognize strengths and potential within, as well as encouraging and guiding the development of these qualities."
>
> Jack Balswick and Walter Wright
> *A Complementary Empowering Model of Ministerial Leadership*, 8

Our readiness to take account of the feelings and values of another is a way of including the other within our world of meaning and concern. At its best, receiving is not unresponsive passivity; it is an active openness. Our reception of another indicates that we are or may become large enough to make room for another within ourselves. Our openness to be influenced by another, without losing our identity or sense of self-dependence, is not only an acknowledgement and affirmation of the other as an end rather than a means to an end. It is also a measure of our own strength and size, even and especially when this influence of the other helps to effect a creative transformation of ourselves and our world. The strength of our security may well mean that we do not fear the other, that the other is not an overpowering threat to our own sense of worth.

The world of the individual who can be influenced by another without losing his or her identity or freedom is larger than the world of the individual who fears being influenced. The former can include ranges and depths of complexity and contrast to a degree that is not possible for the latter. The stature of the individual who can let another exist in his or her own creative freedom is larger than the size of the individual who insists that others must conform to his or her own purposes and understandings.

(Loomer, 18)

This conception of leadership in no way suggests that one refuse to exercise influence and initiative. Rather it includes the additional dimension of being responsive to the efforts of others as they also initiate and influence. Jesus recognized the world's pattern as one of domination and supremacy and commanded us to not "lord it over" one another (Mark 10:42-43). In kingdom living He alone is Rabbi. That kind of dominant authority and power is His. Our role is that of one relating to others as *equals*. "But you are not to be called 'Rabbi,' for you have only one Master, and you are all brothers" (Matt. 23:8). With God as Father we all share in this relationship of equality. That common bond with Him calls us into special relationship with one another as equals. And that unique relationship as children of the one Father makes domination of one another illegitimate. In fact He completes this relational prescription with, "The greatest among you will be your servant" (Matt. 23:11).

The disciples were given this picture when they struggled with the temptation to vie for a position of greatness. Mark locates this incident on the way to the Jerusalem cross which makes their concern even more ridiculous. Jesus corrects them:

> You know that those who are regarded as rulers of the Gentiles lord it over them, and their high officials exercise authority over them. Not so with you. Instead whoever wants to become great among you must be your servant, and whoever wants to be first must be slave of all. For even the Son of Man did not come to be served, but to serve (Mark 10:42-45).

Such radical restructuring pictures a leader as one who is so attentive to followers that he or she acts out leadership as a ministering to the needs observed in others. There is no ego building, no feeling of control or superiority—only a desire to fulfill the other in the relationship. There is an interdependence reflective of the Godhead—each magnifying the ministry of the other. Relational power focuses on being open and responsive to doing what another needs to have done. The Apostle Paul repeats this again and again. "Christ loved the church and gave Himself up *for her to make her holy*" (Eph. 5:25-26). "Husbands, love your wives" *feeding and caring for them* (Eph. 5:25, 29). Likewise, wives are to be *receptive* and *responsive* to the fact that husbands need respect. Children serve by also giving attitudes and acts of *respect to parents* and parents reciprocate by *providing* for children *consistent* and *reasonable boundaries* so they do not face exasperation. Slaves likewise offer *respectful responses* to masters and they in turn are to give *respectful service* to their slaves. As equals regardless of age, social status, or gender, we are absorbed in providing what will build up and enable the other to carry out his or her role as a child of our Father. John pictures Jesus again teaching the disciples by moving to His knees so they could have clean feet. He prefaced this event with "Having loved His own . . . He now showed them the full extent of His love" (John 13:1). This act of awareness and care, a prelude to the theme of the cross, reveals a Christ who was influenced by the need of the disciples without losing His identity as the Son of God. John notes, "Jesus knew that the Father had put all things under His power and that He had come from God" (John 13:3). His own behavior was transformed by the presence of those He loved who ate with dirty feet. Dramatically He demonstrates the function of power—it is initiating and responding through simple acts which honor others as equals in the bonds of relationship (Lee and Cowan, 188–192).

> 〰 "Leadership is an art, something to be learned over time, not simply by reading books. Leadership is more tribal than scientific, more a weaving of relationships than an amassing of information. . . ."
>
> Max DePree
> *Leadership Is an Art,* 3

RELATIONAL LEADERSHIP IN SMALL GROUPS

How is this leadership of relational power exhibited in small group community? As seen earlier, four foundational tasks that appear again and again in group life are the issues of inclusion, power, intimacy, and effectiveness. Each of these tasks offers opportunity to express leadership that initiates out of being influenced by another.

Inclusion

Inclusion is an initial need in the formation stages of a group. It asks the question, "Do I belong? Is there a place for me?" Those knowledgeable in group dynamics know the importance of bonding techniques and security-building formats. The motivation of the Christian exercising relational power is the valuing and nurturing of a brother or sister to an "at homeness" with others of like faith. There is a desire to preserve the uniqueness of the individual as one shaped by God. There is a longing to release that individual to experience the creative freedom of feeling at home with others who bear likeness but also are different.

Relational power expresses itself through provision of safety, knowing names, talking about agendas, allowing others to have a hand in shaping what goes on, and developing boundaries of what the group will and will not do. Servant power makes gentle but helpful inquiry that allows new group members to share who they are in a receptive setting. Their story is heard and their contributions affirmed. Authentic self-disclosure is modeled and encouraged. Care is taken to ensure genuine understanding so the one sharing is truly heard. Everyone is included in the conversation, in the decision-making. The group is portrayed as *our* group, not *my* group, and relational power is comfortable allowing the group to develop its own identity. Honesty is encouraged by asking for feelings and by frequent checking-in questions to be sure all are included. Nonjudgmental attitudes are cultivated so that participants can feel, "It's safe here. You can be yourself." The leader protects those who appear timid, those deviant in comparison to the majority, and those working through their own issues. Inclusion is sometimes questioned when in the course of group life a participant seems "out of step" or "slower to respond." Servant leadership is not only aware of these anxiety producing situations, but also takes steps to initiate acceptance and to allow the deviant to be heard. "It's OK to feel differently on this issue. Let's have Tom help us see things from his point of view."

Power

Power deals with occasions of mutual influence. It asks the questions, "What do I have to contribute? How do I influence what goes on in this group? Does anybody listen to me? What does the group have to contribute to me?" Power concerns run throughout the life of the group. Some do not contribute because they doubt they can influence others. Some struggle with the designated leadership or the traditional patterns and feel unheard. In the stage theory of group development, the stage that follows group formation is primarily marked with power conflicts as persons test out boundaries and struggle to find their roles. "Who's in charge here?" is likely to become a target question the group must settle. Power needs are not always negative. They are a part of developing self-esteem. They may also express creative alternatives where a person seeks to influence the group with a new idea. Even when the power surges appear in the form of attack upon the designated leader's power, they become moments to embrace and foster a new structure of power. Whitehead observes:

> The designated leader is usually in a position of some considerable power when the first questioning of leadership

occurs. If the leader uses that power against the group member who questions, the rest of the group learns that new patterns of power will not be easily won. The message is given that the stakes are high in the process of change. If, however, the designated leader does not respond to this question as if it were a personal attack, a different tale is told. The message here is that power in the group need not be interpreted as a personal possession and jealously guarded from attack. Rather it is a resource of the group that needs to—and can—be examined, accounted for, and even redistributed among us.

(Whitehead, 51)

Influencing and being influenced are a part of maturing. Relational power leaders recognize that they do not have all the influencing potential. In fact, the group becomes unhealthy if only the leader influences and initiates. Servant leadership knows its boundaries, its strengths and limitations, and goes about releasing others to fulfill roles as influencers and initiators. Asking for and taking suggestions, allowing others to assume responsibility, and cultivating ownership of the group purpose by all contribute toward a sense of power and influence as well as a willingness to be influenced. Willingness to be influenced creates trust and breeds a like willingness to listen and hear fairly in the other. A key factor in seeing this task through the lens of being equals in relational power is the awareness that all that is needed in leadership does not reside in the designated leader. Persons protective of their unilateral leadership in groups do not know the freedom of allowing another to become what he or she was called to be. Their development becomes a threat. Their giftedness is viewed as competitive. Their presence is seen as a challenge to subdue. The servant leader does not abdicate leadership but seeks to use it to express the strengths of all, not just the one who is designated leader. Relational power leaders are lavish in cultivating and creating new freedoms for persons to become. They serve by doing whatever is necessary to provide a comfortable and challenging growth climate for group members. In this common area of power, Christian small group leaders have opportunity to live a leader lifestyle that is distinctively Christian, responding counter to the cultural view of leadership which says control, resist threats, establish authority. At the heart of their response is the prophetic vision of Jesus when faced with the Gentile cultural pattern, "It shall not be so with you" (Mark 10:43).

Intimacy

Intimacy "involves negotiating an adequate and appropriate degree of personal closeness among members" (Lee and Cowan, 195). Intimacy both breeds and grows out of trust. Intimacy among Christians should have a distinctive flavor growing out of the fact that those who are believers also share relationship with the same God who alone is trustworthy. It is He who uniquely brings closeness and a willingness to experience vulnerability because God has accepted us. Servant leaders enable members to work through fears and challenges to closeness, realizing that it is not up to them to "fix it" should the hopes of one be unrealized in this area of closeness. Knowing God fosters a sensitivity in a servant leader to stand by others who are working through issues of intimacy. Paul called on his loyal Philippian yokefellow to become this kind of enabler for Euodia and Syntyche who struggled with their relationship (Phil. 4:2-3).

Relational power serves in leading members in loving the normally unlovable. It washes the feet of all, offering acceptance even to the "traitor" in the midst. Relational power is not content to accomplish the task at the expense of broken and ignored individuals. The leader's service is influenced by the cries of group members to be loved. Relational power faces issues of conflict, underground prejudice, ostracism, distancing, and pseudocare. Feelings of estrangement do not generate Christlikeness. God authors intimacy. It is because of His servant leadership that we are brought near. This is our service as leaders with relational power. We have been given the ministry of reconciliation (2 Cor. 5:18). We speak of peace with God and new relationships with God's children.

Effectiveness

Effectiveness speaks of accomplishment. It speaks to the question, "Did we reach our goal?" For those of faith this is never the complete task. It always involves being the people of God and living God's way in the process of completing the task. Satisfaction lies not in the completion alone but in the fulfillment of God's will as we acted. Questions to be answered sound like this: "Were we responsive to God's voice? Did we act in a way pleasing to Him? Did our working through this task enable us to know Him in new ways? Did we grow in our grasp of His perspectives? How did we prove the validity of His ways?

Leadership serves by continually promoting integration of theology and life. As people live together in group community they are doing their theology. And doing their theology is a primary way for the people of God to make their faith meaningful. How does the community in which they unite, the processes they experience, and the experiences they undertake fit into their overall understanding of God at work in and through them?

Leaders related to God operate out of that relationship. Jesus came into the world of Judaism and sacrifice because of His love for the Father. He served the Father's purpose. "My food . . . is to do the will of Him who sent Me and to *finish His work*" (John 4:34). "I have brought You glory on earth by *completing the work* You gave Me to do" (John 17:4). "It is *finished*" (John 19:30).

> "Growing almost always requires a confrontation with one's personal dragons. Those who have been most successful talk of forcing themselves outside of their 'comfort zones.' "
>
> Kerry Bunker
> "Leaders and the Dark Chasm of Learning," 6

A servant leader is not just happy that the goal was reached and the task finished. He or she rejoices in having carried out the wishes of God because that is a mark of relationship and that relationship is of utmost importance. Thus fulfilling God's agenda and enabling group members to fulfill their calling as persons in vertical and horizontal relationships is the "food" of a servant leader. Small groups must be led by such relationship-oriented servants. Skills can be taught. Experience also teaches. But greater insight comes from cultivating relationship with the Source and Purpose of all community.

A COMMUNITY OF LEADERS

Not one but many. It would be contrary to all that has been said of community up to this point to suggest that all that is needed for leadership in a community can reside in the one called "leader." God gives ample evidence of operating out of a community focus—we are one body but made up of many parts. The witness as to who He is comes from many, not one alone. He incarnates Himself in the midst of believers *together* while distributing His Spirit to each. Discernment of His will and ways requires the counsel of *many witnesses*. He chose a nation, a kingdom, a people to represent who He is, *not one individual*. We are joined by clouds of witnesses from ages past and by the church on many continents and in numerous forms. Therefore it is presumptuous to believe that God would expect one person to personify all that is needed by members of a community.

We are a community of equals and each is gifted by God. Each is God's gift to the body and each bears responsibility to enrich the body with what God has given. The designated leader may recognize these gifts and acts of leadership, may evoke them, nurture them, celebrate them. The gifts of group members join with the giftedness of the leader in bringing about the community God has designed. To deny another that influence, to stifle the diversity of the body, to prioritize abilities is against the biblical norm. While culture may lead us to believe that one embodies leadership for the many, Scripture depicts one serving by fostering insight and activity in one realm while another provokes and challenges in another arena. And all serve God and the church by participating with what they have. The great ones are those who *serve*.

> "Roving leadership demands a great deal of trust and a clear sense of our interdependence. Leadership is never handled carelessly—we share it, but we don't give it away. We need to be able to count on the other person's special competence. When we think about the people with whom we work, people on whom we depend, we can see that without each individual, we are not going to go very far as a group. By ourselves we suffer serious limitations. Together we can be something wonderful."
>
> Max DePree
> *The Art of Leadership*, 43

WHAT KIND OF DESIGNATED LEADERS
ARE NECESSARY?

While leadership behaviors may be expressed by anyone in the group, some person or persons must be designated as regularly responsible for certain tasks and actions. The types of designated leaders increase with the size of the small group ministry. Following are listed varieties of these leader roles.

Facilitating Ministers
• Are persons who plan and guide group meetings.
• Usually work best within a predetermined structure where format and materials have been designed for them.
• Often come in different roles such as a *team* made up of process facilitator who plans and leads the discussion, Bible study, or group experience; host(ess) facilitator who cares for logistical and relational details; special events coordinator who initiates outside events; mission coordinator who oversees outside group projects. Other designated roles arise as needed. In larger groups more than one person may fulfill one of these roles. Persons who are gifted in areas other than leadership need to be recognized for their contribution to the upbuilding of the body of believers. To participate is to utilize your gift in the service of others.
• Usually require some form of minimal accountability and equipping in group skills outside of the group.

Entrepreneurial Ministers
• Design or adapt and facilitate their own kind of group based on their concerns or observed needs.
• Create their own group materials.
• Usually have had previous group experience and require in-depth understanding of groups with extensive training.
• Are self-starters who require minimal accountability.

Group Coordinators or Shepherds
• Work with more than one group.
• Provide pastoral care and practical help for group facilitators such as information, problem-solving, and encouragement.
• Facilitate communication.

• Need extensive training and experience in people relations and group skills.

Strategists and Equippers

• Design a church group ministry structure, developing an overall group plan for numerous groups.
• Recruit, train, and channel group facilitators.
• Promote the understanding and ministry of small groups and cultivate awareness of persons and happenings in groups.
• Supervise and train coordinators.
• Integrate small group ministry with other church structures.

Job descriptions for two types of Facilitators (process and host) are included below. These are followed by job descriptions for Coordinators called Shepherds and for a Strategist.

ROLES NECESSARY TO SMALL GROUP MINISTRY

Process Leaders
1. Structure the time frame of the meeting, choosing what to include.
2. Keep things moving, deciding when to move on to the next event.
3. Prepare the content of the group time and "help it happen" by stimulating discussion, introducing new thoughts and questions and closing the study with satisfactory conclusion.
4. Maintain good group process, protecting the sensitive, pulling in the reticent, controlling the over-talker, and so on.
5. Work with the Host Leaders in designing the direction and policies of their group.

Host Leaders
1. Arrange the place of meeting and overseeing preparation.
2. Cultivate a feeling of "warmth" and welcome among members, caring for their needs.
3. Help "social events" happen among members.
4. Promote group attendance and make members aware of where and when.
5. Generate "care" among members when special needs arise such as illness, death, celebration, contacting the church with information on such needs.
6. Support enthusiastically the study time in such ways as "priming the pump" in discussion times, encouraging group response.

---

7. Share with Process Leaders in designing the direction and policies of their group.

In recruiting group leaders it is important to seek out mature persons who are comfortable and effective in one of the above descriptive sketches. You may need to help a person see that he/she has giftedness in these dimensions.

Generally, it works most effectively to allow couples or individuals to select (within guidelines) the person/persons who will be a part of their team.

Shepherd Leaders
1. Be active as a group leader, member of a group or regularly visit the groups of your division.
2. Serve as counselor, resource individual, and troubleshooter for Group Leaders of one particular type of group (i.e., married couples).
3. Make regular contact (usually after each meeting) with group leaders or members under your charge to assess the health of the group, to minister to them, and to encourage accountability. Throughout the year gather leaders in your group division together (by groups or in one group) to encourage them, and to share face-to-face, ascertaining how groups are going.
4. Work with (pastoral or lay) strategist as counselor and adviser to prayerfully evaluate the ministry, to promote the continued development of groups, to set goals for this ministry, to make needed decisions and to establish needed policies, and to aid in recruiting and training of group leaders.
5. Be present and participate in group training events and encourage your leaders to be involved.
6. Once a year, after evaluation, contact present group leaders regarding their commitment to continued ministry and recruit needed new leaders.
7. A Shepherd's commitment to service should be at least for one year, that term going through August to ensure carry-over in setting up new groups for the fall.

Strategists
Giving oversight to the total small groups program is a person in the role of Small Group Strategist. This person may be laity or professional pastoral staff, usually depending upon the size of the program. The larger the number of groups, the more time and effort required

to maintain this kind of ministry. Often this means inclusion of someone on the pastoral staff who specializes in this people ministry.

Responsibilities
1. This is the person who promotes the building of Christian community and enables this community to be implemented within the church structure. He or she is ultimately responsible for pulling together all elements of the program.
2. This includes spearheading the recruitment and training of leadership (Shepherds and group leaders).
3. This individual determines and monitors the schedule for small group meetings and training times, incorporating such within the total church calendar.
4. The Strategist assesses and evaluates the overall small group ministry effectiveness. He or she proposes changes in and new directions for this ministry.

Requirements
1. The Strategist needs to be a person with vision, capable of grasping the overall direction of small groups and setting goals for growth.
2. At the same time he/she is responsible for handling specifics such as designing whatever budget is needed, working through specific scheduling and maintaining accountability from groups.
3. The Strategist is usually the "master equipper" so needs to be familiar with small group process and able to teach such to personnel involved.
4. It is the Strategist who usually leads the model group form of equipping. Since this is a people ministry, the Strategist must be skilled in dealing with and motivating people.
5. In a church situation where seven or fewer groups are involved, this Strategist can usually be a lay person, often a person "good with people" and groups and "careful with details." Such a person can learn techniques of small group process while motivating this ministry and maintaining contact with groups, seeing that they have materials and personnel and making available training opportunities where needed.

A team of facilitators (rather than just one) has the advantage of reflecting community in leadership, sharing responsibilities along strength lines, encouraging the utilization and valuation of many gifts, giving feedback and insight along with support, and offering variety in styles to a group.

HOW CAN LEADERS BE EQUIPPED FOR MINISTRY?

The following formats provide varied means of enabling persons to understand and learn skills in group process.

1. *Training Events* such as a workshop or lab experience. This one-time event usually focuses on helping participants pick up tips in a skill such as communication or leading a discussion Bible study. It is characterized by a presentation followed by opportunity to experience or express what has been learned by trying out the technique or principle taught. It requires a person with expertise in one of these areas to lead the event and participants usually pick up one or two new ideas to improve their leadership techniques. This learning is affected by the expertise and experience the participants bring to the event. Those with more experience will naturally pick up more.

2. The *Conference* or *Retreat Experience* lasts longer than the above event and usually occurs no more than once a year. It may last a full day or a weekend, may be "at home" or require participants to travel to a conference center. It has the advantage of concentrated time to develop an idea or skill more fully in the context of relationship building. This type of equipping is often inspirational and motivational and offers opportunity to experience briefly the "living out" of some changed attitude or behavior. It also can provide a variety of emphases with seminars on several topics from which participants can choose. This variety requires several persons who have effectively experienced and can teach an aspect of group ministry.

3. *A Course* may last over a period of time and require a regular commitment from participants. While it is easy to load a course with *information*, it is important that participants *experience* what is being taught as much as possible. The methods of instruction are most effective when they are those which the participants can reproduce in their groups. The course is most effective when the setting replicates the setting in which the leaders will

function. When participants can take what is learned and try it out in their own groups between class gatherings this becomes an effective means of relating new truth to actual situations. Time commitment—adding this course to group time already committed—is a drawback among time conscious adults.

4. *In-Service Learning* is one of the most effective means of equipping because it deals with live situations in a relational setting. In this model leaders are "grown" within functioning groups. The "discipler" is the actual group leader. Besides functioning as group facilitator, the leader serves as modeler to one or more apprentices who are a part of the group. Their equipping comes in the planning and evaluating with the leader who walks them through the process of assessing needs and actions and provides explanation for behaviors and questions. The apprentice often participates in modified leadership functions thus gaining insight under supervision. The strength of this model depends much on the ability of the supervising leader to recognize and teach at teachable moments and to know how to assess and challenge a learner's growth. It has the advantage of one on one personalized training within relational and actual experience.

5. *Existing Groups* and *Committees* can become learning sites when their regular gatherings include some equipping in group leadership skills. This information and experience is usually brief because it is incorporated within another structure. While it may provide some insight, it is usually only a "spraying" with tips and ideas. Since there is no overt commitment or perhaps even interest on the part of members to serve as group leaders, the effectiveness of learning is highly varied. However, since most persons on a committee may be called upon to lead a group as a part of their responsibility, this instruction can lay some foundations.

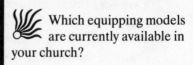 Which equipping models are currently available in your church?

Which have you personally experienced?

Which would you like to lead?

6. The *Leadership Group* model suggests a person with group skills equips others who want to

learn such by modeling good group ministry skills and sharing insight into group situations they experience together. This modeling must be done for ten to twelve weeks. After a positive group experience there follows a period of group members sharing in the leadership of their group and sharpening one another for another eight to ten weeks. The final phase is to provide a system of support as the participants are released to facilitate their own groups. When the members have experienced a trial group they are usually able to replicate a similar group experience for others. This model provides the most in-depth, intensive involvement for leadership training. It also requires the availability of a person who can lead such a training group. And it is highly goal oriented to producing persons who will copy what they have experienced in an intentional way. The longer term investment and commitment allow for more than a temporary, surface adaptation of behavior. Facilitators learn by being good group members first.

IDENTIFYING THE BETTER LEARNERS

Kerry Bunker has given several ways to identify betters learners:

- Even in childhood, better learners seem to engage in constant, on-line evaluation of their learning efforts. They analyze and correct their learning strategies even as the process is unfolding. . . .
- They seem to be more aware than others of how their basic personality drives and personal preferences influence learning. . . .
- They also seem more open to the discomfort that accompanies the use of strategies and tactics they do not prefer. They deliberately pick projects that are uncomfortable and tackle them with their strengths. . . .
- They tend to think of experience in terms of the lessons that can be learned from the experience. . . .
- Finally, the better learners are much more likely to be objective about their strengths and weaknesses. Their frank self-assessment allows them to address their shortcomings with compensating strengths on new ways of framing problems.

WHAT FACTORS DETERMINE WHICH MODEL
I CHOOSE TO IMPLEMENT?

1. Personal factors become determinants such as the amount of time and energy available, what my goals are, what has priority in my concerns, and what is my relationship to the participants?

2. People factors affect my choice. What are the people in my church ready for at this time? Do I have enough functioning leaders or do I start from scratch? What fits into the overall church program? What are church goals? What is an acceptable model to the participants? What are expectations?

3. Timing. Which model is best for beginning to train? What else is being asked of these participants from other church ministries at this time? How does this fit into an emphasis in our church at this time?

4. Resources. What skilled persons are available to help equip? What persons are available for being equipped? What time slots are open? What support will the church leadership give?

5. What are the total benefits and costs of a model? What will be built with this model?

Does one type of personality make a better small group leader than another? No. There is room for all. Some express their service to others in a more authoritative style. This "take charge" directive form of leadership works well especially as a group begins. Others prefer a coaching or supportive style of leadership. They solicit more sharing of leadership and contributions from others. Such a democratic style builds a sense of shared ownership and investment among group members. Others who recognize the aptitude

> Which model would you choose if just beginning a small group ministry?
>
> If you had trained leaders?
>
> Which if you had both experienced and new leaders?
>
> Which two could you run at the same time?
>
> Which could you offer in your church this year?

> "Learning from mistakes is easier and more common than learning from accomplishments. . . . Failure means a rude shock, a striking contrast. The lessons of success are not so obvious; it takes far more insight and motivation to discern the subtle differences in learning that result from success and accomplishment."
>
> Kerry Bunker
> *Leaders and the Dark Chasm of Learning,* 5

and ability of members utilize a delegated form of leadership, serving the group by releasing those members who are mature and capable to participate freely in the group direction-setting and progress.

CHANGING LEADERSHIP ROLE

Initiation

A leader's role changes as the group matures. At the beginning of a group leaders provide a sense of safety and warmth. Their confidence and awareness of where the group is headed breeds confidence in members. Someone needs to be in control of the situation, having planned and now executing that plan. By calling persons by name and by eliciting a proper degree of sharing, leaders develop caring and set norms of communication. More than any other time in the group this initial period, where members vacillate between anticipation and anxiety, calls for a more directive, authoritative stance to provide boundaries and keep the group moving. The leader serves as a protective "fence" and nurturing energizer.

Chaos and Adjustment

During that period when the leader seems to come under attack as members define their positions and test others', the leader must be flexible and not take these skirmishes personally. The expression of servanthood at this time comes in the form of expression of encouragement and understanding for those who struggle. Staying authoritarian here can provoke increased resistance. Persons need to be heard and their feelings acknowledged. However, the leader's stance is never to be perceived as abdication or weakness. There is a solid strength that can allow members to work through issues without feeling threatened and can encourage confrontation and the commitment needed to work through to a positive resolution. A leader at this stage must enable members to be heard, caring for those who suffer anxiety and stress when confrontation occurs and must cultivate open discussion without feeling threat. A vital role is to identify issues of concern among members and to look for ways to blend diverse opinions. The leader becomes the glue the group needs to stay together to work through concerns.

Productivity

When the group enjoys productivity and the freedom of acceptance and risk, the leader's role becomes one of switchboard. Service comes from releasing members to carry out their roles in the group, challenging some to take new risks, supporting their efforts, and helping the group receive feedback and evaluation in terms of goals set. During times of production and enjoyment the leader serves as wise counselor.

Differentiation

In the midst of differentiation where members initiate challenges and changes in terms of themselves or the group as a whole, the leader provides both a steadiness and an openness to explore. As the turbulence of transition is experienced the leader's service is reassuring the anxious while sensitively encouraging an investigation of newness with those impatient for action. The leader's openness to change will be mirrored in the group.

Closure

At termination, leaders are extremely important in their role of "celebrating finisher." By cultivating positive review and reflection leaders develop members' attitudes toward future groups. They bring a sense of closure and appreciation. As guide, leaders recognize the sadness and distancing that take place when a group dissolves. They also become key in preserving the steps taken and growth achieved within the group and within individual members. When members begin to pull away in preparation for dissolution, the leader needs to continue strong in confidence and warmth as exhibited when the group was in initial formation.

With the exception of initiation and termination the leader roles described above will probably recycle several times within a group's life. Service to Christ is expressed by enabling each member at every stage to be all that he/she can be as fulfilling individual parts in the body of Christ. When a person by inexperience or inability lacks something necessary to the fulfillment of wholeness possible at that stage, the leader gives him/herself for the upbuilding of the person and the group. This may be in the form of direction, support, confrontation, challenge, or comfort. It may involve *doing for, coming alongside,* or *releasing and stepping back.* Servanthood comes in doing what is best for the other as a leader in relationship. "Even the Son of Man did not come to be served, but to serve" (Mark 10:45).

WORKSHEET FOR GROUP LEADER

PRAY:
Who are the people coming? What would you pray for each? Pray for the relationships within the group and for the spirit of the group as a whole.

Pray for your role as leader and think through implications.

PREPARE:
Location — Setting — Resources
What arrangements do you need to make for "place" and set up of seating?

What other factors can you work on to help set the group climate?

What resources (Bibles, food, materials, child care, etc.) need to be cared for? Who will care for each of these items? With whom do you need to check to be sure these factors are being thought through?

Discussion Design — Schedule
What game plan have you developed? Is the timing realistic? What could you eliminate if necessary? Actual starting time? Ending time?

What questions or activities do you plan? Time for each? Materials available?

Will anyone be involved in helping you?

How do you plan to build people to people? What will you do to help them build relationships with one another?

GUIDE:
How can you help the group know caring? What can you model? Motivate?

How can you help the group accomplish their purposes?

Keep the discussion moving? Protect from tangents?

How can you build leadership within the group?

Do you give the group a sense of closure on each section?

How can you help each to feel fulfilled by exercising his/her gift?

CARE:
How is care expressed from the moment the first person arrives?

What demonstrates servanthood in your leadership?

Who seems to be exercising care along with you?

Who needs protecting? Stretching? Encouraging?

How do you help persons share with others? How do you get them to talk to new persons?

How do you help them express care for one another? For the group as a whole?

15

TRANSFORMING THE CHURCH: MINISTRY OF SMALL GROUPS

*There is nothing so powerful as
an idea whose time has come.*
Victor Hugo

etworks of community are seen as desirable today whether in society, business, or the church. The February 5, 1990 issue of *Newsweek* magazine devoted its cover story to the plethora of support groups now servicing our needy society—from networks of those who fear riding in elevators to those who cope with codependency in a family relationship. Some 500,000 such groups attract some 15 million Americans every week. MBA's find the cooperative philosophy of support systems and the development of skills for the creation and cultivation of teams to be key elements in their education and subsequent operation as corporate executives. Blame it on increased anxiety and stress, the Japanese influence on management and production, our shrinking world that demands cooperation, or whatever, we are very accepting of groups. In the ecclesiastical realm, church growth with the phenomenal Korean Cho Church paradigm, renewed emphasis on relational style as opposed to professional distance, and the intensifying needs of members for personal care have made the church ripe for the introduction of small group ministry.

In the race to survive, many churches have responded to this

284

phenomenon through curriculum-driven or program-driven group ministries. Because these generic groups were often quickly added to the church's marketable menu without the benefit of deeply rooted theological conviction nor focused on the actual needs of local people, churches who thought this addition to be the remedy for a declining membership found that such groups died as quickly as they had arisen. They did not achieve the hoped-for results and left people feeling disappointed, manipulated, and burned out. They became one more gimmick that didn't work as advertised. Community cannot be programmed nor developed by curriculum alone. Relationships cannot be cheaply bought. Community is not simply one more piece in the ecclesiastical pie.

As related in Chapters 1 and 2, community is at the heart of reflecting and responding to God. Jesus Christ, by placing us in His body, determined that relating to one another become a major facet of our faith. Interdependence is a distinguishable mark of the divine nature on the church. Thinking, acting, and being a person in community is not an addendum to the church's agenda — it is at the very heart of what it means to be the church — His body. The only way to implement the insights of this book within the church is to frame each dynamic with the God-designed priority of becoming a people in community. We evaluate every small group tactic by "How will this develop or enhance community among the people of God?"

Stated in other terms, community must be an integral part of our philosophy of ministry. When subjected to this theological reevaluation, our models of ministry are transformed. We are not simply demonstrating some group dynamic skill — we are responding to our Creator by doing His work among His people. We do not set up groups so that our church will become an up-to-date "full service station" but because we know that persons cannot fulfill God's purpose in their lives without community.

A THEOLOGICAL CONVICTION OF COMMUNITY

For a church to be transformed into community someone must have an awareness of community as a theological conviction. God wants the church to reflect community: to show the world what relationships are to be, to demonstrate that His work is to be relational, not solo, and to consider others, not just self.

When community development is recognized as a response to God and a working guide for how believers are to operate, we reshape our ministries by such questions as, "What will move this board from being an independent committee to an interdependent community?" "What will enable this organization to develop accountable relationships among its members?" "How can this event be redesigned to express our need for and awareness of others in the body?" "How do our leadership models communicate interdependence and the value of diversity?" Without this kind of conviction, groups will remain an independent area of specialized technique that is predominantly skill driven. Some will give themselves to "try out this experience" for a while to determine whether or not they like it. Worship is not something you try out to see if you want to pick it as one of your responses to God. Worship from a biblical framing is living so that our very lives may become acts of worship. Our service, in whatever form, is an expression of worship. In like manner God's kind of relational living must be seen as pervading all we do and affecting all we are. It is a core value in what it means to be Christian.

A VISION FOR COMMUNITY
Such conviction when placed in a local church setting becomes "vision." That vision with its magnitude and constantly growing implications must be resident in the believer who would seek to implement small group ministry in the church. Someone must see the potential for that church in terms of what it can become as it embraces God's patterns for community. It must be a vision that is broad enough to include all, with specifics enough to energize and motivate each segment. Dream the difference that relationships in ministry could develop. Write a mission statement that describes what you see the people of God in your church becoming, what you see them doing, and the values or principles that stimulate and direct this becoming and doing.

Stephen Covey's widely acclaimed book *The 7 Habits of Highly Effective People* suggests that one of those life patterns is to "Begin with the end in mind." By focusing on clear desirable results of what we can become, we begin living and working to fulfill that pattern. " 'Begin with the end in mind' is based on the principle that all things are created twice. There's a mental or first creation, and a physical or second creation to all things" (Covey, 99). An example of this is the blueprint which visually pictures the house before it is constructed. A vision encapsulates clearly realizations yet unseen. Fuzziness affects the production. Envision your church as the people of God living in community. What does it look like? Can you picture it?

INFECT OTHERS

Communicate that vision so that others also begin to understand and want community. Tell and retell it. Enable others to catch the spirit of your dream. An important aspect of building change is to expose those involved to the big picture. Let them see the cause toward which you are moving. Movements of change are swept along by the vision of where they are going. Change processes get immobilized when they become mired down by focusing on the intervening steps which must be taken.

Dreams turn requirements into means. This is best capsulized by the well known illustration of the inquiry addressed to three workmen, "What are you doing?" to which the first replied, "I am laying bricks," and the second responded, "I am building a wall." The third, however, proclaimed, "I'm creating a cathedral!" Trust people with the cause. It shapes their present activities and keeps them from faltering along the way. A clear commitment to that eventual cause will cause them to take in stride the costs for getting there. It is said of Jacob who agreed to work seven years to receive Rachel for his own, "So Jacob served seven years to get Rachel, but they seemed like only a few days to him because of his love for her" (Gen. 29:20). Sharing the vision motivates people to want to be a part of the dream.

As they envision a church that is relationally operating, they automatically begin thinking and talking small group implementation within the spheres of their influence. Like impacts like when it comes to transfer of ideas. "The innovator in any group is likely to be the person in that group who shows the greatest degree of cultural similarity [shared interests, values, situations] with the person from another group who is introducing the innovation. What is more, whether and/or how quickly the innovation will be adopted in the group as a whole will depend in part on whether the innovators are seen by at least part of our group [the early adopters in particular] as being more like 'one of us' or more like 'one of them' " (Singer, 197).

Thus by infecting Sunday School class members with the vision of community building within the church, they will begin to look for ways their class could be shaped by that dream (such as small dinner groups where members get to know one another outside of class or such as inserting into class time an opportunity to share personal concerns in groups of four or five). Through regularly exposing the church board to community convictions and implementing this relational priority in minute ways at their meetings, a few may "catch the spirit" and decide to spend some scheduled time at the annual board retreat in relational groups, sharing with and caring for one another as persons. Let your vision become contagious.

EXPECT RESISTANCE

Even as you begin to sow a new way of thinking and doing small group ministry there will be those who are frightened of the dream. If you are clergy, they may see you as an "outsider" and feel you don't value what they have achieved over years of faithful ministry. The concept of community may cut across comfort zones of privitized and individualized church experience. How can you respond without forsaking the dream or the persons resisting?

A second principle of *The 7 Habits of Highly Effective People* states, "Seek first to understand." This principle helps you in packaging your dream.

> We typically seek first to be understood. Most people do not listen with the intent to understand; they listen with the intent to reply. . . . Empathic (from empathy) listening gets inside another person's frame of reference. You look out through it, you see the world the way they see the world, you understand their paradigm, you understand how they feel.
>
> (Covey, 239–240)

In hearing a person's concerns you restate that value or emotion that is causing them to act. "You are fearful that our church will lose its passion for reaching out if we focus on building community." or "You had a bad experience with a sensitivity group in the '70s and haven't been in a group since." The first person is thinking in "either/or" frameworks while the second fears that groups manipulate one into a psychological striptease, a definitely uncomfortable position for one's self-esteem.

Affirm the reality of the resistor's feelings. Then inculcate your vision for relational living in the value or principle they embrace. Show them how their value is enhanced by community. This is sensitivity to the other's agenda. A "crucially important aspect in the transmission of ideas on innovations from one group to another is the question of translating the idea into language and values that are culturally acceptable to the second group" (Singer, 197).

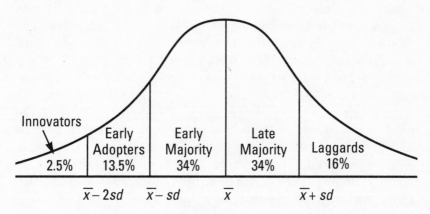

Adopter categorization on the basis of innovativeness. The innovativeness dimension, as measured by the time at which an individual adopts an innovation or innovations is continuous. However, this variable may be partitioned into five adopter categories by laying off standard deviations from the average time of adoption. Reprinted with the permission of The Free Press, a Division of Macmillan, Inc. from *Diffusion of Innovations,* 3rd ed., by Everett M. Rogers. Copyright © 1962, 1971, 1983 by The Free Press.

It is similar to visiting a foreign country where the visitor's currency is not usable until the currency is changed into the currency of the country. Sharing relational principles in terms of what another values is adapting to their "country." God's principles do not contradict each other. Outreach and community are not paradoxical but supportive. For example, "Without outreach, community becomes stale and nonproductive. With community, outreach ministries are strengthened by larger bases of support and renewed as groups respond with creative ways to share their energy." And esteem-building and the valuing of the individual are actually what God's kind of community seeks. So you reply "No one should be forced to live the rest of his/her life with the world's distortions of God's provision for His own. The kind of relationships God projects for groups gives individuals a chance to be themselves in ways fulfilling their role as God's gift of them to the body of Christ."

All persons need time to integrate new directions with old values. "A study on innovation conducted by Everett M. Rogers reveals five categories into which persons in any group fall. The smallest segment are Innovators, most ready to risk and experiment. These persons also were categorized as those in the group having the most ties to other outside groups, a factor which may have conditioned them to more exposure and less apprehension toward new ideas. This subgroup usually comprises 2.5% of the total group. Early Adaptors to innovation make up another 13.5% while the Early Majority and Late Majority each were 34% of the group. Laggards at 16% were the last to "get on board" (Rogers, 3rd ed., Chapter 7). Look for ways to "blend" and mark resistors' concerns as helpful warnings of imbalances and sensitivities to avoid in implementation of groups. Resistors actually help by sharing their agendas and concerns so something can be done about them. Some persons are more cautious by nature and can be won by hearing and valuing their cautions. The strongest resistors have often become the strongest supporters once their concerns are answered.

ATTRACT A TEAM
From this vision painting come those who will want to join you in making the dream come true. These become your "band of men and women" who will flesh out the dream and keep it going. David created the hope of an alternative to Saul. Those who

were disillusioned with the status quo or inspired by the possibilities of David's leadership became his "band of men" who worked to cause the dream to become reality. Jesus chose twelve who committed themselves to carrying the dream to the ends of the earth. Three kinds of persons are extremely helpful on this team: enthusiasts who have referent power, supporters who have expert power, and supporters who are on the periphery of the current system. Why these to communicate the dream and its eventual implementation?

Those who have *referent power* in the congregation are the E.F. Huttons, to whom persons give respect. They have earned credibility and are persons of influence because they are trusted. They may or may not be in positions of organizational leadership currently. Referent power persons lend credibility to the dream and will help you gain wisdom and insight into the congregation if you are an outsider or newly arrived. The Rogers Study quoted earlier showed that "the only times a change was widely adopted was when the 'respectable people,' the 'pillars of their communities,' adopted the change (and became early adapters), then there was some likelihood that others would" (Singer, 197).

Enthusiasts who have *expert power* also lend credibility and build trust through the realization and utilization of their skills. They may be experts in group dynamics, in theological framing, in communication, in some ministry specialization (adult ministries), or in organizational planning. Their expertise strengthens the dream and its development and can complement the giftedness you bring as Dream Instigator.

"Fringe" persons often add creativity and new paradigms to the mix. Because they are new or not presently heavily involved in or motivated by current ministries, these persons do not have encumbering investments in things as they are. Their interest in the community dream allows them to bring together fresh insights and new combinations of relational implementation. Things said in a new way bring hope and excitement to existing institutions.

A smattering of these three types of persons makes a stimulating team of dream propagators and implementers whether they be three or fifteen. Sharing the responsibility and the implementation is a part of fulfilling the dream. Attracting a team models developing relationships to share community relationally.

DECLARE BIBLICAL FOUNDATIONS

People are motivated by vision. They are energized to invest in the vision particularly if it ties in with values already embraced. As members of God's family we are those who value His Word. But most congregations are unaware of basic teaching about community in the Bible. Even passages which are familiar are often interpreted individually instead of corporately. We more often think of God individually than in His corporate interdependence. Knowing that God is the author and modeler of community and stresses a relational lifestyle as integral to life with Him is important for those who would pursue following Him. Create a strong base of biblical material through preaching and teaching God's models, principles, and commands concerning community. Target community passages for exploration in retreat settings. Enable the congregation to see the high priority God places on caring for and working with others in the body of Christ. What biblical material comes to mind as you contemplate doing this?

INVESTIGATE AND EVALUATE WHAT EXISTS

Before you instigate a concrete plan for transformation, it is important to know what you have.

Know Networks Before Negotiating

Become aware of hidden agendas. Networks are always present in a congregation. What official groups already exist? How many and what kind of small group offerings are already available? Depending upon when you enter the life cycle of group ministry, you may have numerous officially operating group experiences in existence or you may have only a few limited to one or two areas. Know well what already composes the image of small groups in your situation. Secondly, what unofficial networks currently exist?

Meaningful relational networks are created through natural contacts and interests. While not officially recognized as a small group, these gatherings of clans, persons in similar circumstances (mothers in the same preschool co-op), social associates, or holders of similar interests (RV camping enthusiasts) knit the larger congregation together and form important links in reaching people and in designing intentional groups. Their focus or bonding is often a springboard for creation of a group to enable each other to grow in Christ. Never attempt to build community from nothing.

Hidden agendas have sabotaged many a change agent who failed to investigate behind the scenes. Reflective listening and questions such as "What has characterized this church (small groups and your experience of them) in the past?" or "What is important to know in thinking of small groups within this particular church family?" are investigative necessities. What you are looking for comes under the colorful labels of "Sacred Cows," "Tattered Dreams," and "Mine Fields." "Sacred Cows" are areas not to be tampered with because they house values not understood or appreciated by you. They are emotion-producing blocks which take precedence over new information and replacement values. Those who are part of the tribal tradition recognize and hold apart these areas with survival tenacity. "Sacred Cows" may be organizations, ways of operating, or time slots. If you meet a "Sacred Cow" on the path, cut a path around it.

"Tattered Dreams" are filled with nostalgia. They are usually unrealistic and have achieved aura with time. They frequently haunt us from the "good old days." An outstanding group ministry that fit the needs of a previous era can become hallowed in perspective and become an unrealistic ideal to be "reinstated" now. Deal with "Tattered Dreams" by affirming the good and showing how that is reincarnated in the new vision. Genuinely rejoice over the effectiveness of ministry to the needs of a former day and challenge the supporters to utilize that same spirit of commitment to examine and reshape a plan that will be even more effective today.

"Mine Fields" also hook into the past—usually a sensitive or negative realm from personal history. Contact with one of these areas sets off a response far greater than the encounter called for. Feelings and patterns of thinking have usually been gunnysacked and whoever or whatever touches the sensitive issue receives the flak and the emotions that were stored up from the past. As with "Sacred Cows," "Mine Fields" are to be avoided. Sensitivity to treat such emotional issues with genuine care and firm assurance of your awareness of them can defuse them. Statements such as this assure persons of your efforts to value them: "We want to think through ways of ensuring that singles don't feel like second-class citizens in our group formation. Charlene can especially help us to do that." Cultivate awareness of hidden agendas. Know networks.

Diagnose Before You Prescribe

Evaluation is also necessary before strategizing a plan. It comes in at least two forms: *Assess needs. Identify (determine) your influence.* While there are many realms available for needs assessment, two are extremely important for the small group change agent. The first is to assess the needs of existing groups and their leaders, the second is to identify the concerns of the church not currently being serviced by the present small group ministry. Always start with people; never with a program. Need awareness grows out of relationships. Build relationships with current small group leaders. Convey the posture of enabling, not controlling; of resourcing, not conforming; of listening, not telling. How do you do that? By hanging around. By asking questions and genuinely listening. By tentatively observing wear spots. "I know you're concerned that only half your group showed up tonight. Has this been happening a lot?" or "Why do you think we have difficulty finding enough small group leaders?" Interviewing group leaders several at a time is an excellent way to discover group concerns and conditions. Surveys that are written are often not very productive in helping to uncover real needs of a group. Questionnaires can be interpreted in many different ways and the answers given become valuable only when accompanied by further explanation.

For issues and needs in the congregation at large the above methods of assessment may be used. In addition, clergy and boards who are aware of congregational health and involvement and counselors (if you have such on staff) can usually target areas where small groups can make a difference. Examples could be an increasing awareness of abuse victims within the congregation, numerous members coping with the care of elderly parents, unemployment trauma, and challenges for executives out of work. The Word of God in revealing life as reality within its pages often suggests needs that are still relevant today. Everyday issues and decisions faced by Christians in the workplace or community concerns that call for involvement are other potential sources of group focus. Groups could target ethics in the market-place, the cry of the homeless, and "Financially Free"—support for credit card addicts. In assessing needs, the novel looks attractive but ask yourself, "Is this condition a common concern, or frequently mentioned among our people?" Should your church become involved in an all-church emphasis with major goals centered in a particular direction, ask yourself how small groups can be created to support and implement this cause. Help members begin to think relationally as they pursue this all-church focus. Equipping believers for serving or for living out their priorities in the marketplace are two examples of this kind of across-the-board emphasis. Always begin with people, not program. Needs lead to ministry with the people of God as ministers.

The second half of Evaluation is focused on spheres of persuasion and your place within the congregation. *Perceive before you attempt to persuade.* Before laying out a strategic plan for small group ministry, it is helpful to recognize the sphere of influence which is available to you. Covey calls this our "Circle of Influence." Our "Circle of Concerns" is usually much wider than our "Circle of Influence"—the things we can do something about in contrast to other things over which we have no real control. He states, "Proactive people focus their efforts in the Circle of Influence. They work on the things they can do something about. The nature of their energy is positive, enlarging and magnifying, causing their Circle of Influence to increase." They are in contrast to Reactive people who create negative energy by placing their focused efforts within the Circle of Concern, often in realms where they have little or no influence, neglecting areas where they do have influence (Covey, 82–83).

Power is given by persons to others for varied reasons. *Referent power* is openness to be influenced by another who is respected or valued. "My teacher says," or "My daddy says," are good examples of referent power that adults have with children. Referent power influences through status, experience, or charisma. Usually this kind of influence takes time and exposure to develop. Because you are a valued member of a Sunday School class you may have received enough referent "tokens" to influence the class to try small groups. Power is like money. It is earned or given in various ways. Members give leaders power to influence them as that power is invested to achieve some outcome through persuasion. This is not a negative use but one that gives another the right to exercise responsibility or influence for or upon another. A person new to the job of Small Group Ministry Strategist will probably have a small sphere of referent power at the start. A helpful guideline regarding referent power grows out of the Rogers' study. "If we want to explore how decisions are made and/or adopted in groups, we had better identify both the innovators and the opinion leaders. If we want to influence some other group to adopt some innovators or to change their attitudes and values, we had better figure out how to change the attitudes and values of the innovators and opinion leaders of the other group" (Singer, 197).

A second type of power currency that influences others is *expert power*. Recognized specialized knowledge, experience, or skills causes some persons to be influenced by expertise. Those who know a little or much about your area of expertise and value it in their lives are ones most likely to be influenced by this kind of power. For example if the church board has experienced little of community and sees community development as "your thing" not theirs, you may find it difficult to influence them toward being more relationally oriented in their sessions. *Legitimate or position power* is much more likely to have clout with such a board. Persons chosen to represent us such as chairpersons or persons we designate with authority and responsibility such as ad hoc committee members are examples of positions where a person is given the right to decide and act for others. Being designated as Small Groups Pastor or Group Ministry Strategist by the pastor, the church, or a committee gives you greater influence. However, even legitimate power may be limited without referent power also attached. Many a position power leader has found that the ability to persuade and influence is dependent upon keeping up referent status as respected and well meaning. Spheres of influence are often conditioned more by those above us. A Senior Pastor who uses his/her legitimate and referent power to provide access to boards and persons in authority and paves the way with visible affirmation of and confidence in the Small Group ministry and Strategist will provide a wider sphere of influence.

Many a new staff person who has been called to "set up small groups" has encountered the reality of a limited sphere of influence for the exercise of this ministry because others saw the ministry as a threat or saw the instigator as unknown and untried in the congregation. Persons assuming only their first or second position as a member of a pastoral team may have to live with a limited sphere of influence for small group ministry. Those who have a track record and some years in ministry to groups may be given access to the whole church as a potential sphere of development. All of this is to provide realistic and not unreachable goals within the strategic plan. "Bloom where you are planted" is good advice and saves frustration and beating your head against the wall when you seek to motivate and care for concerns outside your sphere of influence. Plan well within your boundaries and that positive experience will likely increase your influence.

Sometimes your influence can be broader because of the referent power of those who team with you. Realize that such awareness of influence is not for personal gratification or power grabbing, but only to facilitate the development of a plan that will build credibility in this focus on relational prioritizing.

Choose Specific Target Areas Over Broadside
If you are beginning a small group ministry or "starting over," take note of the target populations that keep cropping up in your all-church assessment of needs. Who appears to be open and responsive to small groups? Who is among the not already over-committed? Whose need would naturally and easily be facilitated through a small group format? Which ministry focus do you wish to respond to? If evangelism or outreach, does a certain target population arise? (many young couples in the community? untapped singles?) If incorporation and congregational bonding, who is naturally hungry for this? (new members, newly married who are looking for a new set of mutual friends) Any target population in transition becomes a good candidate for small group focus (persons moving into the church family, persons changing the status of their lives through marriage, retirement, etc.). If your focus is support or recovery, what areas have been uncovered that reveal pain or struggle and the need for understanding?

If setting up a model group, make it focused toward the kind of group you want reproduced—model an evangelistic outreach group, a service/mission type group, or a prayer or study group. By focusing on a specific emphasis, members will be able to replicate that model and expand that ministry.

With an existing or even flourishing small group ministry, targeting areas for new growth or direction while maintaining the older systems is an important step. Many members may have invested in the old groups and thus remain fiercely loyal. It is important to continue these avenues of support wherever they continue to provide life and to meet the concerns of the congregation. However, new directions may be begun at the same time through your involvement in a new model, targeted to fulfill a new purpose or to set new directions for the small group ministry. Do not seek to pull members away from the existing groups. Find your target population amid those who are unreached by the present groups, and develop new paradigms with this population. This may add to your congregational menu of group offerings or may be the beginning of a new breed that will eventually become the norm for groups in your church. Never try to dissolve groups that are unhealthy except under extreme circumstances. Create healthy models alongside them. Health attracts others. Train yourself to be aware of target areas where small groups can flourish.

Design Goals Before Plan
Goals tell us where we want to be. They are targets that focus the direction of our efforts. Goals may be broad (develop an understanding of community) or they may be specific (equip 12 new leaders in the next two years). The more specific the objectives, the more accountability there is built in.

When setting goals think long-range as well as near future. Plan for three to five years from now as well as the increments that make up the more immediate time frames. If you plan to involve 50% of your congregation in small groups within five years, how many specific groups will need to be formed? How many leaders will need to be trained? How many of these will be needed in year one? Always include goals for existing groups. What does your investigation show they desire as changes? In what ways do you assess they need to grow? What are your goals for the congregation as a whole in regard to relational attitudes and understanding of community? Be realistic and base your projections upon your research and evaluation of present church condition.

Developmental thinking considers phases which impact each other. For example, if your church has suffered deterioration in the small group ministry or is generally apathetic toward involvement in groups, your goal of rebuilding or changing attitude may require a year of reorientation and the creation of one new model rather than setting a goal to begin 10 new groups. Attitudes and understandings must always precede actions and both of these take time to process. Writing goals in terms of what the people will do often gives an awareness of steps that must be taken before that goal is achieved. For example, setting a goal that the adult Sunday School classes will regularly incorporate relational interaction in their classes causes awareness that the members must be motivated to want this and understand the necessity of it for their growth and personalization of content. That response necessitates that previously the leadership becomes aware of and desirous for this priority as well as becoming knowledgeable in a variety of ways to sell and develop a relational lifestyle. Such a step requires relational networking with that leadership as well as teaching them the values and principles of small group sharing experiences.

Networking requires gaining access to that leadership and negotiating contact time to achieve the above. Working backward from the desired outcome enables an awareness of the steps needed to bring it to reality.

> People who do not know where they are going will almost certainly reach a destination, but they won't know when they do."
>
> Donald K. Smith, 96

Without goals a small group ministry will have difficulty moving forward. Without a focused plan the ministry of groups will develop uneven focus and can become sidetracked on nonessentials.

Decide On Models and Design a Plan

The models of small group ministry available offer variety and adaptability. Some churches use one of the alternatives given below; some combine elements from both. What model choices are in existence?

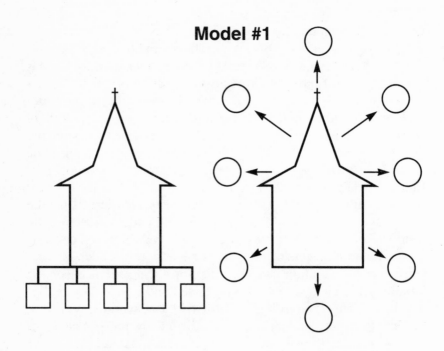

Model #1

1. Central Control   vs.   Central Motivation

Church perceptions on the role of the professional staff and the role of the laity will probably determine this choice. This perception is largely determined by the leadership—both paid and unpaid. Central Control focuses the power to determine, initiate and control the small group ministry within the official church structures. The paid staff assumes responsibility and the congregation is supportive. Central Motivation places the power to determine, initiate, and maintain the ministry of groups within the congregation and makes the paid staff supportive. Character-istics of each model follow.

Central Control

- Designs goals and groups after assessing needs
- Recruits leadership
- Sets up specific number and kinds of groups
- Assigns or enables group members to enter groups
- Groups by contract/age level usually
- Aware of curriculum – often supplied, often uniform, often sequential/thematic
- Guides and supports group leadership and members
- Organizes groups around church year

Central Motivation

- Pastor models/calls persons to construct and become involved in community
- Allows persons to design groups according to their motivation/ interests
- Provides minimal enablement
- May group by contract (task/purpose oriented) or by time available (emphasis on being in group for community sake)
- Minimally aware or unaware of specific curriculum used
- Curriculum usually highly varied
- Staff aware of purposes – often unaware of groups – number, etc.
- Groups function primarily on their own
- Groups are organized spontaneously

Most Small Group Ministries across the country follow the Central Control philosophy. Bruce Larson, while pastor at University Presbyterian in Seattle, embodied the Central Motivation model. He states,

We simply model the importance of this [small group] experience and let people sort themselves out. . . . For example, two of our members . . . picked up on something I'd preached about in Acts 5:12-16, where it tells about the early Christians meeting in a place called Solomon's Porch, and whole crowds came there for healing. This was a public place, not a church building. So they said, "Why couldn't there be a place for people to just drop in and be with Christians?" They settled on a Burger Chef, and every Friday noon this group gets together to laugh, cry, share, and set one another free.

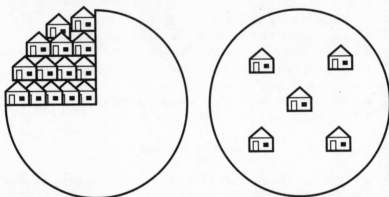

2. Geographically Assigned   vs.   Member Selection

This model focuses on how members enter groups. When desirous of keeping members together in manageable locations so they can be attended to by an elder, deacon, or other, some churches assign persons to groups according to where they live. Since location is the common denominator, interest and commitment may be less in these groups with the level of sharing often not as intimate as when the members can select the persons with whom to associate. Advantages include saving travel time, getting to know your neighbors, and identification with the area.

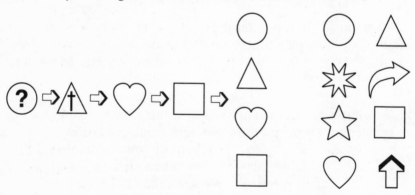

3. Predetermined Menu   vs.   A La Carte

The Church as a
Transformational Growth
System

Equipping the Saints

STAGE I MISSION	STAGE II MOORING	STAGE III MOLDING	STAGE IV MOBILIZING	STAGE V MINISTRY
Evangelism	Enfolding	Equipping Educating Enriching	Empowering	Enabled & Equipped

Pre-evangelism

Entry

Home
Neighborhood
Marketplace

○ Education
○ Social
○ Evangelism
○ Music
○ Pastoring
○ Missions
○ Counseling
○ Etc.

| INQUIRERS- NEW MEMBERS CLASS GROUPS | FELLOWSHIP (LAMBS) GROUPS | NURTURE – DISCIPLE – GROWTH BIBLE STUDY GROUPS | EQUIPPING CLASSES & GROUPS | SPECIAL INTEREST GROUPS | OUTREACH MINISTRY & MISSION GROUPS |

SPECIAL SUPPORT GROUPS

CONVERT TO CHRIST	CONVERT TO COMMUNITY	CONVERT TO TELEIOS IN CHRIST	CONVERT TO MINISTRY

MENDING AS OUTREACH

MENDING THE SAINTS

SANCTIFICATION PROCESS

Dr. Gary R. Sweeten, Equipping Ministries International, Inc.,
4015 Executive Park Drive, Suite 309, Cincinnati, Ohio 45241 (513-769-5353)

To enable believers to progress toward becoming well-equipped mature persons the Predetermined Menu organizes groups around developmentally sequenced goals to provide balance and growth. This incremental strategy is usually designed to be experienced in a definite order with the goal in mind of experiencing growth or transformation by moving through the stages of groups. Some choose to include certain tracks or segments of predetermined group emphases within their small group ministry offerings. These groups usually proceed from basic to advanced, from exposure to understanding to implementation or through some similar sequence. Following these requirements the members then move into elective small groups.

The A La Carte model offers a plethora of offerings from which any member may select according to interest or need. An illustration of the Predetermined Menu model is found in the "Equipping the Saints" plan designed by Gary R. Sweeten on page 303. Following is the four-fold emphasis of Evergreen Baptist Church, Rosemead, California spelled out through their goals and then fleshed out through four types of groups as designed by Arlene Inouye (see pages 305–306).

Disciples who Grow to Go that Others might Come and See

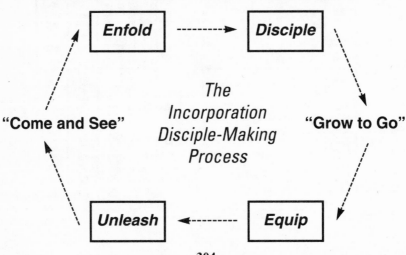

EVERGREEN'S INCORPORATION PROCESS

Purpose: "*Grow to Go...*"

Primary Goals:

Enfold → Disciple → Equip → Unleash

Secondary Goals:

Enfold

The church will seek to help the individual to:

1. Feel welcome and cared for.

2. Develop at least seven friendships with those in the congregation.

3. Participate in worship services 2-4 times a month.

4. Join and participate in a small group that meets his or her perceived needs.

5. Explore the Christian faith and grow in his or her understanding and commitment to God and His Word.

6. Make a decision to accept Jesus as Savior and Lord, if he or she has not yet done so.

Disciple

The church will seek to help the individual to:

1. Participate in a small group which fosters development toward spiritual maturity, including how to integrate faith and everyday life.

2. Identify with Evergreen's vision, mission, and goals.

3. Find a ministry task or role for which he or she can be responsible and find meaningful.

4. Make a decision regarding becoming a member of the church.

5. Understand biblical stewardship, including tithing, and tithe regularly.

Equip

The church will seek to help the individual to:

1. Participate in a small group that fosters continued development toward spiritual maturity and emphasizes reproduction of disciples.

2. Discover his or her calling and spiritual gifts for ministry.

3. Find a ministry area that matches his or her giftedness.

4. Develop his or her leadership potential through training and discipling.

Unleash

The church will seek to help the individual to:

1. Receive on-going training that will increase his or her ministry effectiveness in the area he or she has been "unleashed."

2. Participate in a small group that fosters continued development toward spiritual maturity and emphasizes reproduction.

3. Meet the need for on-going support and encouragement as he or she is directly involved in ministry and missions.

4. Encourage non-Christians to "Come and See" at Evergreen in the hope that they also will come to "Grow to Go."

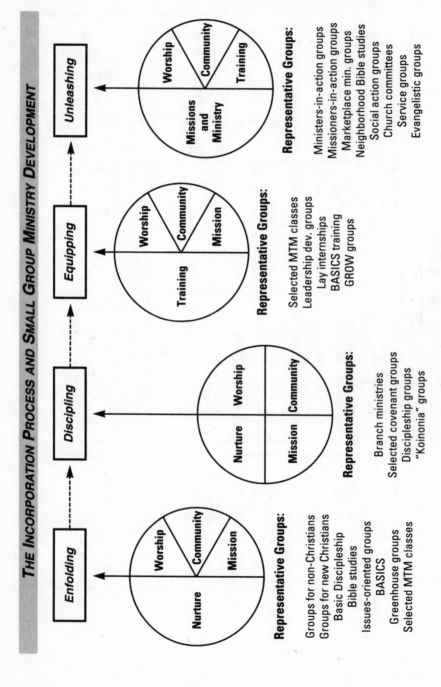

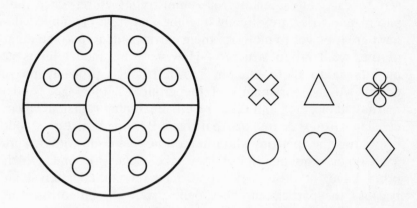

4. Likeness–Same Elements   vs.   Diversified Types

Some models emphasize every group's incorporating certain generic elements regardless of its emphasis. Often called Koinonia or Discipleship groups, this three-focus agenda usually includes Fellowship, Bible study and Prayer while most four-focus groups include some form of Prayer, Care, Study, and Mission. Diversified models may choose to include any one or more of the above elements without having to incorporate the others.

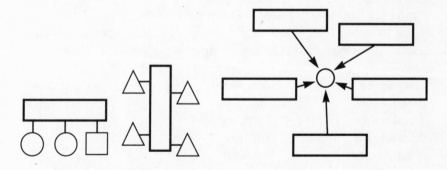

5. Groups within   vs. Groups Across or Apart
Existing Structures   from Existing Structures

Forming Groups under the umbrellas of established ministries such as Sunday School classes or missionary association is a good way to ease into a small group ministry structure. Since these parent ministries are already ongoing and have credibility, they have great power to motivate their participants to become a part of the small group structure. However, this model limits acquaintance to those already known (though probably not in depth), to the parameters of the group whether age, gender, marital status, etc., and often results in cloning rather than variety. The Groups Across or Apart from Existing Structures Model brings together persons who often do not associate with or know each other. This may mean they take longer to bond. On the other hand, because they are formed on mutual interest and because the participants have deliberately chosen to associate, they may blend more quickly and with higher enthusiasm over involvement.

Variety of Purpose in Groups

The categories of purpose for which small groups may be designed are numerous. Several major agendas are noted below with representative types of groups who carry out the primary goal.

Groups for Belonging	*Groups for Knowing*	*Groups for Healing**
Outreach	New Believer	Support
New Member	Study	Recovery Awareness
House Church	Discipleship	Self-help Recovery

Groups for Serving	*Groups for Enriching*
Leadership Training	Covenant
Mission/Ministry	Affinity
Task/Project	Worship

*Coleman and Scales present a helpful distinction between these two need-oriented groups:

> *Support Groups:* The purpose of the group is primarily to share your experience about something you all have in common.

Recovery/Healing Groups/Awareness Groups: The purpose of the group is primarily to gain more information about something that you may or may not be involved in. This is not a therapy group. This is a group in which you investigate the issue that is a problem in our society and may have a personal connection to you. Out of this group experience a person may wish to seek personal counseling or enroll in a self-help recovery group, such as Alcoholics Anonymous.

SUPPORT GROUPS	RECOVERY/HEALING GROUPS
1. Engaged couples	1. Alcoholism
2. Newly married	2. Nicotine addiction
3. Parents of young children	3. Codependent relationship (self-worth)
4. Parents of adolescents	
5. Single parents	4. Compulsions (eating problems, etc.)
6. Blended families	
7. Divorce	5. Addictions (work, sex, gambling, etc.)
8. Grief/loss	
9. Aging parents	6. Assertiveness
10. Life-threatening illness	7. Victims of abuse (sexual, physical, etc.)
11. Midlife crisis	
12. Career change/ unemployment	8. Emotions (depression, anger, etc.)
	9. Phobias/Fears
	10. Adult children of dysfunctional families
	11. Obsessive relationships
	12. Pornography

Lyman Coleman and Mary Scales, *Serendipity Training Manual for Groups,* Serendipity House. Used by permission.

CRITERIA FOR SELECTING A MODEL

What factors influence the selection of one model over another? The following questions can serve to point out factors that could lead to selection of one model as priority over another.

1. What convictions, experience, vision, and goals do I have?

2. What is our church's philosophy of ministry? What priorities are emphasized? Not seen as priority?

3. What is the role of the laity in our church? What role is expected of the clergy?

LIFE CYCLE OF A MINISTRY

1. **Exploration**
   —Trial Experiences
2. **Initiation**
   —Focusing Model
3. **Assimilation**
   —Gathering to Model
4. **Expansion**
   —Try Secondary Models
5. **Confidence-Comfort**
   —Sustaining Central Model
   —Developing Support Structures
6. **Consolidation**
   —Refocusing Central Model
   —Focusing Secondary Models
7. **Controversy-Crisis**
   —Model Limitations
   —Model Problems
   —Model Conflicts
   —Leadership Frustrations
   —Conflicts of Interest
8. **Consultation-Collapse**
   —Evaluation and Assessment
   —Inside Outside Help
   —Roadblocks to Change
   —Denial
9. **New Cycle**
   —Change Agency
   —New Plan Trials
   —Conflicts of Values
   —Reformation

1. Pre-Contracting

2. Orientation

3. Power-Control

4. Trust

5. Differentiation

6. Termination
   New Start

Gareth Icenogle. Used by permission.

4. Where is the church in the lifecycle of small group ministry? (Gareth Icenogle has designed the following schema showing phases of a small group ministry. The congregation is probably open to new models of groups and needs a pioneer type of leader at stages 1, 4, 8, and 9. If you enter the picture at stage 2, 3, 5, you must be prepared to buy into the existing model. Stages 7 and 8 are crucial for the future of small groups in the church and require leadership that can listen and absorb while maintaining a new vision.)

5. What are people ready for? Cautious beginnings? Risk to change? Conserving the current norms? How does timing of other major emphases or events affect small group plans? (looking for a senior pastor? Entering a building program? Responding to a financial crisis?)

6. Are many persons at the same stage of growth? Many new believers? Primarily young couples? Is the church in a new area so that outreach is prime? The presence of many homogeneous units can suggest a small group emphasis focused on that area as "ripe" for community building. What is the history of groups in our congregation? Anything to avoid? To embrace and enlist?

7. What are congregational needs at this time? Do we require open groups so persons can get acquainted with us as a church? Or an interchurch focus to build security and depth? Or an equipping focus to send members out to live their faith in the marketplace? Or all three in balance?

8. What are the leadership's stated goals? Congregational stated goals? A life of discipleship? Building in new persons?

9. What is the role of groups in conjunction with other agencies in the church? A substitute for adult classes? An extension of congregational worship?

10. What leaders of groups are available? What equipping have they had? Do we have leadership available for different types of groups?

11. What kind of support and development system is available

for groups and leaders? From the clergy? From the congregation? From the boards and committees? Any support from existing agencies in the church?

12. What has God clearly called us to be and do? What is He motivating in our midst at this time? What is it we simply must do to keep faith with what has been revealed to us?

Design a three-to-five year plan based on the above assessments, choices, and desirable goals. Include training, special events, steps to be taken in the support of existing groups and the formation of new groups, and a timeline.

PROPOSAL

It may be helpful to develop a proposal for sharing your goals and plan with persons who need to catch the vision and cause it to happen.

Guidelines for writing a proposal

1. Succinctly state what it is you plan to do. "Establish a discipleship small group ministry at First Church." "Expand the small group ministry to include recovery and mission groups."

2. Briefly relate this projection to the theological and expressed values of the leadership and the church. Show how it will support or carry out value. "This small group emphasis will strengthen the goal of living your faith in practical ways of service within the church and in the marketplace. It will involve believers in carrying out the work of Christ in the world and will strongly support our stated goal of 'Every member a minister.' "

3. State your goals and the strategy to carry them out.

4. Project objections or questions, and answer them.

5. Note who will be involved. Who will take responsibility? How will these persons be trained or prepared?

6. Share a timetable of projected emphases and events.

7. List resources that will be required. Costs? Budgeted? Facilities? Personnel? Timing in terms of existing ministries.

8. Summary. End with a rousing exhortation to adopt the proposal and enjoy the benefits.

Such a proposal, if it is to be grasped quickly, should be no longer than two to three pages but needs to give evidence of having been well thought through and full of conviction.

A sample timeline can be found on page 314.

Prepare Personnel and Purchase Resources
After securing approval and sharing your strategy with key people, implement recruiting and training as noted in your strategy. It may be that you will simply recruit members for your model group where you will share the process in a life setting of group experiences. If you expect others to lead groups, offer informational and experiential sessions to give them security and a sense of purpose and competence. (See *A Training Manual for Small Group Leaders,* Victor.) Prepare any other needed leaders such as co-ordinators. All of this preparation is best accomplished with the involvement and guidance of the Ministry Team who early on caught the spirit of community and bought into the vision.

When using a printed curriculum, purchase copies far enough ahead to allow leaders time to familiarize themselves with the material. (See GroupBuilder Resources, Victor.) If persons are new to the curriculum or to leadership, offer an informational seminar on how to use the material to greatest advantage. Give an overview of the series and suggest ways to personalize the curriculum to your church's needs. If you allow leaders to choose their own curriculum, make available several series from which to choose. Having material available early gives a feeling of security especially to those who like to plan ahead. There are numerous types of curriculum on the market for all kinds of groups. As strategist you are better able to review and select possible curriculum series. Do not expect lay leaders untrained in knowing what to look for to do this task. For a comprehensive overview of the many small group resources available see *The Curriculum and Small Group Resource Guide* (NavPress) compiled by Judy Hamlin.

Good PR — Publicize, Recognize
Small group ministry must be kept before the congregation not only so they realize what is available but also to highlight the priority of community in the congregation. Pulpit interviews, brochures describing the ministry, and newsletters describing who is involved and what is happening make this relational emphasis

EXAMPLE OF TIMELINE

	YEAR 1				YEAR 2
	1–4 weeks	5–20 weeks		21–29 weeks	1–4 weeks
GROUPS: Goal 1 — In three years to have at least 25% of our active members involved in some type of small group within the church.	Publicize Send out survey to congregation	Begin to talk through contracts and how to write one Divide into teams Set up three small groups	Begin small groups Bring in leaders with one other person with leadership potential for viewing and evaluation of small groups.	Make list of those desiring to be involved in small groups Set up six small groups Contract in groups	Begin small groups Add small groups as leaders are trained and available
LEADERS: Goal 2 — By the end of the first year at least 3 teams of leaders equipped, by the end of the second year at least 10 teams, and by the third year at least 15 teams of leaders.	Collect survey Look for prospective model group members	Model group time Note: I will lead the first 8 weeks. The remaining 12 weeks will be delegated to various members		Weekend retreat Recruit six teams of leaders from last year	Set up 2 seminars Strategize in order to recruit new leaders
EVALUATION: Goal 3 — For three years every six months conduct an evaluation of the progress of the small group ministry. Also report back to the committee every six months.		Evaluate and prepare report for committee	Observe small groups and prepare report Set up program for Year 2 Plan September retreat	Find and contact speakers for seminars	Evaluate progress

visible. Of course the best publicity are the enthusiastic group participants who tell others of the benefits.

Honor those in the church family who serve as ministers in this vital area. The church in general is often known for using people and then forgetting them. Those who invest their lives and gifts need to be affirmed. Gratitude is a quality of the Christian that God frequently extols. How have churches done this? Commission group personnel at some period in the church year. Regularly mention them in prayer in public. Publish the names of those who are giving themselves to this ministry. Reward faithfulness with certificates and a dinner for those who lead. Care for their needs and enable them to grow through regularly planned support and training events.

Recycle, Reevaluate, Readjust the Plan with the Ministry Team

Regular evaluations of the ministry plan give opportunity for reflecting on what is taking place within the small group ministry, for adjusting in areas where the "fit isn't quite right," and for adding new dimensions. This team becomes invaluable in developing operational policies, setting new goals, and helping to implement the plan through recruiting new leadership, caring for present leadership, sharing in the training of leadership, and publicizing community. They grow because you are investing community insights in them and giving them responsibility for the ministry. These persons are the energizers and implementers. They also become the strategists and equippers. Eventually they will be able to carry the primary responsibility for the small group ministry enabling you to become consultant and to move into new and creative forms of community development.

Pray

God is the author of community. It is not man-made nor organizationally developed. From the beginning, prayer tunes you and others in to what God intends to bring about through relational

> "We are not human beings having a spiritual experience. We are spiritual beings having a human experience."
>
> Teilhard de Chardin

commitments within your local church body. Prayer is the price of a formational ministry of small groups. What are you and your church willing to invest to know life together as God designed it?

16

GROUPS ACROSS CULTURES

One of the greatest stumbling blocks
to understanding other peoples within or without
a particular culture is the tendency to judge
others' behavior by our own standards.
James Downs

Any way you look at it, we live in a multicultural world. That "other" culture may be a different ethnic group, urban versus suburban, a generation that is not ours, a portion of the country different from where we live, or simply another small group or family. "A culture is a particular way of living which is shared among a group of human beings" (Lee and Cowan, 63–64). It is made up of shared values, beliefs, symbols, and behaviors. And "its patterns provide coherence in the lives of its participants by orienting them toward a common set of meanings which give order and purpose to their existence" (Lee and Cowan, 64). Any group pattern of perceptions and norms of behavior has its own culture.

Some cultural norms are easily accepted and adapted to. For example, upon entering a high-class restaurant you quickly learn that you will be seated and served. At another type of eating establishment you pick up some items while being served others. In a smorgasbord or salad bar you may be required to pick up everything and to be served nothing. It seems easier to accept the dining culture's rules than to put up with another group's way of running their group time differently.

Being different does not equate with being inferior nor are cultural values in themselves moral values. Persons may use cultural values for good or for evil. The importance of looking at groups from a cultural approach is so that we may learn to see, hear, understand, care, benefit from, and adapt to another's way of perceiving and behaving. We then can communicate truth and acceptance more clearly.

In learning to accept a person from a different cultural pattern Marvin K. Mayers in his excellent book *Christianity Confronts Culture* suggests that "acceptance of a person does not imply acceptance into one's life of all that the other person does, says, or believes. . . . Even though we do not need to accept [believe] what a person believes, we can still accept [respect] what a person is and does and believes" (Mayers, 48–49).

In accepting others we free them and us to grow. Our relationships with those encountered in different cultures—whether ethnic or small group variety—will be enhanced by affirmative responses to the following questions.

1. Can I, in some way which will be perceived by the other person as trustworthy, be as dependable or consistent in some deep sense? Do I realize that being trustworthy does not demand that I be rigidly consistent but that I be dependably real?
2. Can I be expressive enough that what I am will be communicated unambiguously?
3. Can I let myself experience positive attitudes toward this other person—attitudes of warmth, caring, liking, interest, respect?
4. Can I be strong enough to be separate from the other? Can I be a sturdy respecter of my own feelings and needs, as well as his? Can I acknowledge my own feelings and, if need be, express them as something belonging to me and separate from his feelings?
5. Am I secure enough within myself to permit him his separateness? Can I permit him to be what he is—honest or deceitful, infantile or adult, despairing, or over-confident?
6. Can I let myself enter fully into the world of his feelings and personal meanings and see these as he does? Can I step into his private world so completely that I lose all desire to evaluate or judge it? Can I enter his private world so sensitively that I can move about in it freely, without trampling on values that are precious to him?

317

7. Can I receive him as he is and communicate that attitude? Or can I only receive him conditionally—acceptant of some aspects of his feelings and silently or openly disapproving of other aspects?
8. Can I act with sufficient sensitivity in the relationship so that my behavior will not be perceived as a threat?
9. Can I free him from the threat of external evaluation?
10. Can I meet him as a person who is in the process of becoming, or will I be bound by his past and by my past?

Marvin K. Mayers, *Christianity Confronts Culture: A Strategy for Cross-Cultural Evangelism*, Grand Rapids: Zondervan Publishing House, 1974.

CULTURAL TERMS

The term *cross cultural* signifies the comparison of variables across two or more cultures. Persons in a culture tend to take for granted the worldview embraced by their culture. They operate out of it and only become conscious that it exists when another worldview presents a different reality or when their worldview fails to operate. Ethnocentrism is a tendency to place one's own group at the center of reality and to evaluate and interpret all other situations according to the norms and values of your own culture. It becomes judgmental of "out-groups" in thinking, *"We* do it right. *You* do it differently. *You* must be wrong." The in-group's ways seem logical, and thus appear to be superior.

When encountering experiences different from her own the cultural exclusivist asks: "What does this mean to me? How can it be said or done so that it is meaningful to me? How can others see life as I see it? How can I make the other person be more like me?" (Mayers, 241) The culturally open observer asks: "What is the person with whom I am communicating like? What can I say or what can I do to know that there is complete understanding on the part of the other? Can we both stand back and evaluate the communication to be sure we fully understood each other?" (Mayers, 242) An example of placing one's own perspective in the dominant role is seen in that the United States covers only a part of two continents called America and yet has taken over the name America and American. Citizens are taught that the "American way of life"—including democracy, capitalism, individualism, and a spirit of independence—is superior to any other system.

Small groups are subject to this one-way perception of reality and operate out of the standards—both personal and social—consciously or unconsciously affirmed by the group. "Cultures are communities of memory and expectation" (Lee and Cowan, 67). Interpretations are made on the basis of the history of the group and norms for present and future ways of behaving and being are interpreted by the group. In fact, there are no uninterpreted facts for creatures of culture (Lee and Cowan, 66). They are always colored by the perceptions of the culture.

PERCEPTIONS

Viewing the world from a "different perception" can seem strange and wrong. Perceptions become the ways that we experience and, therefore, behave toward the world. Following the 1992 riots in Los Angeles, Thomas Kochman, professor of communications and theater at the University of Illinois and author of *Black and White, Styles in Conflict,* was interviewed by *USA Today* (May 4, 1992) regarding social and cultural differences that lead to conflicting styles and misunderstandings.

When ased why so many blacks say racism was involved in the Rodney King verdict while many whites didn't see it that way, Kochman replied:

This is what I call socially based patterns of difference. Whites start from a premise that a situation is not racist until we prove it is. Blacks start from a premise that the situation is until you prove it's not. ... I think the Anglo culture sees racism as acts of commission and blacks see racism as acts of omission—what you're not doing. And in this case, the whole issue of how protected are people in society and how vulnerable are they. What it suggests is that some lives are worth more than other lives. ...

Whites wish to believe that a situation is not racist because if they had to concede that it was, they'd have to do guilt over it—and whites don't want to do guilt. That's why you get constant denial on the white side when blacks say: "This is racist. ..."

It's easier for a black person to shout racism and blame the system than to admit personal fault. Whites try to avoid guilt, and blacks try to avoid shame.

The importance of culture is seen in the fact that practically every communication we receive will be directly or indirectly influenced by the conditioning of the cultural constructs in which we exist. Unfortunately, those perceptions may be inaccurate or skewed by the context around them. The Muller-Lyer line illusion shown below illustrates how surrounding material affects our interpretation of line length.

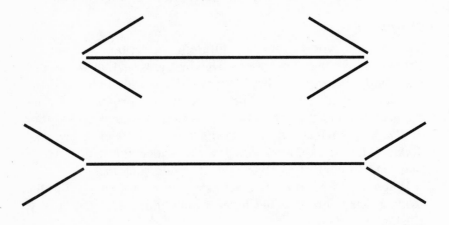

The Muller-Lyer illusion. From *New Horizons in Psychology* edited by Brian M. Foss (Penguin Books, 1966) copyright © Penguin Books, Ltd. 1966.

Both center lines are the same length even though the one in the lower drawing appears longer. We perceive out of our experience. Marshall Singer presents the following symbols to illustrate different interpretations of the same stimuli.

In numerous testings various individuals saw the first symbol as signifying a cross, a plus sign, crossroads, hands of a compass, Red Cross insignia, Swiss flag, sacrifice, eternal life – to name only a few. Confusion and misinterpretation of data surrounding this symbol naturally follow in communication when two different cultures or individuals assign different meanings to the same symbol. When the symbol is a word concept, an action or behavior, nonverbal expression or gesture, persons from within the *same* group may interpret the communication in entirely differ-

The Role of Culture and Perception in Communication

Singer, Marshall R. *Intercultural Communication.* Englewood Cliffs, NJ: Prentice–Hall, Inc., 1987, p. 17.

ent ways. How much greater the likelihood of miscommunication and misunderstanding across *two different groups.* For example, students of Chinese cultural background saw the symbol as the Chinese number ten (Singer, 16–17). "We tend to assume that almost everyone perceives what we perceive, and that we perceive everything (or almost everything) that everybody else perceives. . . . The two exceptions to this rule usually are people who look very foreign (or don't speak our language) and people who are specialists in fields about which we know nothing" (Singer, 20).

TRY THIS CULTURAL RESEARCH
Notoriously difficult for foreigners are cultural idioms, phrases interpreted in a special way by the in-group. Think through any special meanings attached to phrases in your family's experience. For example, in my family we once misplaced an item and dili-

gent searching over several days was fruitless. Feeling frustration and having exhausted our sources one family member suggested, "Maybe Erin took it," referring to the little girl next door who had been over for a visit. When we later found the lost article we laughed over the suggested alternative that Erin had been the culprit. To this day when an article seems "unfindable" we release our tension with "Maybe Erin took it." What phrases have special meaning for your family or group?

Variance in perception of meaning across cultures can cause disagreements which are called pseudoconflicts. "In pseudo-conflict [incompatible] concerns do not *actually* exist but instead are *perceived* as existing. In cross cultural pseudoconflict the mistaken perception that a conflict situation exists out of cultural differences in how people process information and communicate" (Borisoff, 120). A person who is silent or who refuses to look the communicator in the eye may be seen as respectful in one culture and as surly and belligerent in another. Arriving late may be interpreted as showing little value and create conflict or may be accepted as the norm depending upon the cultural context.

> Chevrolet was baffled when its Nova model did not sell well in Latin American countries. Officials from General Motors finally realized the problem: In Spanish, *no va* means "does not go."
>
> Adler and Towne
> Looking Out, Looking In, 85

Working with groups that cross or mix various ethnic and national cultural backgrounds presents a challenge to understanding and interpretation in light of the context of the person or groups involved.

CULTURAL DIFFERENTIATION

Edward T. Hall devised a simple differentiation of cultures based on the predominant communication style: High-context and Low-context communication.

A high-context culture is made up of people who pay special attention to the concrete world around them. Everything in the physical setting communicates something significant: the atmosphere of the room, sounds, smells, expressions on people's faces, and body language. High-context people tend to remember people's names and details about events. . . .

A low-context culture, on the other hand, is made up of people who pay special attention to ideas and abstract concepts. They may remember a conversation about an important topic but not remember the name of the person involved in the conversation. The specific words communicate more than the tone of voice used in making the statement. Low-context groups emphasize the details and analysis of ideas.

(Plueddemann, 118)

Gudykunst and Kim cite the programming of a computer as an example of low-context where in order for the program to run everything must be specified in the program (Gudykunst and Kim, 13). High-context may be illustrated by a couple who have lived together for fifty or more years and who communicate with abbreviated sentences, words, and glances.

While no culture is purely high-context or low, one of these two types of communication predominates in a culture. On a continuum of low to high the Swiss, Scandinavian, German, and U.S. cultures are considered lower in context while most Asian cultures such as Japanese, Chinese, and Korean may be located toward the high-context end. For example, if wishing to look up a Chinese character in the dictionary, one must know the context in which it is used because that context affects its meaning (Gudykunst and Kim, 13). This does not mean, however, that all Chinese are high-context and relational nor all Americans low-context and individualistic. In the same way, no small group is purely one type. However, some groups that focus strongly on schedule keeping, following a specific format, or

> What evidences of culture have you become aware of in your group?
>
> What would happen if a low-context leader were assigned to a high-context culture group?
>
> What adaptations would a high-context leader have to make when leading a group predominantly low-context in culture?

323

working primarily with ideas and knowledge of facts lean more toward low-context as their basic value system. Members who accent caring for needs and building relationships in a relaxed person-centered atmosphere lean more toward the high-context end.

Researcher Hall sees context as affecting everything about how we communicate. He sees high-context communication as "a long-lived, cohesive force," slow to change, and unifying the group using it while low-context communication changes rapidly and leaves the users to function as separate entities (Hall, 98). In terms of groups we can expect high-context group members to be belongers not easily moving from group to group, having a special bondedness with the "insiders" within the group, and expecting more of these fellow members than low-context groups would.

> How would the cultural values mentioned here affect what goes on in a group made up of Korean-Americans and other Americans?
> How could it affect decision-making? Self-disclosing? Group commitment? Contracting?
> What other factors reflect changing values that occur as one moves from group cultures at one end of the continuum to the opposite end, and how are these likely to impact a group?

Another researcher identifies cultures as individualistic or collectivistic, low-context being identified with the former and high-context becoming the latter (Hofstede, 1980, 1983). Low-context, individualistic cultures accentuate personal development, personalized relationships, and rights of the individual as well as the importance of verbal self-assertion. Group harmony and taking time to cultivate social relationships are priorities for members of the high-context collectivistic cultures. Persons in individualistic cultures cultivate specific friendships while persons in collectivistic cultures develop predetermined friendships that grow out of solid relationships formed in early years of life (Gudykunst and Ting-Toomey, 41, 68, 70).

Behavior often becomes understandable when the values of a culture are uncovered. Consider how the following values will shape group cultures.

VALUE: PERSPECTIVE ON TIME

Time as a resource is viewed differently by different cultures. For some it is to be harnessed and utilized by scheduling, and by beginning and ending at definite points. For others, time is to be expended according to the needs of the moment and the needs of the person take precedence over the domination of a set time frame. Jim and Carol Plueddemann have summarized this aspect of time according to perspectives of high- and low-context groups.

High-Context Small Group	Low-Context Small Group
Many things can happen at the same time. It may be difficult to begin and end on time, or isolate one activity at a time.	The group will begin and end on time. Events can be scheduled in an orderly sequence. People will want to stick to the passage.

(Plueddemann, 120)

Time may also be focused on the past, the present, or the future in certain cultures. Past-orientation cultures value tradition and roots. Present cultures see only the "now" as important and real while future-oriented cultures usually value change highly and see the future as enabling that. Bible history and savoring the stories of those who form the history of Israel and our Judeo-Christian heritage will be favored by groups with a bent for the past, while the didactic passages which lead to present or future active involvement in living out the teachings of Christ in a changing world will appeal to the future-orientation group. Resulting behavior patterns of Time-Oriented and Event-Oriented value systems are suggested by Mayers.

1. Time-Oriented
   a. A time-oriented person will be concerned with the time period in terms of seconds, minutes, and hours, not years and multiyears.
   b. For the time-oriented person, the time period will be a certain length depending on the intent or purpose of the time spent. It cannot be too long nor too short in

relation to this intent. It will be carefully planned to accomplish the most possible in the time allotted.

c. The time-oriented person will be concerned with the "range of punctuality" at the beginning and end of each timed session.

d. The time-oriented person sets long-, middle-, and short-range goals that are related to some type of time period. He feels most comfortable when he has planned ahead in this manner.

e. The time-oriented person will attempt to condense into a given time period as much as he can of that which he considers worthwhile.

f. The time-oriented person will have in his mind a time/dollar equivalence, or a time-spent/production equivalence in his way of life. If he spends a certain number of hours studying for a test, he expects a certain grade.

g. The time-oriented person will not fear the unknown too greatly. It will be quite predictable due to temporal control.

h. The time-oriented person will recall and try to reinforce certain times and dates.

2. Event-Oriented

a. An event-oriented person is not overly concerned with the time period.

b. The event-oriented person will bring people together without planning a detailed schedule and see what develops.

c. The event-oriented person will work over a problem or idea until it is resolved or exhausted, regardless of time.

d. The event-oriented person lives in the here and now and does not plan a detailed schedule for the future. Therefore, he is not interested in, nor is he much concerned with, history.

e. The event-oriented person trusts his own experience rather than the experience of others.

VALUE: FOCUS OF ACTIVITY

Cultures often divide along the lines of doing and being orientations. The former appears to be more external and measurable. Expression is given to concepts in tangible ways. "What can we do?" or "What have we accomplished?" are important extensions of this value (Gudykunst and Kim, 45). Being or becoming is less tangible and often issues in an integration or holistic inner perspective, a development of character, or lifestyle response. What am I thinking? Who am I becoming? What is my identity? indicate the more reflective concerns of the being orientation.

VALUE: SCOPE OF RESPONSE

Some cultures respond to others or to objects in a holistic way. For example: they see a tradesperson as a whole person, not just a plumber or beautician. Others respond to the specific role or orientation given and think of a waitress as only that (Gudykunst and Kim, 48). "In collectivistic cultures, the tendency is for people to treat others as whole persons, while in individualistic cultures, the tendency is to treat people depending upon the unique identities they perform" (Gudykunst and Ting-Toomey, 55).

The holistic framework extends to ideas and methodology as well as persons. The Plueddemans suggest, "Leaders from low-context cultures should not be surprised when high-context members skip around between observation and application questions. It may seem to a low-context leader that the group members don't have the ability to stick to the point, when in actual fact they may see things more holistically. Peter Chang explains the difference with this analogy: 'In an American meal, one has steak, potatoes, and peas placed separately on the plate; whereas in chop suey everything is mixed together. The latter is not without organization, but only organized differently' " (Pleuddemann, 122). How would this value affect group interaction? In a variation of the "unique identity" or specialized value view of life, Mayers lists potential behavior implications for group members who lean toward a dichotomizing or two-polarized view, seeing one aspect as contrasting to another. He also notes behavior for the member who sees life holistically.

Dichotomizing
1. A dichotomizing person will tend to polarize life in terms of black and white, here and there, me and the other, right and wrong, etc.
2. A dichotomizing person will tend to evaluate the other (person, program, or idea) on the basis of his dichotomies.
3. A dichotomizing person must feel that he is right, that he is doing the right thing and thinking the right thoughts, to be satisfied with himself.
4. A dichotomizing person will tend to adapt well to computers, which are based on binary conceptualizations. However, for some, fear of computers may result from seeing them in terms of "the other."
5. A dichotomizing person is likely to be highly systematized in classifying and organizing people, experiences, and ideas in his mind.
6. A dichotomizing person finds that his organization of where he fits in life and where others fit provides him security.

Holistic
1. For the holistic person, the parts will only have a vital function within the whole.
2. For the holistic person, no consideration can be given any part unless it is also considered within the whole. Situations in which one must consider one part without respect to the whole produce frustration.
3. A holistic person when faced with such frustration will utilize some defensive measure as the "mock" which strikes at the whole scene.
4. A holistic person derives his satisfaction through integration of thought and life, whether planned or unplanned.
5. The holistic person feels very insecure whenever he/she is placed in a category.

VALUE: PURPOSE OF INTERACTION
Interactions with persons can be seen as means to other ends or as ends in themselves. In the latter the interactions themselves

are important and valued. In the United States, interactions with others usually help us reach some other desired goal. We join groups in order to make friendships, network, or profit from one another's insights and expertise. We have lunch to do business. Arab and Latin American cultures value friends and conversations for their own sake. American groups are predominantly instrumental, using interactions as a means to another goal (Gudykunst and Kim, 49). Targeting the focus of group goals the Plueddemanns write:

High-Context Small Groups	Low-Context Small Groups
The purpose of the group will be to build interpersonal relationships. Group will be people-oriented.	The group will be task-oriented. Group will want to cover a specific number of verses or finish particular projects.

(Plueddemann, 121)

Goal-Conscious (Object as Goal)
1. A goal-conscious person is concerned with a definite goal and with reaching that goal. Achieving the goal becomes a high priority. He will dedicate all that he is and has for the sake of attaining the goal.
2. A goal-conscious person forms his deepest friendships with those who have goals similar to his. When necessary he will go it alone.

Interaction-Conscious (Person As Goal)
1. An interaction-conscious person is more interested in dealing with people than achieving a goal. He will sacrifice a goal for the sake of talking with or helping a person.
2. The interaction-conscious person will break rules or appointments if they interfere with his involvement with another person.
3. The interaction-conscious person will find his security within the group by getting to know the people in the group and being involved with them.

VALUE: CONFLICT PERCEPTION

Researcher Stella Ting-Toomey is convinced that members from low-context cultures are more likely to perceive conflict as a means to an end rather than an end in itself. In contrast, conflict among members of high-context cultures is an end—the process is valued (Gudykunst and Kim, 57–58). Persons in low-context cultures are likely to hold a confrontational attitude that deals with conflict directly while members of high-context groups will be nonconfrontational and seek to use indirect methods to preserve harmony (Gudykunst and Kim, 58).

> Effective interaction means giving of yourself—trying to see the world of others and to respect their life ways. It means not forcing your ways on them. Yet at the same time, it means being true to yourself and your ways. To be really effective, interaction must be a two-way street or, of course, it is not interaction at all. That is, all interacting individuals should be doing so from the basis of awareness, understanding, and knowledge.
>
> Clarence C. Chaffee

"Indirect" means appealing to other values such as "caring for the person" or to careful placement of persons in subgroups so as not to promote occasions of conflict. What other implications could this value have in small groups?

High-Context Small Groups	Low-Context Small Groups
Indirect resolution is sought through mutual friends. Displeasure is shown through non-verbal, subtle communication. Conflict resolution may be avoided for as long as possible.	Resolution is sought through direct confrontation. People will meet face-to-face and explain the difficulty verbally. Speaking the truth will be emphasized.

(Plueddemann, 120)

VALUE: RELATIONSHIPS AND ROLES

Asian and many African cultures see role relationships in hierarchical terms with rigid rules about how those credited with higher status are to be treated. In Japan the language provides different verb endings for addressing persons of higher status, equal status, or lower status. Students in strong hierarchical cultures would not consider challenging a professor's ideas with questions. Should a teacher from a hierarchical culture avoid answering a question because such seems "out of line," a student from a more equal status setting may assess the teacher as lacking knowledge and expertise (Gudykunst and Kim, 72–73). Expert power is highly respected in the non-hierarchical culture while position power seems more important in the former.

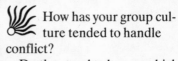 How has your group culture tended to handle conflict?
Do they tend to be more high or low-context in conflict attitudes and resolution?

Prestige-Ascribed

1. A prestige-ascribed person will show respect in keeping with the ascription of prestige determined by society.

2. The prestige-ascribed person will expect others to respect his rank and standing in the community.

3. The prestige-ascribed person will play the role his status demands and will associate with those of his own prestige or rank.

Prestige-Achieved

1. A prestige-achieved person will tend to ignore formal credentials and consider rather what the person means to him.

2. The prestige-achieved person will struggle constantly to achieve prestige in his own eyes and will not seek to attain a particular status in society.

These elements connected with role will have a definite effect on the power structure and leadership perspective found within small groups.

High-Context Small Groups	Low-Context Small Groups
Prestige is given by the group and becomes almost permanent. Others will be expected to respect rank. Formal credentials are important and need to be established.	Authority is earned by individual and personal effort. It is temporary and dependent on continued performance. Formal credentials are not as important as performance.
Leadership is usually highly controlling in order to maintain group harmony and conformity. Leader often has charismatic personality. Leaders reward loyalty to the group.	Leaders will allow each person to have significant input into decision making. Group members are more likely to question the ideas and decisions of the leader. Leaders respect individual initiative from group members.

(Plueddemann, 120)

VALUE: COMMUNICATION, WHAT'S IMPORTANT?
The way something is said may be more important than the content in some cultures. Diligence in being personable, and correctness of intention and of procedure can be more valued communication than content or conveyance of an idea. This view can be frustrating or confusing to one who believes that receiving a clear, correct image is the priority, not good intentions, elaborate forms of correct procedures, or being seen as a sincere person. How has this value been expressed in groups you have experienced? When have you felt irritation over a group not communicating according to your priority?

Persons in high-context cultures "expect the person to whom they are talking to know what is on their mind. People in high-context cultures will talk indirectly about what is on their mind, giving the other person all

In which settings have you seen each of the above cultures exercised in groups?
Can you think of leaders who reflect each of these positions?
Which seems to fit you best?
In what ways would you need to "adapt" your style if dropped into the opposite culture or were given a group that felt most at home in the culture different from yours?

the necessary information except the 'crucial' piece. Figuring out the final piece and putting it all together are the responsibility of the other person" (Gudykunst and Kim, 78). Both listener and speaker bear responsibility for understanding. The listener in this culture must intuit the meaning and read the nonverbals responding to the whole person. The chapter on communication refers to "hinters" who embrace many of the same values as high-context cultures.

In regard to communication style within small groups:

High-Context Small Groups	Low-Context Small Groups
Communication will be indirect, with emphasis on nonverbal messages. Tone of voice, posture, and facial features will have group meaning.	Communication will be direct, either spoken or written. The concept being discussed will be more important than the feelings behind the statement.
	(Plueddemann, 120)

VALUE: FOCUS ON SELF OR OTHERS?

Individualistic cultures foster goals that allow the individual to become all he or she can become. Collectivistic cultures focus more on group goals and inclusion of all. Fairness for those related interpersonally in collectivistic cultures is interpreted as everyone being rewarded regardless of what each has contributed. As David gave equal spoils to those who guarded possessions and established this as a norm in Israel, so all are included. Fairness in an individualist culture is framed as getting what you deserve based on what you have done. This is a self-oriented perspective while the former is an other-oriented view (Gudykunst and Ting-Toomey, 63). Likewise in giving to those who have given to you, individualistic cultures emphasize the voluntariness of reciprocating while collectivistic cultures teach the obligatory nature of giving back to another in an interdependent way. Much of the basis of these relational

> What interesting dilemmas arise as you envision (or recall experiencing) a group in which these two cultural norms come together. Why are both needed?

interactional styles involves factors that compose "face-enhancing and face-saving." It is building esteem and protecting that esteem from criticism and rejection. In individualistic cultures "face" is enhanced by "being your own person" and by being in control of self and others. In collectivistic systems "face" is gained by being an integral part of the highly valued group and to be rejected or disloyal to that structure causes loss of face. This driving value of face shapes our behavior and our mindset. Ting-Toomey has summarized her analysis of culture and facework in the following table. As you survey it think of ways persons in groups have acted out the cited processes to create "face" within the framework of their cultural norms.

Summary of Low-Context and High-Context Face-Negotiation Processes

Key Constructs of "Face"	Individualistic, Low-Context Cultures	Collectivistic, High-Context Cultures
Identity	emphasis on "I" identity	emphasis on "we" identity
Concern	self-face concern	other-face concern
Need	autonomy, dissociation, negative-face need	inclusion, association, positive-face need
Suprastrategy	self-concern positive-face and self-concern negative-face	other-concern postive-face and other-concern negative-face
Mode	direct mode	indirect mode
Style	control style or confront style, and solution-oriented style	obliging style or avoidance style, and affective-oriented style
Strategy	distributive or competitive strategies	integrative or collaborative strategies
Speech Act	direct speech acts	indirect speech acts
Nonverbal Act	individualistic nonverbal acts, direct emotional expressions	contextualistic (role-oriented) nonverbal acts, indirect emotional expressions

William Gudykunst and Stella Ting-Toomey, *Culture and Interpersonal Communications,* © 1988. Reprinted by permission of Sage Publications, Inc.

The Pleuddemanns summarize the context focuses found in small groups as follows:

High-Context Small Groups	Low-Context Small Groups
Testimonies and sharing of needs are emphasized. Application of biblical passages is important.	Bible study is the focus, with an emphasis on understanding and interpreting the major ideas of the passage.
Major Difficulties encountered: Has problems relating life needs to the objectived truth of the Bible. Can lead to heresy.	Has difficulty relating objective truth of the Bible to the problems of life. Can lead to dead orthodoxy.
Major strengths included: Builds empathetic relationships. Christian commitment is fervent and caring.	Builds a solid understanding of God's truth. Places a healthy emphasis on personal ownership and responsibility.

(Pleuddemann, 121)

Becoming aware of cultural values allows us to build trust within community and shows value for persons who are "different" from us in their orientation. It enhances communication and reminds us that we are all "pilgrims" in progression toward community.

Try this:
On a set of cards write various group settings: task group, support group, Bible study, committee, etc. On another set of cards write one of the previously noted values on each card, e.g., one card "values self-individuality." Ask a person to draw one "setting" card and two "value" cards. Allow the first drawn value card to take priority over the second. (Be sure to include both aspects of the value, each on a separate card, e.g. "treats people and objects holistically" and on another card "treats people and objects according to unique characteristics and roles or idiotomistically, polarizing characteristics. Using the three cards, describe a group situation that illustrates the impact of these basic values on the group. If two values are drawn from the same set, treat it as a mixed culture group.

IDENTIFYING CULTURE BY OBSERVING ROUTINES AND RITUALS

When we enter an organization, Frank and Brownell recommend we observe the following:

1. *The activities in which individuals regularly participate.* These activities do not themselves contribute to the organization's productivity, but rather reinforce "the way things are done." Included in this category are such events as company retreats, picnics, parties, and recognition ceremonies.

2. *The chain of command.* What are the formal and informal communication networks like in actual practice? Who gives direction to whom? Important information can be gained concerning who the decision makers are and how company politics operate. This information provides insight into the company's power structure and basic mode of operation.

> As Christians we are all cross-cultural. We live in this world, but are only sojourners, for our citizenship really is in heaven.
>
> Akiko Kugita,
> *AIM Journal*

3. *Group membership.* We can observe what groups operate within the organization and ask ourselves questions such as: Who is a member of this group? How is membership determined? What specific function does each group serve? How is it recognized and reinforced within the organization? How cohesive is it?

4. *Routinized methods for taking care of everyday concerns.* This category includes such behaviors as allocation of resources, performance appraisal, reward systems, and coordination of various activities.

(Frank and Brownell, 217)

17

INTERGENERATIONAL GROUPS: MINISTERING TO THE FAMILY IN GROUPS

During the next decade, the importance of ministry that addresses the issues faced by families — from child-raising to marital problems — will escalate. Parents are interested in organizations and resources that can help them in their struggle to understand and master the responsibilities of parenthood. Most women work today. This has dramatically altered the ability of women to cope with the pressures of nurturing their young. The Nineties, when compared with the Sixties, possess a more complex and comprehensive series of social problems in which young people are entangled.
George Barna

G roups that include the family may be one of the most promising arenas of outreach and growth in the future of small group ministry. Churches who formerly divided the family into age related units are considering group adventures in intergenerational experiences.

The generation gap disclosed in the Sixties caused anxiety and disappointment along with a realization that from now on there must be intentionality in our efforts to build one generation to another. This gap remains with us. Absent are the bindings that laced former families to one another across age lines. The natural amalgamations and lifestyle inclusions developed by earlier agricultural and economic circumstances are gone forever. Even sporadic family reunions are rare now because of distance and time. The support system found in intergenerational communities within the church serves as an extended family, providing models and experiences that are seldom experienced anywhere else today. Intergenerational groups often provide a framework for one era of persons to educate and enrich another. The relationships of individuals within the nuclear family are also strengthened and refocused. "In some cases, small groups develop such an importance and closeness that a virtual counterculture is created, a way of life that aids the family in the nurturing of its youth" (Sell, 231).

> Mother wrote, "When I was a little girl, I loved Louisa May Alcott's books: *Little Women, Eight Cousins.* As I look back now I can see the similarity in my life and *Eight Cousins.* There were always plenty of children to play with, aunts and uncles to run to for comfort. Life more or less revolved around St. John's Church, and at the four corners of the church lived four great uncles and their large, multi-generational families."
>
> Madeline L'Engle
> *Summer of the Great-Grandmother,* 198

WHERE IS THE FOCUS OF FAMILY GROUPS?

Two intergenerational possibilities present themselves: intra-family or inter-family. Groups that focus on *intra-family* limit the group to the members of one nuclear family and facilitate the growth of that family unit. *Inter-family* groups consist of several families together within a group. The gathering becomes "intergenerational" when it is made up of two or more generations. A generation may be defined as a period of life. Although exact ages may differ slightly the usual stages break along the following approximate age lines: 0–12 Childhood; 13–21 Youth; 22–44 Young Adulthood; 45–64 Middle Adulthood; 65+ Senior Adulthood. A third type of family group is often called *Family Support Systems.* Though usually not intergenerational, this group contributes to the strengthening and coping of the family by gathering together persons from different families who are experiencing similar needs. Examples of Family Support Systems would be groups for parents of teenagers or for persons facing decisions about elderly parents, a group for single parents or for widows and widowers who are coping with the recent death of a spouse.

For the most part, an intergenerational group is envisioned as one made up of inter-family constituencies.

WHO IS INCLUDED?
Four to five family units usually comprise an inter-family group. A "family unit" can be the two parent family or the single parent family or singles, never married or formerly married, or the couple either with no children or grown children.

WHAT PURPOSES CAN THESE FAMILY GROUPS ACHIEVE?
As in any group, the purpose may be focused or broad with several of the purposes mentioned below as targets of the group. The goal for participating families may be:

• To learn information and to gain insight and understanding of truth. Such teaching may be biblical in nature, life-related, or value or attitude slanted.
• To process and apply scriptural principles. These groups seek to uncover lifestyle implications and to actually practice while together the truths they know about relational living.
• To gain or improve skills such as competence in communication or esteem building or Bible study.
• To strengthen the family's networking and support systems by teaming together with other families to share and work on growth issues. For example, families impacted by natural disasters or who share similar circumstances such as blended family conditions can often aid each other in working through family concerns.
• To experience worship together. This group may be together for celebration—often short-term around Advent or Lent, or long-term as a house church.
• To enjoy fun and socializing as a family. Often the easiest group to introduce families to intergenerational experiences, this group purpose enables them to rebuild relationships and cut through barriers that have arisen as they have developed a separated lifestyle.
• To evangelize pre-Christians by placing them in a group with Christian families who are seeking to live out their

faith. The family becomes the attractive reality that enables pre-Christians to see how life in Christ is experienced. Another way of expressing this purpose is to support one another as families as you seek to share the Gospel with neighbors on the block.

• To carry out service projects as families in ministry together. This type of group can serve on a regular basis as to a shelter for the homeless or can work together on a short-term project such as designing a family event for the larger church family.

Purpose is probably the most important decision to be made. Out of the purpose grows the plan—including size of group, what will happen when together, how long it will be together, and who will be the participants.

WHAT ARE UNIQUENESSES OF FAMILY SMALL GROUPS?

With family units involved these intergenerational groups become distinct from most other kinds of groups. They are set apart by their assets and by their liabilities. What pluses and minuses come to mind as you think of groups made up of several families together?

WHAT DO WE HAVE WORKING FOR US IN A FAMILY GROUP?

A tremendous asset is the fact that networks have already been built between many persons in the group. Usually when a typical group forms, it takes a minimum of four to five meetings primarily focused on helping persons get to know each other so they can begin to trust one another. Families usually have that trust when they come into a group. Knitting those families to other families therefore becomes the focus of relationship building. But from the start the individual family units can break into subgroups to work on a target zone.

Another plus is the fact that parents are aware of the age level of their own (and often others') children. They strive to help the group communicate at a level the children can understand.

The variety that comes from mixing generations can be refreshing and challenging to one who is used to learning with his or her own age group. The comments of a child have been known to penetrate an adult's heart and mind with an impact that surpasses the eloquent. Likewise, the wisdom and experience of older generations often impresses the younger. The interesting variety that accompanies mixed generations can be stimulating and disarming.

All of us experienced family. It is a lifestyle grouping more closely related to everyday existence and thus more likely to be realistic in its challenges and to be transferable in its learning. While we can put forth an image in small groups, we are forced to be real with our families present.

WHAT ARE HURDLES TO BE ADAPTED TO?

A main concern is that family groups bring with them family baggage in the form of hidden agendas and established patterns of relating and responding. Each family has its own rituals and routines which become norms, never to be questioned. Now these norms may come into conflict with another family's norms. Another "bag" to be unpacked is the expected roles family members play without question in their own families. Dad's way of responding may be customary for his family, but in a family group he suddenly realizes he is exposed to an audience made up of more than his family. This can cause him to change in the presence of these "strangers" and his change in behavior affects his whole family because they are a system. What they have become accustomed to as dad's behavior, is no longer predictable and this throws off the whole system (Vance, 257–59). Families are used to one way of doing things as "the way we do it." This can be hard to change. "This is the way it works in our family" is a piece of their family baggage.

Another hurdle is the comparative/competitive syndrome. A teenager may feel resentment when he compares his parent to another in the group family. Because we have so much invested in our family relationships their behavior becomes high stakes in the comparison game. Competition and peer pressure can cause parents or children to want to look good in front of others and to unleash anger at the family member who makes them look bad.

Major among the challenges of whole families in groups is the difficulty in finding content and activities that will interest and involve all. Reading skills may still be forthcoming for a member of one family so that is something to be considered. Abilities and interests range widely from one age to another. A hurdle to avoid is that of gravitating to one age level and ignoring the rest. Adults can dominate the discussion, or everything can be child-oriented while the rest of the group is bored.

Size can become unmanageable or prevent closeness. Even four families of four or five members each can create a large small group.

George Koehler, a strong proponent of intergenerational learning, faces the realities of such an experience and adds these comments: "Any kind of across generational experience will take a lot of planning. It is often difficult to get all family members to attend. Some youth and children would rather be with their peers—they want to get away from adults. Some parents want to get away from their kids" (Koehler, 17–18).

These hurdles make the development of an intergenerational group ministry anything but easy. However, the benefits that come from promoting groups with families include exciting trans-formations of individuals and whole households. Intergeneration-al groups are an active expression of the Family of God becoming to one another community in its finest sense.

WHAT ARE BENEFITS OF USING THE GROUP FORMAT WITH FAMILIES?

Insight
Increased learning and understanding tops the list. New insights and new awarenesses are cultivated by this community experi-ence of learning together. It was no accident that Jesus trained the twelve together through lifestyle experiences.

Bonding
Development of family ties takes place just by spending quality time together. The fact that all family members are focused together in this event can rekindle relationships and give them something in common about which to communicate. Family groups, unless they are run by a professional counselor, assume the presence of basically healthy families, not those needing ther-apy. Healthy families can profit from sharing occasions and activ-ities in common.

Belonging

Groups create a sense of belonging. For those firmly "cemented in" and those who may feel like outsiders in their family, interfamily groups give participants a sense of being a part of something important and nurturing—they find identity in a community.

Influence and Perspective

Groups can provide boundaries and structure—affirming, encouraging, rewarding positive behavior, and correcting negative behavior. With families joining forces together they develop greater power to establish values. They can call the deviant to consider others or give a sense of equality to the taken-for-granted or ignored. Seeing how others respond can provide positive models for family living and can give a sense of perspective. It can create a desire for change as families actually see how they compare with other families.

Transformation

Research has shown that groups are effective systems in helping persons change. Individuals are likely to change if they see others changing. Openness, self-disclosure, and taking a risk are more likely to occur in structured situations. Families often learn something about a member in a group situation that was unexpressed at home (Hoopes, et al., 47).

WHAT MUST CHARACTERIZE ACTIVITIES IN A FAMILY GROUP?

Examine the activities listed below. Evaluate the use of them in a family group experience of some kind. If they would be good to use with families, mark with a G, if poor mark with a P, if usable when qualified mark Q. After identifying each as G, P, or Q, think back to the qualifiers or principles that enabled you to make your choice.

___ Write your own paraphrase of Mark 4:25.
___ Fingerpaint a picture of creation by families.
___ Play Red Rover.
___ Prepare mimes of household appliances (e.g. toaster) by family units.

___ Hold a contest for the most realistic sand sculpting of a castle.

___ Debate the pros and cons of paying allowances for doing household chores.

___ Share an unfinished story asking, "What would you do?"

___ Create a play that demonstrates your understanding of "faith."

___ Act out a Bible story.

___ Share riddles and puns.

___ Visit a shelter for homeless and distribute food packages you've made.

___ Prepare a talent show.

___ Collect newspaper clippings on self-centeredness.

What principles for family activities conditioned your choices above? What guidelines complete the statement below?

"Choose activities that. . . . "

Compare your list to the following:

1. Include activities that are designed to involve *all* in active learning. Viewing a film isn't active intergenerational learning. Talking about it afterward in groups can be. We learn more by being active participants than by being passive onlookers or listeners.

2. Select activities that strengthen interpersonal dynamics. Avoid those that require specialized, individualized actions. The goal is to build persons together, not to give limelight to the superstar. If only one person is involved, she must be the best, the fastest, the most artistic, etc.

3. Choose actions that are non-competitive and non-comparative. Your purpose is thwarted if every family member is angry with the six-year old who wasn't as fast as the other group's eight-year old. Make completion of the event by everyone reaching the goal, not finishing first. You can also take away competition and make activities fun by awarding prizes for different

strengths—"the craziest looking," "the most beautiful," "the silliest," "the cleverest," etc.

4. Pick or redesign activities to fit all age levels. Guard that no one is left out. Some activities can be shaped so that each age level contributes something challenging for that age.

5. Make sure each activity is simple—understandable by all, concrete. Avoid conceptual for literal-minded younger children, "doable"—can families accomplish it? and varied—so nobody gets bored because "we always have *discussion.*"

6. Plan to change activities on the average of every 15 to 20 minutes so younger children will remain interested. If it's longer than 20 minutes, it's probably too complicated for the whole family.

Experiences in family groups work from two major sources. Situational experiences occur within the family units outside the group time. They provide illustration, reflection, and interaction within the group and become a means of insight and growth. Structured experiences are those that are intentional activities designed to be "lived out" within the group and then made the resource of insight and sharing as members talk about what happened and what was gained. Such learning is called experiential education. Jesus used this methodology to teach His disciples new values and the heart of old truths. He healed and then made the healing a shared source for learning new principles. He washed their feet and then explained to them the significance of their feelings and his message. Charles Sell has included in his work on Family Ministry Margaret Sawin's procedural guidelines for this kind of educating. They outline the framework for this kind of learning with families.

THE ROLE OF THE EXPERIENTIAL EDUCATOR

The Role of the Experiential Educator is to stop the event. (This is never easy since most people are conditioned to go on experiencing— to dismiss the event as unimportant.)

1. Identifying—selecting a specific portion of an experience to be recalled. Questions might be: What really happened? To whom? How? The aim is to be concrete and specific, e.g., "When you said . . . " and "When I did . . . " and "I felt. . . . "
2. Analyzing—moving beyond the first date to deepen the group's understanding of the chosen date: looking at the nature of the event itself. Questions might be: What was helpful? What hindered or blocked the process? How were you affected by this experience?
3. Generalizing—moving into a possible future situation with questions: What will I do differently another time? What learning can I extract that I can transfer to new behavior? This process is called E I A G-ing: Experiencing—Identifying—Analyzing—Generalizing.

In Family Cluster Education:
1. The leader attempts to set an *experience* in which all ages of family members can participate. Therefore, you utilize many techniques and experiences often thought of as child-centered but which really are experience-centered: role-playing, clay modeling, finger painting, simulation games, collage making, form-model building, fantasizing, questionnaire-responding, interviewing, etc. If experiences are real and authentic, most people will respond and have feelings in response that become part of the learning experiences in the group. It is helpful for the leader to move around, observe forms of body behavior, check who is speaking—controlling whom, check lack of response, move in to facilitate people to "do" comfortably, etc.
2. The leader leads the group in *identifying* quickly, and children will usually "hang in there" when the experience has been real enough and meaningful enough for them. Sometimes the leader needs to help children "zero in" on what they would recall rather than leave it to the adults, as different age level people see the experience in different ways. People also have to be helped to learn how to talk about their feelings . . . to acknowledge their feelings.
3. The leader allows children the freedom to leave the group if it gets too "heavy," too talkative, too discussion-oriented at the *analyzing* point. Many times this is where parents begin to get insights, and they will often want to discuss them at more length. Preadolescents and young adolescents are often ready for this type of discussion in an adult setting when they are ready to understand more abstract ideas.
4. The leader can often help children *generalize* into their future hopes of utilizing this learning—as well as the adults—by sorting out the relevant ideas of children and reinforcing them. This is the point

where the leader can sometimes repeat the child's contribution in adult language and use nonverbal language to communicate a child's learning to an adult.

We do not learn by words alone but by the kinds of behavior that are elicited from us and how significant people respond to those behaviors.

From a paper by Margaret Sawin, "The Role of the Experiential Education," pp. 1–2 (Distributed by Family Clustering, Inc., P.O. Box 18074, Rochester, NY 14618).

WHAT ARE WAYS TO ORGANIZE FAMILY SMALL GROUPS?

In Terms of Time

Choice must be made between a voluntary short-term setting or a regular on-going time frame. The voluntary limited time frame seems to predominate so that participants can maintain age-level contacts. A four or six week commitment seems much less intimidating and demanding. "Ninety percent of intergenerational education takes place in elective, short-term situations" (Sell, 240). Having a choice as to whether to go intergenerational or not and realizing that choice is temporary will free persons to "try out" family small groups for a period of time. If inserted into a regular existing group ministry where there is no choice (dividing a class into intergenerational groups), plan to do so on a short-term basis. The temporary nature of this commitment as well as the wide age span will definitely impact the level the group achieves.

Occasionally some families will want to spend a year committing themselves to being together as a family, meeting with other families on a regular nine to twelve month basis. One church offered the choice of attending a family oriented "Circle of Concern" small group community which specialized in building families for a nine month commitment. Another church offered an equipping group called "Family Core" which met twice a month for meals, recreation, and family interaction experiences for a six month period. These families were being equipped to implement family ministry in the church as a whole and to lead family-oriented events offered by the church to the congregation. Generally, however, the group emphasis will be limited to a briefer period, such as choosing the summer to introduce family fun groups or the holidays to offer intergenerational small group celebrations. Churches who have already experienced the above "tastes" of intergenerational experiences or who are concerned in a major way about a family life emphasis to meet the need of the congregation may wish to design these groups as regular options for families to choose. Further suggestions for a variety of settings may be found under "Intergenerational Settings in the Church School" by George Koehler in Appendix A.

In Terms of Specific Emphasis

Purpose determines the plan. Some groups are designed for families to *learn knowledge and information* together. This may be biblical content, awareness of mission fields, or practical living insights such as media impact on family relationships. Emphasis is on teaching and learning something new. Generally the way of learning such knowledge will be refreshing especially for adults because it will likely be more right-brained that the typical adult curriculum, and taught in an experiential manner. For a sample of this type of design see Griggs' "Creation and Creativity" from *Generations Learning Together* in Appendix B.

Other groups will target *enrichment* which is the experiencing of some idea already known or the processing and applying of principles within the family relational circle. Emphasis is on transformation of the individual and the group as they actually practice known truths. Often a biblical principle such as "A gentle answer turns away wrath, but a harsh word stirs up anger" (Prov. 15:1) or "Honor one another above yourselves" (Rom. 12:10) becomes the basis for a group's activities for a session. Through games, role plays, or expressive media, "gentle answers" or "ways of honoring" are explored and tried out. Family persons are given opportunity to know the "wonder" of those words from others or to share the consciousness of being recognized and honored. Called "enrichment," such modeling provides exploration of feelings and habit development within interpersonal relationships. For a taste of the enrichment design look over the "Family Core" design on "Commitments" in Appendix C.

Family *skill-building* groups focus on the development of certain abilities through cultivating awareness of how to do something along with actually trying out that suggested pattern. Often in the communication realm, families work on goals such as giving accurate feedback to one another—"Do you mean you want me to ask you more questions?" or identifying feelings before giving solutions—"You're feeling frustrated because I asked you to be there?" Skills can be targeted toward specific needs such as "How can we handle the death of a family member?" "the loss of employment by a major wage earner?" Other skills equip for new achievements—"What does it mean to entertain others in a godly way?" or "How do you run a family council?" Check out the sample session entitled "Living With Anger: Yours and Theirs" in Appendix D.

Family *support models* are sharing oriented. Members of this group share a common need and identify with one anothers' dilemmas and feelings. Whether death, divorce, illness, addiction, rebuilding relationships, or other concerns, these groups usually need some person to lead who has been through the concern and developed a maturity to walk through the issue with others. Severely traumatized persons need a professionally led group. Members can provide support for each other, however, in the normal stress moments of life such as several families banding together to support one another through the ups and downs of adolescence and the family transitions accompanying such movement.

Some intergenerational groups focus on working together on a *service project*. In such groups someone must have some knowledge regarding the need and how to meet it, or the group will find it difficult to go anywhere. Since this is easily seen as a task or achievement oriented group, regular intentional efforts to maintain relationships while carrying out the project are vital. Also, every age level must buy into the project and be able to contribute something worthwhile, or it settles into a "typical family chore" syndrome.

Fun times together are difficult for families to experience today. So *family recreation or socializing* can be a big plus for some intergenerational groups. All need to be involved and esteem building can be a major emphasis along with relationship strengthening. The non-competitive game books available today offer great ideas for doing things in unusual and satisfying ways.

One other type of group for families is the *"at-home model"* which comes together to share what has been done "at home" or outside the group. Each has worked on some research or implementation within their nuclear family unit and comes to share findings and raise questions for further insight. Commitment must be high for this kind of group because the group session depends on the homework done outside and accountability is hard to enforce. However, this group's transfer of learning is usually higher because participants are required to carry out the purpose "on their own" in their lifestyle setting.

Family clusters are the specialized approach developed by Margaret Sawin. "Designed to help the entire family communicate, make decisions, and work out internal squabbles, clustering is an educational effort through which the participating families hope to prevent major crises from occurring" (Sell, 246). Clusters, made up of whole family units, usually meet for two to three hours at a time for an eight to twelve week period. Clustering requires leadership that is trained and experienced. For those who have not had considerable educational or group counseling experience, Family Clustering, Inc. offers this in a thirty-hour workshop and week-long Training Laboratory. Further information on clustering will be found in Appendix E.

In Terms of People-Grouping

What choices are available for placing persons together in intergenerational groups? A common way of structuring membership is to match the ages of children within a group. Families with grade school children are matched with others who have children of that age. Some intergenerational groups will have a representative of each category: a senior couple or person, two or more singles, one or more single-parent families, two or more two-parent families. Because of the complex scheduling of so many people, some groups are formed according to the times families can meet. Some families form natural networks and tend to form their own groups.

Within the group time, grouping has many varied possibilities. At times participants may group by age, by activity, by families, by interest, by sex, by interage groups representing two or more generations or grouping may be random (Koehler, 66).

Contracting is important not only within the intergenerational groups but also with individuals and family units. Where it is important for a whole family unit to be present, it becomes vital that the entire family contract to be there for an agreed-upon period of time.

What characterizes *leadership* in a family group? At times you may simply want to appoint a mature couple or person within the group to serve as catalyst person. The best leaders of intergenerational groups are aware of and skilled in group dynamics. They are also aware of age-level dynamics and levels of understanding. ("How does a first-grader think and how does he learn best?") Finally, it is valuable to be aware of family dynamics in leading this kind of group. Intergenerational groups present unique challenges and rewards to those called to lead.

Special intergenerational groups known as *house churches* embody distinctives that set them apart from typical intergenerational groups. House churches always include the element of worship and often celebrate the sacraments. They see themselves as the church. The major emphasis is that of pastoral care, and each house church requires spiritually mature individuals or couples who will model, disciple in, and exercise this role (Barrett, 19).

The term "house church" implies size: it must be small enough to meet in a house. It implies level of participation—all must be involved. There are no observers: children, youth, and adults all contribute though preschoolers may require a separate focus. Uniquely house church implies a certain quality of relationship—a whole person focus. Banks would describe it "as if family together." Members are treated as part of a household. Relationships blur as person A's children become the joy and the responsibility of the whole church who serve as extended family.

Adults see each other as relatives in the Body. The house church lifestyle is a shared one from the happenings at work to the participative counsel in decision-making. The house church seeks to become a lived experience of the New Testament image of being the body of Christ and family of God.

Intergenerational groups present unique challenges and promise great potential. Futurist George Barna in a paper on the unique dynamics of the '90s and beyond predicts:

Churches will grow in size, not only because of brilliant marketing strategies, superior preaching or teaching capabilities, or an improved sensitivity of churches to the existing needs of the population. They will do so because of an increasing emphasis on ministry to the family unit, as a consequence of people's growing need for such attention. The American people are hungry for meaningful relationships. . . .

God designed and instituted both the family and the church. They were to provide community for those who reflected His image.

> *"It is not good for persons to be alone —*
> *self-sufficient, individualistic."*
> *Your Heavenly Father*

THE LAST WORD

What life have you if you have not life together?
There is no life that is not in community,
And no community not lived in praise of GOD.
T.S. Eliot, "Choruses from "The Rock," The Complete Poems and Plays,
1909–1950, Harcourt Brace Jovanovich Inc.

L ife begets community. And community makes life liv-
able. What distinctively identifies the followers of Jesus
is their treatment of one another. It was this element
that Jesus seized to urge upon His disciples before He left them.
Community is distinctively Christian. Its development requires a
person with a vision who works commitedly with the Divine
Enabler to carry out His design. This God wants to make us like
Himself and thus calls us into relationship.

Building community is much like the children's folk tale in
"Stone Soup" by Ann McGovern. In her story a young man who
has walked all day comes to the house of an old woman and begs
for food. The woman replies that she has no food. The young
man then asks for a stone to make soup. The old woman is
intrigued.

Purposefully, the young man next asks for a pot, followed by
requests for onions, carrots, beef bones, seasonings. The two
eventually decide the soup is fit for a king. And it all came from
a small stone.

May you, the reader, continue writing the story of community
today as you search out the implications of community in a day of

353

acclaimed individualism. In *Megatrends 2000,* Naisbitt and Aburdene affirm, "The great unifying theme at the conclusion of the 20th century is the triumph of the individual." But "He died for all, that those who live should no longer live for themselves but for Him who died for them and was raised again. So from now on we regard no one from a worldly point of view" (2 Cor. 5:15-16) We are His body—interconnected, caring for one another, called to reflect and serve Him through our varied gifts and ministries and seen as one community by the head of the church.

See you at the consummation of community—when we celebrate the marriage supper of the Lamb! Until then—

Let me be your servant,
and pray that I have the grace to
let you be my servant too.

APPENDIX A

INTERGENERATIONAL SETTINGS IN THE CHURCH SCHOOL

1. Elective, short-term settings:
   - A six-week Sunday morning class for those children, youth, and adults who care to enroll
   - A four-week Sunday evening school of missions for elementary children through adults
   - An eight-week cluster of families exploring family communication
   - A five-night sex education course for senior highs and their parents
   - A weekend retreat for single parents and their children
   - A Wednesday evening Advent or Lenten study for families
   - A summertime weekly fun-and-learning night for youth and older adults
   - A six-day family camp
   - A family vacation church school
   - A five-week youth-adult discussion with the pastor following the sermon
   - A five-week Tuesday night exploration of an urgent community issue by youth and adults
   - A twelve-Saturday training program for service by youth and adult volunteers in a community center

2. Elective ongoing settings:
   - A weekly Wednesday evening supper-learning-celebration for all ages
   - A monthly Sunday evening fellowship for families
   - A quarterly weekend outing for families with handicapped members

3. Basic, short-term settings:
   - A one-quarter Sunday morning class for all 4th–6th graders and their parents

Community That Is Christian

- A Lenten Sunday church school class for all youth and adults, replacing the usual classes
- A five-week Sunday evening study of the congregation's mission to the community for all youth and adults
- A summertime Sunday morning learning center for all ages, replacing age-level classes
- A one-Sunday, five-hour learning-and-celebration festival for the congregation's anniversary
- A special congregational meeting for study and intentional planning in response to a personal or social crisis
- A youth and an adult class which agree to meet jointly for one quarter

4. Basic, ongoing settings:
- A continuing intergenerational Sunday church school class
- An intergenerational Sunday church school in the small church
- A midweek intergenerational church school
- A monthly or "fifth Sunday" intergenerational Sunday morning setting in place of other classes

Taken from *Learning Together–A Guide for Intergenerational Education in the Church,* George E. Koehler. Discipleship Resources, 1977, pp. 18–20.

APPENDIX B

CREATION AND CREATIVITY

A. INTRODUCTION
The sessions included in this unit could be rearranged in a variety of ways. The sessions could be used as single experiences without any connection to each other. The sessions could be developed all together through the use of learning centers. Single sessions from this unit could be added to other units. Or, the four sessions could be presented together in a sequence of four weeks.

B. UNIT OBJECTIVES
Each session has specific objectives which are stated as a part of the session. In addition the following are some objectives that may be accomplished as a result of experiencing the whole unit.

At the end of this unit participants should be able to:

1. Express their own concepts of God's work as creator.
2. Describe ways that they are participants in and benefactors of God's creative work in the world.

C. MATERIALS NEEDED
The following materials will be needed for two or more of the sessions:

1. Bibles and/or *Good News for Modern Man*
2. Concise Bible Concordances
3. Paper, pencils, felt tip markers
4. Creative Activity Materials

D. SEQUENCE OF SESSIONS AND ACTIVITIES
First Session: Psalm 95 and Hands
Introduction
In teaching this session it is important for teachers to have re-

hearsed in their minds all of the procedures of the session. There are a variety of teaching activities and resources recommended. The pace of the session moves quickly and the teacher needs to be prepared for spontaneous responses, questions, and suggestions which may arise from the students.

Objectives
At the end of the session the participants should be able to:

1. State their understanding of the Psalmist's concept of God and His meaning of the word "Hand" in Psalm 95.

2. See and feel the importance, power, and creativity of their own hands.

3. Express creatively their individual responses to Psalm 95:1-7 and God's Trombones.

Room Arrangement and Teacher Preparation
It would be helpful to divide the room into two parts. For the biblical study, discussion and listening, place the chairs in a circle. Have one Bible per chair. Place a screen or bulletin board so that it can be seen by everyone. Also, place the phonograph so that it can be reached easily by the leader and heard by the whole class. In the other part of the room (either around the perimeter of the circle or in the other half of the room) have tables (one for each six persons) covered with newspaper or butcher paper. It is best to have chunks of clay already available at the places around the table. Also, provide a dishpan of water and paper towels. It is much more satisfactory to use moist potter's clay available in red, grey, or tan from most art supply stores. Plan for about one to two pounds per student.

ACTIVITY ONE – Discussion
Have the students discuss in pairs the following assignment.

Everybody has some used-to-thinks. Used-to-thinks are those things you used to think and now don't think any more. We are going to discuss some of our used-to-thinks about God. Share with each other some of the things you used to think about God and don't think in the same way anymore.

Allow about five minutes for this.

ACTIVITY TWO—Read and Discuss Psalm 95
Have the class work in groups of four to six persons to do the following:
  a. Read Psalm 95:1-7

  b. Discuss two questions:
    1. *What is the writer's idea, image, or concept of God? What does he think God is like?*
    2. *What is the significance or meaning of the words "hand" and "hands"?*

Allow five to eight minutes for this, then provide an opportunity for the small groups to share with the whole class some of their ideas.

ACTIVITY THREE—Focus on Hands
There are many ways to focus on Hands. The teacher's own creativity, available resources, and time will determine what is possible.

Some suggestions are: (Don't try to do them all. Try your own approach.)

A. Have everyone look at his/her own hands then respond spontaneously as a group to the following questions:

  1. What are some things that are important or fun that you do with your hands?
  2. What would it be like to be without hands?
  3. Why do you think the Psalmist used the word "hands" as a key part of this Psalm?

B. Do some nonverbal creative expression with hands by encouraging persons to communicate feelings of the following:

1. Show anger or frustration
2. Show sadness or loneliness
3. Express friendship to another person
4. Communicate happiness or joy with hands
5. Show you need someone else's help
6. Play a game with another person using hands
7. Shake hands with several people showing them you are glad to see them.

C. Look through magazines to find pictures of hands expressing feelings and actions of hands. Make individual or group montages.

D. Mount several significant pictures or photographs on the tack-board to use as illustrations of feelings that are expressed with hands.

E. Use a print of Michelangelo's painting "Creation of Adam" showing the creation of man where the hands of God and man are outstretched toward each other. Prepare ahead of time a mask to cover over the whole painting except for a small square which reveals both hands.

ACTIVITY FOUR – Sing Together
Have the group stand in a circle holding hands.

The leader could ask for students to report how they feel as a group now in a circle holding hands compared to when they first came into the room. Or, the leader could express some of his/her own feelings then ask for some responses.

After a minute or two ask if anyone thought of the song "He's Got the Whole World in His Hands." Sing the song encouraging students to suggest words to create new verses to the song. Suggest clapping hands to keep the rhythm.

With the group in a circle holding hands or possibly putting hands and arms around each other's shoulders or waists the feeling of closeness is communicated. Our hands bring us closer to

Appendix B

each other. This then would be a natural time for prayer to express thanksgiving for hands and commitment to use our hands for continuing God's creation.

ACTIVITY FIVE – Share a poem
Encourage the group to sit down. Allow a minute or two for brief, spontaneous conversation in small or larger groups.

Then describe what is to follow.

1. *We are going to listen to a poem.*
2. *After hearing the poem we are going to go to a table where there is clay.*
3. *Play and create with the clay in any way that expresses your feelings in response to what we have done or to the poem you will hear.*

(These instructions are helpful **before** the poem so as to avoid having to give any instructions between the hearing of the poem and the moving to work with the clay. Instructions at that point would be an interruption of the thinking and creating process.)

Read the poem from the book "I'll Make Me a World" – James Weldon Johnson's *Story of the Creation,* Viking Press, 1955, and Hallmark Cards, 1972. The poem is also available in the filmstrip titled "Creation" produced by Broadman Films, Nashville, Tennessee.

Encourage the students to listen for all the times when hands or arms are mentioned and what actions they perform.

ACTIVITY SIX – Create with Clay
Everyone spends 15–25 minutes creating and playing with the clay. Teachers could participate also. Conversation will most likely be informal.

After time for creating, persons can circulate to see what others have done.

The leader may want to "wrap-up" the session by asking the students to reflect upon the day's experience.

How did it feel to use hands to communicate and create? What was learned about Psalm 95?

Spend a few minutes sharing with each other the products of creating with the clay. Even if a person doesn't have anything to "show" he/she could share some feelings about working with the clay.

From Donald Griggs, "Unit 5. . . . Creation and Creativity," *Generations Learning Together*, Abingdon Press, 1976.

APPENDIX C

COMMITMENT

GOAL: The purpose of this session is for families to understand better the concept of commitment and to project ways each family member can be more committed to members of the family.

MATERIALS NEEDED: Mime slips
Placemats, designs, markers, paints and spray
Family copies of commitment game
Family puppets for pre-school families

6:00–6:30	Families eat dinner together
6:35–6:55	Fun with mimes
6:55	Children leave for activity
6:55–7:30	Parents talk about commitment
7:35	Children return
7:40	Family Experience Groups
7:55	Prayer and dismissal

6:00	Families share a potluck supper, eating in family groupings with children and parent staff included as extended family.
6:35	Family Fun—Give each family a slip on which is written the name of an appliance (toaster, vacuum, etc.) Ask each to prepare a mime, demonstrating that appliance by incorporating all family members. Each then shares their "production" while the audience guesses the appliance.
6:55	Children leave to work with children's staff to make placemats on which they have illustrated their commitments (promises made to persons in the family because they love them). Parents talk together about commitment.

7:00
PARENT GROUP:
Commitment today is loosely defined. It is acceptable to break
promises for the most trivial of reasons. Commitments are easily
broken whether in major or minor circumstances. Persons sign
up for a church dinner and then don't show up. They accept
responsibility but fail to carry it out. They accept responsibility
but fail to carry it out. They drop out of groups with flimsy
excuses. They abandon persons for their own pursuit of happiness. In what ways do you see commitments as "endangered
species" today?

Commitment is one of the strongest themes of Scripture. We are
assured that God is fully committed to us. He would not bow out
in the Garden. He would not come down from the Cross to save
Himself. Romans 8 declares, "If God is for us—who can be
against us." "Nothing can separate us from the love of God
which is in Christ Jesus"—peril, sword, pain—no circumstance
nor condition.

But Jesus had to teach that kind of commitment to His disciples.
His initial words to His disciples embody commitment, "Follow
me!" He then proceeded to use three years of His life to teach
them what that commitment meant. The words of commitment
are easy to say. The living out of those promises show the extent
of our commitment. "Marry me" and "I do" are not difficult to
say. But we spend a lifetime discovering what that means. Commitment is always being fleshed out in new ways. As the wife of a
retiree declared, "I took him for better or for worse, but not for
lunch every day."

Families are glued together by commitment. What are ways that
parents teach commitment? What are ways parents teach commitment to God and the people of God? What are ways parents
teach commitment to each other—ways they support and respond to each other's needs in the family?

Commitment may be defined as "a love promise you carry out (to
a person) because you've made him/her special in your life."

Share with your spouse right now some ways you know he/she is committed to you. Sometimes it is the little, taken-for-granted things done faithfully and consistently that demonstrate to us another's commitment.

While we are here your children are learning the meaning of 1 John 3:18. "Let's stop just saying we love people; let us really love them and show it by our actions."

In the week to come will you talk together about the questions on this sheet? As family value engineers ask yourselves:

"What commitments do we want to teach our children?" Then choose one of these and think through "What are ways we plan to teach this commitment in our family?" Bring this project next time, and we will encourage each other in this vital area of teaching commitment to our children.

In a few minutes your children will return. We have prepared for your family times some learning materials which you can use right now and during the week to talk about commitment with your children. For grade schoolers there is a game depicting what commitment is and isn't. You can add your own pertinent cards. Or you can discuss the Good Samaritan and use the attached questions to relate it to your family. Preschool families have a verse, an everyday study called "Talk is cheap" and hand puppets to respond to commitment choices. What you don't use here, you may take home for some night this week.

7:40
FAMILY GROUPS:
Grade School

"When dad told mother he loved her and wanted to marry her, he made a commitment to her. What do you think a commitment is?"

"How does dad show he loves mother?" or "mother show she loves dad? Or our family?"

Share verse: 1 John 3:18. We show love by our actions.

Game: "How can we show we are committed to each other as a family? To God and His people? Turn over a card and read the words so we can talk about it."

OR

Story: Read about the Good Samaritan, Luke 10:30-35 and talk about ways he showed commitment (time, compassion, action, offering to take care of his needs).

Commitment shows itself in: (pick one or more)
Time – What are ways we show love/commitment by the gift of our time?

Feelings – What are ways we show love/commitment to another family member by showing we understand their feelings?

Actions – What are ways we can show love/commitment to each other by offering help? How would you like to be helped?

Encouragement – What are ways we can show love/commitment by encouraging and building up each other?

Preschool
Loving shows in a family. The Bible says, "We know we love the children of God if we love God and do what He says. We know we love God if we love the people around us" (1 John 5:2).

Some people don't know about this kind of love. They promise something and then don't do it. We call them "Say and do nothing people." They say, "I'll be there – you can count on me." And then they don't show up.

Read story: "Talk Is Cheap"

Hand out puppets, each matching the role that person plays in the family. On one side they are smiling, which means they want to do what they say. On the other side they are frowning which means they won't do what they say.

Read what is happening and hold up the side that shows what this person is like — a "Say and Do Person" or a "Say and Do Nothing Person."

Jane: "Mother, I love you," called Jane. Then she ran off and left her game scattered all over the floor.

Dad: "I'll bring you a surprise from the grocery store." "Here are your gummy bears."

Mother: "Sure I love you, but I don't feel like fixing lunch — we'll just skip it."

Jim: "Daddy, we love you." (Next morning Dad sleeps in. Jim and Dick are yelling and making their model trucks roar in the family room while Dad tries to sleep."

7:55
PRAYER BY FAMILY UNITS

How does He show us we are a "special people" to Him?	Oh no, those same vegetables again.
	    What do you *FEEL* like saying or doing?
	    What do you *REALLY WANT* to do to show your commitment/ love to Mom for fixing the meal?

How can we show commitment/ love to God?	What's one way our family can show commitment/love to each other at dinner time? Let's act it out.
Finish the following sentence: I show commitment/love to Dad by	**THE COMMITMENT GAME**
You've been making models all morning in your room. This afternoon you are supposed to meet some friends for ball practice at 1 o'clock. Your family is having company tonight. You don't have time to pick up your room before it's time to play.	One family member thanks God for these people:
Act out how Mom feels when she sees the mess in your room and knows you broke your commitment to her. (Didn't show love to her.)	_____ (a child, brother, sister) shows his/her commitment/love to me by
Who are some persons we as a family are committed to love?	How does Jesus show us commitment/love?

APPENDIX D

LIVING WITH ANGER: YOURS AND THEIRS

Topic: Anger in family life

Educational Objective: To teach families how to express their angry feelings in a constructive manner

Biblical Reference: Ephesians 4:15

Materials Needed: Paper, pencils, workbooks

Schedule:
15 minutes: Warm-up
20 minutes: Presentation of the lesson
25 minutes: Exercise No. 1, Primary and Secondary feelings (foster families)
10 minutes: Break
25 minutes: Exercise No. 2, The R.D.A. Exercise (family groups)
15 minutes: Wrap-up

Warm-up:
Build a story. As families arrive, it is fun to build a story together with those who are present. Have one person start by offering one word. Then go around the room, each person adding one word to those already given, thus repeating the story up to that point, then adding a word of his or her own. You will probably be able to go around the room several times, and the stories do get crazy.

Introduction:
Present the "Introduction" material to the class. Use your own words, illustrations, and examples as you wish. Utilize the blackboard to write the capitalized phrases or other key points.

Exercise #1: Primary vs. Secondary Feelings
Form the class into their foster families. It is preferable to utilize the same foster families as in the previous two sessions, but not necessary, especially if there are some absent families this week.

Ask each family to make a circle. Select one family member to be in the center of the circle. He or she will be the protagonist or the receiver. The people around the circle are the speakers.

In the workbook there is a brief description of this exercise and a list of various situations. Make sure that each group has a workbook or you may want to make a list of the situations on the blackboard for all to see. Select situation no. 1. Instruct the group to give in turn a typical anger response to this situation. Speak to the person in the center of the circle. Go around the circle once or twice.

Then immediately go around the circle again, and this time have each person give a response to this same situation from what might be their primary feeling.

For example, in situation no. 1 the person in the center of the circle is a child who almost got hit by a car in the street after being told several times not to play in the street. The people around the circle are speaking as if they are the child's parents. Giving angry responses, they might say things like, "You stupid kid. You almost killed yourself." In giving primary feeling responses, they might say things like, "That sure scared me. You almost got hit."

After going around once with the anger response and once with the primary feeling response; do it again with situation no. 2.

After a couple of situations, give the person in the center an opportunity to say how he or she is feeling. How did the two types of responses feel? Is your self-esteem high or low? Do you feel loved or unloved?

Now switch roles. Let another person go into the center of the circle and do a couple more situations.

Finally, give anyone who wants a turn a chance to be in the center.

This exercise needs some extra structuring. If you have a leadership team, have each team member facilitate one or two groups. If you don't have enough help, write the instructions out on the blackboard and then monitor the groups as best you can.

Exercise #2: The R.D.A. Exercise
The purpose of this exercise is to give families a structured and safe way of expressing their angry feelings. This highly structured exercise is especially good for families that tend to be explosive with their anger. Instead of exploding, the weekly use of this formalized and written approach releases most of the anger in less destructive ways. Not every family will need a highly structured approach, but then again, all families may need it sometimes.

The first phrase of the exercise is primarily pencil and paper work. Participants can write in their workbooks or on separate sheets of paper.

Make three columns, labeling each "R," "D," and "A." The steps are outlined in the workbook.

Step One: "R" stands for resentment. List in the first column all of the resentments that you feel toward any people other than your immediately family. I repeat, in this classroom practice, the exercise is to be done only in relation to non-family members or situations. Later, at home, families can expand this exercise to include family situations.

Step Two: "D" stands for demand. In the second column list specific behavior that you want someone to do differently, behavior that will resolve your resentment. The key point here is to make it specific and behavior oriented. Do not generalize with phrases like, "I want her to treat me better," or "I want his attitude to improve." Challenge the class to get specific. Otherwise there is no chance that a potential listener will know what he or she is to do.

Step Three: "A" stands for appreciation. Take the top four resentments and list in column three an appreciation behind or in each resentment. This is hard for many people. For example, my resentment might be that my boss is always demanding too much from me. My hidden appreciation in that resentment is that I appreciate and respect his high standards, or I'm glad that he has that job and not me. Another example: I resent it when truckers run me off the road (I drive a Volkswagen), yet I appreciate the fact that I can drive. Another example: I resent it that my uncle died last year, yet I appreciate and I am grateful for the happy times that we had together. Do you get the idea? Challenge them to find the hidden appreciation in every resentment.

The second phase of this exercise is to invite the families to share with each other their written materials. Each person is to take a turn and share one resentment, their demand, and their hidden appreciation. Since these resentments will have to do only with non-family situations, most families will not get involved in an argument. Nevertheless, remind them to be accepting of each others' feelings. Do not evaluate or judge what you hear. Ask only clarifying questions.

In this session on anger, the boundary between therapy and education becomes the most difficult to maintain.

Alternative Exercises
Classes vary widely in their degree of functioning with anger. Some families find these anger exercises mild; others get out of control immediately. Again, I remind you that the purpose of this program is not family therapy, but rather it is to learn a skill. People cannot learn skills if they get emotionally upset. This is why we use foster families and why we limit the R.D.A. exercise at first to non-family situations. By neutralizing any potential conflicts, people are free to learn the skills. Then they can go home and continue to practice these exercises without limits, but hopefully with new skills.

You will have some sense of your class from the first two nights. You can then judge as to whether or not they can handle this session as written. If your class is unusually volatile, drop the R.D.A. and substitute a generalized discussion of the questions following the introduction in the workbook.

Wrap-Up:
Refocus the entire class back on you. Invite each family to share with the entire class what they have learned, experienced, or seen in a new light. Re-emphasize some of the themes from the lesson. Explain again to them that the point of this session was not to resolve conflicts but simply to learn some new skills. It is now up to them to apply these skills to their own family situation. There is a new Family Time (homework) assignment for them in their workbooks. They may also wish to try R.D.A. again as a family at home.

Close with a prayer or whatever the Spirit leads you to do.

From R. Scott Sullender, "Living with Anger: Yours and Theirs," *Family Enrichment Workshops,* 1982, pp. 24A–24D.

APPENDIX E

COOKING UP A FAMILY CLUSTER

If you could peek into all the family cluster groups which have met together over the years, you would see a great variety of group size, composition, goals, and activities. Some would be all families with no singles; some would include children only if they are first grade or older; and others would include everyone from infants to great-grandmas. Some would eat and sing together; some would do art projects and cook together; others would study the Bible together. None of these "recipes" for a group is sacred; each has been designed to meet certain needs.

Like a good cook, you can choose from an array of ingredients, varying the proportions as you wish, to create your own recipe for a group that works for you, one that meets the needs and reaches your goals for your group. You and your co-leader will set up this format yourself before the first group meeting. Most of your participants will not be able to tell you what they want in a family cluster group because they have never experienced one before. They probably need to taste it first to see what they like.

If you will be leading a group that contains people who have been in a family cluster before, you can use their input in choosing your format.

GROUP INGREDIENTS:
Who will be in this group?
3–4 families plus young and older singles?

4 families—with children of a designated age group?
Many clusters include only children of reading age—usually first grade plus.

4 families with children of all ages?
This makes planning much harder unless you plan to remove preschoolers during part of the time. But this plan includes many more families of our church.

Whichever format you choose, you will want to try to include one single-parent family; the parent and the kids need an extended family as much or more than the rest of us do!

LESSON PLANNING:
Every Family Cluster meeting has a beginning, middle, and end. Be sure to include:

1. Opening the session
   This could be only 1 or 2 minutes or it could include 25 minutes of games and icebreakers. It is the most important part of the activity of the session because it sets the tone for everything that will follow.

2. Presenting the subject
   Sometimes some basic information is needed about the theme of the evening before the group dives into action. Sometimes the subject can be presented through a game, a song, a reading, or even a sharing question—but it should whet their appetites for what will follow.

3. Exploring the subject
   Time to get to work—usually in smaller groups or as individuals—by discussion, reading Scripture, sharing questions, etc.

4. Responding creatively
   Learning is reinforced as group members participate in simulated or direct experiences including role plays or creative writing or in artistic responses such as painting, modeling in clay,. etc.

5. Ending the session
   Close in a way that helps group members sense a completeness to all the experiences of this session. Group prayer, a song, or large group sharing are some possibilities.

POSSIBLE SUBJECTS FOR CLUSTERS:
When choosing a theme topic for a unit, consider topics that

would be common to all the ages present. Choose a theme that can last about 6 or 7 weeks, allowing yourself 1 or 2 weeks within your 8 week period for social activity or ending celebration.

Some groups have used the following themes:

communication	meals
family histories	work
treasures (values)	Holy Spirit
interpersonal relationships	school
feelings	enemies
play games	memories
losing	love
winning	church
self-esteem	worship
conflict resolution	growing
creative problem solving	death
decision making	parents
dreams and hopes	friends
prayer	mistakes
Advent	Passover
other Christian holidays	other Jewish holidays
Thanksgiving	secular holidays

You may want to use these subjects or use your group's ideas for the agenda for some of your meetings.

Developed by Kathy Sizer. Based on Griggs, *Generations Learning Together,* pp. 16–34.

BIBLIOGRAPHY

Adler, Ronald B., and Neil Towne. *Looking Out, Looking In.* 6th ed. Ft. Worth: Holt, Rinehart and Winston, Inc., 1990.

Adler, Ronald, and George Rodman. *Understanding Human Communication.* 4th ed. Ft. Worth: Holt, Rinehart and Winston, 1991.

Anderson, Leith. *Dying for Change.* Minneapolis: Bethany House, 1990.

Anderson, Ray S. *On Being Human.* Pasadena: Fuller Seminary Press, 1982.

Argyris, Chris. "Interpersonal Barriers to Decision Making." *People: Managing Your Most Important Asset.* Boston: Harvard Business Review (1990): 121–34.

Ashbrook, James B., and James D. Glasse, *Ministerial Leadership in Church Organization.* Boston: Boston University, May 1967, 1–36.

Baird, John Jr., and Sanford B. Weinberg. *Group Communication: The Essence of Synergy.* 2nd ed. Dubuque, IA: Wm. C. Brown Co., 1981.

Bales, Robert Freed. *Personality and Interpersonal Behavior.* New York: Holt, Rinehart and Winston, 1970.

Banks, Robert, *Paul's Idea of Community.* Grand Rapids: William B. Eerdmans, 1988.

Banks, Robert and Julia. *The Church Comes Home.* Australia: Albatross Books, 1989.

Baranowski, Arthur R. *Creating Small Faith Communities.* Cincinnati: St. Anthony Messenger Press, 1988.

Barker, Larry L., Kathy J. Wahlers, Kittie W. Watson, and Robert J. Kibler. *Groups in Process.* 4th ed. Englewood Cliffs, NJ: Prentice–Hall, 1991.

Barker, Steve, Judy Johnson, Jimmy Long, Rob Malone, and Ron Nicholas. *Small Group Leaders' Handbook.* Downers Grove, IL: InterVarsity Press, 1982.

Barna, George. "Seven Trends Facing the Church in 1988 and Beyond." Nation and International Religion Report.

——————— . *The Frog in the Kettle.* Ventura, CA: Regal Books, 1990.

Barrett, Lois. *Building the House Church.* Scottsdale, PA: Herald Press, 1986.

Bast, Robert L. *Attracting New Members.* co-published by New York: Reformed

Church in America and Monrovia, CA: Church Growth, Inc., 1988, 32.

Baxter, Leslie A. "Strategies for Ending Relationships: Two Studies." *The Western Journal of Speech Communication* 46 (Summer 1982): 223–41.

Beebe, Steven A., and John T. Masterson. *Communicating in Small Groups: Principles and Practices*. 3rd ed. Glenview, IL: Scott, Foresman/Little, Brown Higher Education, 1990.

Bellah, Mike. *Baby Boom Believers*. Wheaton, IL: Tyndale House, 1988.

Bellah, Robert, Richard Madsen, William Sullivan, Ann Swidler, and Steve Tipton. *Habits of the Heart: Individualism and Commitment in American Life*. Berkeley: University of California Press, 1985.

Benjamin, Alfred. *Behavior in Small Groups*. Boston: Houghton Mifflin, 1978.

Bennis, W.G., and H.A. Shepard. "A Theory of Group Development." *Human Relations* 9 (1956): 415–37. Reprinted in G.S. Gibbard, J.J. Hartman, and R.D. Mann, eds. *Analysis of Groups*. San Francisco: Jossey–Bass, 1974.

Berkowitz, Leonard. "Group Standards, Cohesiveness, and Productivity." *Human Relations*, 509–19.

Bertelson, David. *Snowflakes and Snowdrifts: Individualism and Sexuality in America*. Lanham: University Press of America, 1986.

Bettinghaus, Erwin P., and Michael J. Cody. *Persuasive Communication*. The Dryden Press, New York: Holt, Rinehart and Winston, 1987.

Birkey, Del. *The House Church*. Scottsdale, PA: Herald Press, 1988.

Bittner, John R. *Understanding Each Other*. Englewood Cliffs, NJ: Prentice–Hall, 1983.

Bloom, Allan. *The Closing of the American Mind*. New York: Simon and Schuster, 1987.

Blumberg, Herbert H., Paul A. Hare, Valerie Kent, and Martin F. Davies, eds. *Small Groups and Social Interaction*. vol. 2, New York: John Wiley and Sons, 1983.

Bock, Lois, and Miji Working. *Happiness Is a Family Time Together*. Old Tappan, NJ: Revell, 1975.

Boff, Leonardo. *Ecclesiogenesis: The Base Communities Reinvent the Church*. Maryknoll, NY: Orbis Books, 1986.

Bolton, Robert. "Listening Is More Than Merely Hearing." *Bridges Not Walls*. 4th ed. John Stewart, ed. New York: Random House, 1986.

Borisoff, Deborah, and David A. Victor. *Conflict Management*. Englewood Cliffs, NJ: Prentice–Hall, 1989.

Bradford, Leland P., ed. *Group Development*. 2nd ed. San Diego: University Associates, Inc., 1978.

Bradshaw, John. *Bradshaw On: The Family*. Deerfield Beach, FL: Health Communications, Inc., 1988.

——————. *Healing the Shame That Binds You*. Deerfield Beach, FL: Health Communications, Inc., 1988.

Brehm, Sharon S., and Saul M. Kassin. *Social Psychology*. Boston: Houghton Mifflin, 1990.

Brilhart, John K., and Gloria J. Galanes. *Effective Group Discussion*. 6th ed. Dubuque, IA: Wm. C. Brown, 1989.

Bruce, A.B. *The Training of the Twelve*. Grand Rapids: Kregel, 1971.

Bryce, J. *The American Commonwealth*. vol. III. repr. of 1888 ed. New York: Macmillan, 1888.

Buffington, Perry W. "The Art of (Silent) Persuasion." *Sky: Delta Airlines*. (September 1989).

Buscaglia, Leo. *Loving Each Other*. Thorofare, NJ: SLACK, Inc., 1984.

Canary, Daniel J., and Brian H. Spitzberg. "Appropriateness and Effectiveness Perceptions of Conflict Strategies." *Human Communication Research*. vol. 14., no. 1 (Fall 1987): 93–118.

Carnes, Patrick J. *Family Development 1: Understanding Us*. Interpersonal Communication Programs, Inc.

Carr, Jacquelyn B. *Communicating and Relating*. 3rd ed. Dubuque, IA: Wm. C. Brown, 1984.

Chesto, Kathleen O. *Family Centered Intergenerational Religious Education*. Kansas City: Sheed and Ward, 1988.

Cho, Paul Yonggi, and Harold Hostetler. *Successful Home Small Groups*. Plainfield, NJ: Logos International, 1981.

Coleman, Lyman, and Marty Scales. *Serendipity Training Manual for Groups*. Littleton, CO: Serendipity House, 1989.

Condon, John C., and Fathi Yousef. *An Introduction to Intercultural Communication*. New York: Macmillan, 1975.

Conrad, Charles. *Strategic Organizational Communication.* 2nd ed. Ft. Worth: Holt, Rinehart and Winston, 1990.

Corey, Gerald, Marianne Schneider Corey, Patric J. Callanan, and J. Michael Russell. *Group Techniques.* rev. ed. Pacific Grove, CA: Brooks/Cole Publishing Company, 1988.

Corey, Gerald and Marianne S. *Groups: Process and Practice.* 3rd ed. Monterey, CA: Brooks/Cole Publishing Company, 1987.

Covey, Stephen R. *The Seven Habits of Highly Effective People: Restoring the Character Ethic.* New York: Simon and Schuster, 1989.

Crabb, Larry. *Men & Women, Enjoying the Differences.* Grand Rapids: Zondervan, 1991.

Critelli, Joseph W., and Karl F. Neumann. "An Interpersonal Analysis of Self-Disclosure and Feedback." *Social Behavior and Personality.* 6 (1978): 173–77.

DePree, Max. *Leadership Is an Art.* New York: Doubleday, 1989.

Derlega, Valerian, and Barbara A. Winstead, eds. *Friendship and Social Interaction.* New York: Springer–Verlag (1986): 82–95.

Dimock, Hedley G. *Groups: Leadership and Group Development.* San Diego: University Assoc., Inc., 1987.

Downs, Perry G. "Baby Boomers' Ministry Needs." *Christian Education Journal.* vol. XI, no. 1, 25–32.

Doyle, James A., and Michele A. Paludi. *Sex and Gender.* 2nd ed. Dubuque, IA: Wm. C. Brown, 1991.

Dyrness, William A. *How Does America Hear the Gospel?* Grand Rapids: Eerdmans, 1989.

Egan, Gerard. *Face to Face.* Monterey, CA: Brooks/Cole Publishing Co., 1973.

Elgin, Suzette Haden. *The Last Word on the Gentle Art of Verbal Self-Defense.* New York: Prentice–Hall, 1987.

Emerson, Ralph Waldo. *Essays and Lectures.* New York: Library of America, 1983.

——————— . *Selected Essays.* New York: Penguin, 1982.

——————— . *The Works of Ralph Waldo Emerson: Essays First Series.* New York: Fireside Edition, 1883.

Fablo, Toni, and Letitia Anne Peplau. "Power Strategies in Intimate Relationships." *Journal of Personality and Social Psychology.* vol. 38, no. 4 (1980): 618–28.

"Finding Friends—For a Fee." *Newsweek*. (February 12, 1990).

Fisher, B. Aubrey. *Small Group Decision Making: Communication and the Group Process*. New York: McGraw-Hill, 1974.

Fisher, B.A., and D.G. Ellis. *Small Group Decision Making: Communication and the Group Process*. 3rd ed. New York: McGraw-Hill, 1990.

Fitzpatrick, M., and J. Winke. "You Always Hurt the One You Love: Strategies and Tactics in Interpersonal Conflict." *Communication Quarterly*. 27, no. 1 (Winter 1979): 3–11.

Fluegelman, Andrew, ed. *The New Games Book*. New York: Doubleday, 1976.

_____. ed. *More New Games and Playful Ideas*. New York: Doubleday, 1981.

Forsyth, Donelson R. *Group Dynamics*. 2nd ed. Pacific Grove, CA: Brooks/Cole Publishing Company, 1990.

Fowler, James W. *Weaving the New Creation*. San Francisco: Harper, 1991.

Frank, Allan, and Judi Brownell. *Organizational Communication and Behavior*. New York: Holt, Rinehart and Winston, 1989.

Freedman, Jonathan. "A Positive View of Population Density." *Psychology Today* (September 1971): 58–61, 86.

Friedman, Leslie J. *Sex Role Stereotyping in the Mass Media*. New York: Carl and Publishing, 1977.

Gaede, S.D. *Belonging*. Grand Rapids: Zondervan, 1985.

George, Carl F. *Prepare Your Church for the Future*. Tarrytown, NY: Fleming H. Revell, 1991.

Gibb, Jack R. "Defensive Communication." *Bridges Not Walls*. 4th ed. John Stewart, ed. New York: Random House, 1986, 255–60.

Gibbard, Graham S. "Bion's Group Psychology: A Reconsideration." Unpublished paper, Psychology Service, Veterans Medical Center, West Haven, October.

Gibbard Graham S., John J. Hartman, and Richard D. Mann, eds. *Analysis of Groups*. San Francisco: Jossey-Bass, 1974, 177.

Gillette, Jonathan, and Marion McCollom, eds. *Groups in Context: A New Perspective on Group Dynamics*. Reading, MA: Addison-Wesley Publishing Company, 1990.

Gilligan, Carol. *In a Different Voice*. Harvard: Harvard University Press, 1983.

Glazer, M., and R. Glazer. "Techniques for the Study of Group Structure and Behavior: Empirical Studies of the Effects of Structure in Small Groups." *Psychological Bulletin* 58 (1961).

Goodall, H. Lloyd, Jr. *Small Group Communication in Organizations.* 2nd ed. Dubuque, IA: Wm. C. Brown, 1990.

Gorman, Cinda Warner. *Growing Up Christian in a Sexy World.* Brea, CA: Educational Ministries, Inc., 1989.

Gorman, Julie A. "Commitment." Unpublished programs for Family Core.

Grayson, Curt, and Jan Johnson. *Creating a Safe Place.* San Francisco: Harper Collins, 1991.

Griffin, Em. *Getting Together: A Guide for Good Groups.* Downers Grove, IL: InterVarsity Press, 1982.

Griggs, Donald. "Unit Five . . . . Creation and Creativity." *Generations Learning Together.* Nashville: Abingdon, 1976.

Grove, Theodore G. *Dyadic Interaction: Choice and Change in Conversations and Relationships.* Dubuque, IA: Wm. C. Brown, 1991.

Gudykunst, William, and Stella Ting-Toomey. *Culture and Interpersonal Communication.* Newbury Park, CA: Sage Publications, 1988.

Gudykunst, William B., and Kim Young Yun. *Communicating with Strangers: An Approach to Intercultural Communication.* New York: Random House, 1984.

Hacker, H.M. "Blabber Makes and Clams: Sex Differences in Self-Disclosure in Same-Sex and Cross-Sex Friendship Dyads." *Psychology of Women Quarterly.* 5 (1981): 385–401.

Hadaway, C. Kirk, Stuart Wright, and Francis M. DuBose. *Home Cell Groups and House Churches.* Nashville: Broadman Press, 1987.

Hagberg, Janet O. *Real Power.* Minneapolis: Winston Press, 1984.

Hall, E.T. *Beyond Culture.* New York: Doubleday, 1976.

——————— . *The Dance of Life.* New York: Doubleday, 1983.

——————— . *The Silent Language.* Garden City, NJ: Doubleday, 1950.

Hall, Judith A. *Nonverbal Sex Differences: Communicating Accuracy and Expressive Style.* Baltimore: The Johns Hopkins University Press, 1984.

Halley, Richard D. "Distractibility of Males and Females in Competing Aural Messages Situations: A Research Note." *Human Communication Research.* 2 (1975): 79–82.

Hansan, Paul D. *The People Called: The Growth of Community in the Bible.* San Francisco: Harper and Row, 1987.

Hare, Paul A. *Handbook of Small Group Research.* 2nd ed. New York: The Free Press, 1976.

Harrison, Albert A. *Individuals and Groups: Understanding Social Behavior.* Monterey: Brooks/Cole Publishing Company, 1976.

Hatch, Nathan O. "The Christian Movement and the Demand for a Theory of the People." *Journal of American History.* 673 (December 1980).

Hauerwas, Stanley. *A Community of Character.* South Bend, IN: University of Notre Dame Press, 1981.

Hearn, G. "Leadership and the Spatial Factor in Small Groups." *Journal of Abnormal and Social Psychology.* 54 (1957): 219–72.

Hemphill, John K. "Relations Between the Size of the Group and the Behavior of the 'Superior' Leaders." *Journal of Social Psychology.* 32 (1950): 11–22.

Heshka, S., and Y. Nelson. "Interpersonal Speaking Distance As a Function of Age, Sex, and Relationship." *Sociometry.* 35: 481–98.

Hestenes, Roberta, and Julie Gorman. *Syllabus. Building Christian Community in Small Groups.* Pasadena: Fuller Theological Seminary, 1992.

Hocker, Joyce L., and William W. Wilmot. *Interpersonal Conflict.* 2nd ed. Dubuque, IA: Wm. C. Brown, 1985.

Hoffman, Virginia. *Birthing a Living Church.* New York: The Crossroad Publishing Company, 1988.

Hofstede, G. *Culture's Consequences: International Differences in Work-Related Values.* Beverly Hills: Sage, 1980.

_____ . "Dimensions of National Cultures in Fifty Countries and Three Regions." In J. Deregowski, S. Dzuirawiec, and R. Annis, eds. *Explications in Cross-Cultural Psychology.* Lisse. The Netherlands: Swets & Zeitlinger, 1983.

Hoopes, Margaret H., Barbara L. Fisher, and Sally H. Barlow. *Structured Family Facilitation Programs: Enrichment, Education, and Treatment.* Rockville, MD: Aspen Pub., 1984.

Horton, Michael Scott. *Made in America: The Shaping of Modern American Evangelism.* Grand Rapids: Baker, 1991.

Iacocca, Lee, with William Novak. *Iacocca: An Autobiography.* New York: Bantam Books, 1984.

Jacobs, Marion, Alfred Jacobs, Garry Feldman, and Norman Cavior. "Feedback II – 'The Credibility Gap': Delivery of Positive and Negative and Emotional and Behavioral Feedback in Groups." *Journal of Consulting and Clinical Psychology*. 41, no. 2 (1973): 215–23.

Johnson, David W. *Reaching Out: Interpersonal Effectiveness and Self-Actualization*. Englewood Cliffs, NJ: Prentice–Hall, 1972.

Johnson, David W., and Frank P. Johnson. *Joining Together*. 4th ed. Englewood Cliffs, NJ: Prentice–Hall, 1991.

Kaplan, Sidney, and M. Roman. "Phases of Development in an Adult Therapy Group." *International Journal of Group Psychotherapy*. 13 (1963).

Kegan, Robert. *The Evolving Self: Problem and Process in Human Development*. Cambridge: Harvard University Press, 1982.

Keirsey, David, and Marilyn Bates. *Please Understand Me*. Del Mar, CA: Prometheus Nemesis Book Company, 1984.

Kell, Carl L., and Paul R. Corts. *Fundamentals of Effective Group Communication*. New York: Macmillan, 1980.

Kellerman, Henry, ed. *Group Cohesion: Theoretical and Clinical Perspectives*. New York: Grune and Stratton, 1981.

Kemp, C. Gratton. *Perspectives on the Group Process*. 2nd ed. Boston: Houghton Mifflin, 1970.

Kimball, Don. *Power and Presence*. San Francisco: Harper & Row, 1987.

Kleisser, Thomas A., Margo A. LeBert, and Mary C. McGuinness. *Small Christian Communities: A Vision of Hope*. New York: Paulist Press, 1991.

Knapp, Mark L. *Interpersonal Communication and Human Relationships*. Newton, MA: Allyn and Bacon, Inc., 1984.

Knox, Alan B. *Adult Development and Learning*. San Francisco: Jossey–Bass Publishers, 1983.

Koehler, George. *Learning Together*. Nashville: Discipleship Resources.

Kraus, C. Norman. *The Authentic Witness*. Grand Rapids: Eerdmans, 1979.

Kroeger, Otto, and Janet M. Thuesen. *Type Talk*. New York: Dell Publishing, 1988.

Larson, Bruce. "None of Us Are Sinners Emeritus." *Leadership*. (Fall 1984): 3–13.

Larson, Jim. *A Church Guide for Strengthening Families: Strategies, Models, Pro-*

grams and Resolutions. Minneapolis: Augsburg Fortress, 1986.

——————— . *Teaching Christian Values in the Family.* Elgin, IL: Cook, 1982.

Lechner, Bettye. *Empowering Families.* National Marriage Encounter.

——————— . *Manual for Family Days.* National Marriage Encounter.

Lee, Bernard J., and Michael A. Cowan. *Dangerous Memories.* Kansas City: Sheed and Ward, 1986.

LeFever, Marlene D. *Creative Teaching Methods.* Elgin, IL: Cook, 1985.

Leonard, Joe, Jr., ed. *Church Family Gatherings.* Valley Forge, PA: Judson Press, 1978.

Lesly, Philip. *How We Discommunicate.* New York: AMACOM, 1979.

Lohfink, Gerhard. *Jesus and Community.* Freiberg: Herder Verlag, 1982.

Lont, Cynthia M., and Sheryl A. Friendly. *Beyond Boundaries.* Fairfax, VA: George Mason University Press, 1989.

Loomer, Bernard. "Two Kinds of Power." *Criterion.* (Winter 1976): 11–29.

Louv, Richard. *Childhood's Future: Listening to the American Family.* Boston: Houghton Mifflin, 1990.

Luft, Joseph. *Group Processes: An Introduction to Group Dynamics.* 3rd ed. Mountain View, CA: Mayfield Publishing Company, 1984.

Lukes, Steven. *Individualism.* New York: Harper and Row, 1973.

MacIntyre, Alasdair. *After Virtue: A Study in Moral Theory.* 2nd ed. South Bend, IN: University of Notre Dame Press, 1984.

Mader, Thomas F., and Diane C. Mader. *Understanding One Another.* Dubuque, IA: Wm. C. Brown, 1989.

Mallison, John. *Growing Christians in Small Groups.* London: Scripture Union, 1989.

Marty, Martin E. *The Pro and Con Book of Religious America: A Bicentennial Argument.* Waco: Word, 1975.

Mayers, Marvin K. *Christianity Confronts Culture: A Strategy for Cross-Cultural Evangelism.* Grand Rapids: Zondervan, 1974.

McBride, Neal F. *How to Lead Small Groups.* Colorado Springs: NavPress, 1990.

Meisels, M., and C.J. Guardoc. "Development of Personal Space Schematas." *Child Development*. 40: 1167–78.

Miles, M. Scott. *Families Growing Together*. Wheaton, IL: Victor, 1990.

Miller, G.R., and M.A. Hewgill. "The Effect of Variations in or on Fluency on Audience Ratings of Source Credibility." *Quarterly Journal of Speech*. 50 (1964): 36–44.

Miller, Hal. *Christian Community: Biblical or Optimal?* Ann Arbor: Servant Books, 1979.

Miller, Paul M. *Group Dynamics in Evangelism*. Scottsdale, PA: Herald Press, 1958.

Miller, Sherod, Daniel Wackman, Elam Nunnally, and Phyllis Miller. *Connecting with Self and Others*. Littleton, CO: Interpersonal Communication Programs, Inc., 1988.

Moltmann–Wendel, Elisabeth, and Jurgen Moltmann. *Humanity in God*. New York: Pilgrim, 1983.

Morgan, Edmund, ed. *Puritan Political Ideas*. New York: The Bobbs–Merrill Co., Inc. 1965.

Morrison, Thomas. "Members' Reaction to Male and Female Leaders in Two Types of Group Experience." *The Journal of Social Psychology*. 125, no. 1 (1984): 7–16.

Morton, T. Ralph. *Community of Faith: The Changing Pattern of the Church's Life*. New York: Association Press, 1954.

——————— . *The Twelve Together*. Glasgow: The Iona Community.

Murren, Doug. *The Baby Boomerang*. Ventura, CA: Regal, 1990.

Naisbitt, John, and Patricia Aburdene. *Megatrends 2000*. New York: William Morrow & Co., 1990.

Napier, Rodney W., and Matti K. Gershenfeld. *Groups: Theory, and Experience*. 4th ed. Boston: Houghton Mifflin Co., 1989.

——————— . *Making Groups Work: A Guide for Group Leaders*. Boston: Houghton Mifflin, 1983.

Neighbour, Ralph W., Jr. *Where Do We Go From Here?* Houston: Touch Publications, Inc., 1990.

Nichols, Ralph G., and Leonard Stevens. "Listening to People." *People: Managing Most Important Asset*. Boston: Harvard Business Review, 1990, pp. 95–102.

Orlick, Terry. *The Cooperative Sports and Games Book.* New York: Pantheon Books, 1978.

Otto, Herbert A., ed. *Marriage and Family Enrichment.* Nashville: Abingdon, 1976.

Palazzolo, Charles S. *Small Groups, an Introduction.* New York: D. Van Nostrand Co., 1981.

Pearson, Judy C. "The Effects and Setting and Gender on Self-Disclosure." *Group and Organization Studies.* (Sept 1981): 334–40.

Pearson, Judy Cornelia, and Brian Spitzberg. *Interpersonal Communication.* 2nd ed. Dubuque, IA: Wm. C. Brown, 1990.

Pearson, Judy Cornelia, Lynn H. Turner, and William Todd-Mancillas. *Gender and Communication.* 2nd ed. Dubuque, IA: Wm. C. Brown, 1985.

Peck, M. Scott. *The Different Drum.* New York: Simon and Schuster, 1987.

Pedersen, Paul B., Juris G. Draguns, Walter J. Lonner, and Joseph E. Trimble. *Counseling Across Cultures.* Honolulu: University of Hawaii Press, 1989.

Peterson, Jim. *Evangelism As a Lifestyle.* Colorado Springs: NavPress, 1980.

Petronio, Sandra, Judith Martin, and Robert Littlefield. "Prerequisite Conditions for Self-Disclosing: A Gender Issue." *Communication Monographs.* 51 (September 1984): 268–73.

Phillips, Gerald M., Douglas J. Pedersen, and Julia T. Wood. *Group Discussion: A Practical Guide to Participation and Leadership.* Boston: Houghton Mifflin Co., 1979.

Piper, William E. "Cohesion As a Basic Bond in Groups." *Human Relations.* 36, no. 2 (1983): 93–108.

Pippert, Wesley G. "The Revival of Religion in America: Editorial Research Reports." *Congressional Quarterly, Inc.* (1988): 366–75.

Plantinga, Cornelius. "The Perfect Family." *Christianity Today.* (March 4, 1988): 24–27.

Plueddemann, Jim, and Carol Plueddemann. *Pilgrims in Progress.* Wheaton, IL: Harold Shaw, 1990.

Powell, John. *Why Am I Afraid to Tell You Who I am?* Chicago: Argus Communications, 1969.

Prior, David. *Parish Renewal at the Grass Roots.* Grand Rapids: Francis Asbury Press, 1983.

Reardon, Kathleen K. *Where Minds Meet.* Belmont, CA: Wadsworth Publishing Company, 1987.

Reich, Charles. *The Greening of America: The Coming of a New Consciousness and the Rebirth of a Future.* New York: Bantam, 1971.

Rickerson, Wayne E. *Good Times for Your Family.* Ventura, CA: Regal.

Robinson, H. Wheeler. *Corporate Personality in Ancient Israel.* Philadelphia: Fortress Press, 1980.

Rosener, Judy B. "Ways Women Lead." *Harvard Business Review* (Nov.–Dec. 1990): 119–25.

Ross, Raymond, and Mark Ross. *Relating and Interacting: An Introduction to Interpersonal Communication.* Englewood Cliffs, NJ: Prentice–Hall, 1982.

Rupp, Anne N. *The Family Car.* Brea, CA: Educational Ministries, Inc., 1986.

Rupp, George. *Commitment and Community.* Minneapolis: Fortress Press, 1989.

Russel, Cheryl. *One Hundred Predictions for the Baby Boom: The Next Fifty Years.* New York: Plenum Press, 1987.

Sawin, Margaret M. *Family Enrichment with Family Clusters.* Valley Forge, PA: Judson Press, 1979.

Sayles, Leonard. "A 'Primer' on Cultural Dimensions." *Issues and Observations.*

Scheidel, Thomas M., and Laura Crowell. *Discussing and Deciding: A Desk Book for Group Leaders and Members.* New York: MacMillan, 1979.

Schein, Edgar H. *Organizational Culture and Leadership.* San Francisco: Jossey–Bass, 1991, 185–209.

Schriesheim, J. "The Social Context of Leader-Subordinate Relations: An Investigation of the Effects of Group Cohesiveness." *Journal of Applied Psychology.* 65 (1980): 183–94.

Schultz, B. "Communicative Correlates of Perceived Leaders in Small Group." *Small Group Behavior.* 17, no. 1 (February 1986): 51–65.

Schultz, Charles. *Things I Learned After It Was Too Late (and other Minor Truths).* New York: Holt, Rinehart and Winston: 1981.

Schutz, William C. *FIRO: A Three-Dimensional Theory of InterPersonal Behavior.* New York: Holt, Rinehart and Winston, 1958.

Sell, Charles M. *Family Ministry: The Enrichment of Family Life Through the Church.* Grand Rapids: Zondervan, 1981.

Sikora, Pat J. *Small Group Bible Studies*. Cincinnati: Standard Publishing, 1991.

Singer, Marshall R. *Intercultural Communication*. Englewood Cliffs, NJ: Prentice–Hall, 1987.

Sizer, Kathy. "Cooking up a Family Cluster" Unpublished paper. Fuller Theological Seminary, Christian Formation and Discipleship Department.

Smith, Dennis R., and L. Keith Williamsen, eds. *Interpersonal Communication*. Dubuque, IA: Wm. C. Brown, 1985.

Smith, Donald K. *Creating Understanding. A Handbook for Christian Communication Across Cultural Landscapes*. Grand Rapids: Zondervan, 1992.

Smith, Kenwyn, and David Berg, eds. *Paradoxes of Group Life: Understanding Conflict Paralysis, and Movement in Group Dynamics*. San Francisco: Jossey–Bass, 1987.

Snyder, Howard A. *The Problem of Wineskins*. Downers Grove, IL: InterVarsity Press, 1975.

——————. *The Radical Wesley*. Grand Rapids: Francis Asbury Press, 1980.

Stech, Ernest, and Sharon Ratcliffe. *Effective Group Communication: How to Get Action by Working in Groups*. Lincolnwood, IL: National Textbook Company, 1985.

Stewart, John, ed. *Bridges Not Walls*. 4th ed. New York: Random House, 1986.

Stewart, Lea P., and Stella Ting-Toomey, eds. *Communication, Gender, and Sex Roles in Diverse Interaction Contexts*. Norwood, NJ: Ablex Publishing Corporation, 1987.

Stowe, Robert. *The Love Feast*. Brea, CA: Educational Ministries, Inc., 1987.

Sullender, R. Scott. *Family Enrichment Workshops*. Brea, CA: Educational Ministries, Inc., 1982.

Swindoll, Charles R. *Dropping Your Guard*. Waco: Word, 1983.

Tannen, Deborah. *That's Not What I Meant*. New York: William Morrow and Company, 1986.

——————. *You Just Don't Understand*. New York: William Morrow and Company, 1990.

Thelen, Herbert. *Dynamics of Groups at Work*. Chicago: The University of Chicago Press, 1954.

Thompson, James. *Our Life Together*. Austin: Journey Books, SPC Publications, 1977.

Ting-Toomey, S. "A Face-Negotiation Theory." Y. Kim and W. Gudykunst, eds. *Theory in Intercultural Communication.* Newbury Park, CA: Sage, 1988.

Tournier, Paul. *The Gift of Feeling.* Atlanta: John Knox Press, 1979.

Trenholm, Sarah, and Arthur Jensen. *Interpersonal Communication.* Belmont, CA: Wadsworth Publishing Company, 1988.

Tubbs, Stewart L. *A Systems Approach to Small Group Interaction.* Reading, MA: Addison–Welsey Publishing Company, 1984.

Tuckman, B. "Developmental Sequence in Small Groups." *Psychological Bulletin.* (1965): 384–99.

"Unite and Conquer." *Newsweek.* (Feb. 5, 1990): 50–55.

Vance, Barbara. *Planning and Conducting Family Cluster.* Newbury Park, CA: Sage Publications, 1989.

Verderber, Kathleen S., and Rudolph F. Verderber. *Inter-Act: Using Interpersonal Communication Skills.* Belmont, CA: Wadsworth Publishing Co., 1986.

Verderber, Rudolph F. *Communicate!* 4th ed. Belmont, CA: Wadsworth Publishing Company, 1984.

Voges, Ken, and Ron Braund. *Understanding How Others Misunderstand You.* Chicago: Moody Press, 1990.

Wakefield, Norman. *Listening: A Christian's Guide to Loving Relationships.* Waco: Word, 1981.

_____ . *You Can Have a Happier Family.* Ventura, CA: Wadsworth Publishing Company, 1984.

Walker, Georgiana, ed. *The Celebration Book: Fun Things to Do with Your Family All Year-Round.* Ventura, CA: Regal.

Watson, David Lowes. *Accountable Discipleship.* Nashville: Discipleship Resources, 1986.

Weaver, Carl H. *Human Listening: Processes and Behaviors.* New York: Bobbs–Merrill, 1972.

Wheeless, L., V. Wheeless, and F. Dickson Markman. "A Research Note: The Relations Among Social and Task Perceptions in Small Groups." *Small Group Behavior.* 13 (1982): 373–84.

White, James. W. *Intergenerational Religious Education.* Birmingham: Religious Education Press, 1988.

Whitehead, Evelyn, and James Whitehead. *Community of Faith: Models and Strategies for Developing Christian Communities.* San Francisco: Harper & Row, 1982.

Whitehead, Evelyn, and James Whitehead. "Community of Faith." *Journal of Psychological Type.* 9 (1985): xx

Whitman, Walt. *Complete Poetry and Collected Prose.* J.E. Miller, Jr., ed. New York: Houghton Mifflin, 1972.

Williams, Mel, and Mary A. Brittain. *Christian Education in Family Clusters.* Valley Forge, PA: Judson Press, 1982.

Williams, Robin M., Jr. *American Society: A Sociological Interpreation.* 2nd ed. New York: Alfred A. Knopf, 1960.

Williamson, David L. *Group Power.* Englewood Cliffs, NJ: Prentice–Hall, 1982.

Willis, F.N. "Initial Speaking Distance As a Function of the Speaker's Relationship." *Psychonomic Science.* 5:221–22.

Wilson, Gerald L., and Michael S. Hanna. *Groups in Context.* New York: Random House, 1986.

Wilt, Joy, and Bill Watson. *Relationship Builders Ages 4–8.* Waco: Word.

——————. *Relationship Builders Ages 8–12.* Waco: Word.

Winstead, Barbara A. "Sex Differences in Same Sex Friendship." *Friendship and Social Interaction.* Valerian Derlega and Barbara A. Winstead, eds. New York: Springer–Verlag, 1986.

Winstead, Barbara A., V. Derlega, and P. Wong. "Effects of Sex-Role Orientation on Behavioral Self-Disclosure." *Journal of Research in Personality.* 18 (1984): 541–53.

Winter, Dorothy A., and Samuel B. Green. "Another Look at Gender-Related Differences in Leadership Behavior." *Sex Roles.* 16 (1987): 41–56.

Winthrop, John. "A Model of Christian Charity." *Puritan Political Ideas, 1558–1794.* Edmund S. Morgan, ed. Indianapolis: Bobbs–Merrill, 1965.

Wolff-Salin, Mary. *The Shadow Side of Community and the Growth of Self.* New York: Crossroad, 1988.

Wolvin, Andrew, and Carolyn Gwynn Coakely. *Listening.* Dubuque, IA: Wm. C. Brown, 1988.

——————. *Listening.* 3rd ed. Dubuque, IA: Wm. C. Brown, 1982.

Woodbridge, John D., Mark A. Noll, and Nathan O. Hatch. *The Gospel in America: Themes in the Story of America's Evangelicals.* Grand Rapids: Zondervan, 1979.

Wright, G. Ernest. *The Biblical Doctrine of Man in Society.* Philadelphia: Trinity Press, 1954.

Wuthnow, Robert. "Evangelicals, Liberals, and the Perils of Individualism." *A Journal of Reformed Thought Perspectives.* Grand Rapids: Reformed Church Press (1991): 10–13.

Yankelovich, Daniel. *New Rules: Searching for Self-Fulfillment in a World Turned Upside Down.* New York: Bantam, 1982.